ATLANTA
GREEKS

ATLANTA GREEKS

AN EARLY HISTORY

Stephen P. Georgeson

THE
History
PRESS

Published by The History Press
Charleston, SC
www.historypress.net

First published 2015

Manufactured in the United States

ISBN 978.1.46711.950.4

Library of Congress Control Number: 2015949281

Notice: The information in this book is true and complete to the best of our knowledge. It is offered without guarantee on the part of the author or The History Press. The author and The History Press disclaim all liability in connection with the use of this book.

For:

My parents, Paul and Christine Georgeson.

My petherika, Mike and Eva Chaknis.

Valine, Alexis and Alex, Vickie and Brian and Zachary and Megan.

My grandchildren, Amalia and Theodore, the newest generation.

Nothing is more likely to forward this object [of self government] *than a study of the fine models of sciences left by* [your countrymen's] *ancestors; to whom <u>we</u> also are all indebted for the lights which originally led ourselves out of Gothic darkness. No people sympathize more feelingly than ours with the sufferings of your countrymen, none offer more sincere and ardent prayers to heaven for their success…*

I have thus, dear Sir, according to your request, given you some thoughts on the subject of national government…. They are yet but outlines which you will better fill up, and accommodate to the habits and circumstances of your countrymen. Should they furnish a single idea which may be useful to them, I shall fancy it a tribute rendered to the Manes of your Homer, your Demosthenes, and the splendid constellation of sages and heroes, whose blood is still flowing in your veins, whose merits are still resting, as a heavy debt, on the shoulders of the living, and the future races of men. While we offer to heaven the warmest supplications for the restoration of your countrymen to the freedom and science of their ancestors, permit me to assure yourself of the cordial esteem and high respect which I bear and cherish towards yourself personally.

—letter of October 31, 1823, sent by Thomas Jefferson to Greek scholar and revolutionary leader Adamantios Korais at the beginning of the Greek War of Independence

…I believe that no one of said aliens is an idiot, or insane person, or a pauper, or is likely to become a public charge, or is suffering from a loathsome or a dangerous contagious disease, or is a person who has been convicted of a felony or other crime or misdemeanor involving moral turpitude, or a polygamist, or an anarchist, or under promise or agreement, express or implied, to perform labor in the United States, or a prostitute…

—from the standard affidavit of the commanding officer of a ship carrying immigrants and entering the Port of New York

CONTENTS

ACKNOWLEDGEMENTS

I t's my great pleasure to thank the many individuals who have assisted me in making this history possible.

I first want to recognize the late Mary Mousalimas for the inspiration she provided to me and many others to preserve our community histories. Mary was the grand lady of Greek-American history for many years and a model for all, me especially. I also want to thank Steve Frangos for his early encouragement to pursue this project and for his support of non-academicians in researching and recording these local histories. I also want to give special thanks to Christine Gabrielides, whose professional and faithful translation of several hundred pages of documents in the original Greek allowed significant portions of this history to be told through the voices of the individuals whose lives were central to this history.

Several individuals within the Atlanta Greek community provided help to me in many ways. The late Mary Farmakis, one of the community's centenarians, met with me on several occasions to provide information on these early years and about her father, Gerasimos Algers, one of the preeminent leaders of the Atlanta Greek community. Some of the oldest photographs used in this book were given by her to the church archives. Many of the photographs in this book are provided courtesy of the Greek Orthodox Cathedral of Atlanta. Nick V. Economy has collected over many years almost all of these photographs in the church archives from which this book's selections were made. Chris Savas graciously offered his professional expertise in cleaning up for publication several of the old photographs. Tassie

Portulas, Themis Cramer, Cleo Janoulis Edwards, Rose Barton and Penny Paris assisted in identifying numerous individuals in the photographs. Vickie Klemis, Zoe Pamfilis, Mary Ann Hiett, Andrea Camp and Harriet Chaknis all helped locate a wonderful photograph of their father/grandfather, a volunteer in the Balkan Wars. Helen Pantelis provided information regarding several of the early Brown men in the community. David Goumenis made available for my research several important documents and books from the collection of his father, the late Father Homer P. Goumenis, the long-serving dean of the Atlanta Annunciation Cathedral. Special thanks go also to Father Paul Kaplanis, Father Christos Mars, Elias Lampropoulos and His Eminence Metropolitan Alexios for help in securing many pages of important files from the archives of the Archdiocese of Greece in Athens. Metropolitan Alexios was able to get from the Greek archdiocese within ten days documents that I had unsuccessfully sought on my own for almost a year. Panos Constantinides offered his legal skills in reviewing and interpreting archival documents and acquiring property transfer information involving the early church. Maria Mandekos Sharp provided original nineteenth-century Greek census information otherwise unavailable to me.

Father Nephon Tsimalis helped in my research of the archives of the Ecumenical Patriarchate at the Phanar in Istanbul and in obtaining photographs of Patriarch Joachim III.

Bill Samonides, a professional historian and scholar who has undertaken important research on the early Greek Orthodox priests in America, graciously made available his work that was important in providing biographical information on the Atlanta priests. Nikie Calles, director of archives for the Greek Orthodox archdiocese of the United States in New York, provided both photographs of the early Atlanta priests as well as some of their original autobiographical information.

Critical information about the early Atlanta priests was given by several sources, including their descendants. I want to thank my *symbetheri*, Tony and Irene Diamond, for putting me in touch with Helen Tsintolas and Malcolm and Daphne Ross in Washington, D.C. Helen is one of the unofficial historians of the St. Sophia Greek Orthodox community, where Father Basil Lambrides served for many years after leaving Atlanta, and she shared with me much information about him. Daphne Ross is Father Lambrides' granddaughter and likewise provided much information and several photographs. Aleck Janoulis, the grandson of Father Demetrios Petrides, was very generous with his time in meeting with me and answering numerous questions and in providing photographs. Likewise, Nick Demetry, the grandson of Father Constas Hadjidemetriou, gave me extensive information about Father Constas and his family and provided the photograph of them used in this book.

I visited the Atlanta History Center on numerous occasions and spent scores of hours conducting research there. Throughout these visits and unending requests, I received patient and knowledgeable assistance from the center archivists, Sue VerHoef and Melanie Stephan. Andy DeLoach and Jada Harris were kind in granting me permission to use six of the photographs from the center's archives in this book. Likewise, Steve Engerrand and Gail Miller DeLoach allowed me to publish a photograph from the collection of the Georgia Archives. Both Cynthia Wells and Janel Woods in the office of the Clerk in Fulton County Superior Court were indispensable in locating and making available to me one-hundred-year-old records of the church and other Greek community organizations. Lynette J. Stoudt, the research center director for the Georgia Historical Society, made research material available to me online for my review. I want to thank Toni Hetzel, Emmanuel Petkas and Monica Matthews for their assistance in identifying potential publishers.

Many thanks are owed to my editors at The History Press: Ryan Finn, Alyssa Pierce and Chad Rhoad. They have been patient, encouraging and supportive. I appreciate all of their assistance in getting this history published. I also want to recognize Kyle Kessler. His invaluable research and expertise in the early history of downtown Atlanta made possible the identification of the correct Whitehall Street address of the commercial space first used by the community for its church services.

I want to give special thanks to my wife, Valine Chaknis Georgeson, an Atlanta native whose family has roots in the Atlanta Greek community reaching back to its earliest days. She has guided me through the thicket of the interrelated Atlanta Greek families, provided suggestions for interview sources, identified several helpful published sources that are part of the bibliography of this book and shared with me her professional knowledge of the publishing world. Her encouragement for me throughout this process was always appreciated, if never adequately acknowledged.

Anna Comnena, in writing *The Alexiad*, an account of the reign of her father, the Byzantine emperor Alexios I, famously described the writing of history as "a great bulwark against the stream of Time" that "checks this irresistible flood" and "holds in a tight grasp whatever it can seize floating on the surface and will not allow it to slip away into the depths of Oblivion." To the extent that the much more modest history that follows achieves this purpose, profound thanks are owed to the clergy and parishioners of the

Greek Orthodox Church of Atlanta, who for more than one hundred years have carefully preserved all of the original records of the church community. As early as 1917, the Church Council recognized the importance of "preserving these records which will be handed down from one Council to the next." Thankfully, these records have been carefully handed down to us. This history could not have been written without access to them, which the early community's care has allowed later generations to enjoy.

NOTES ON NAMES
AND SOURCES

The only consistency regarding the surnames of these first Greek immigrants is inconsistency. The immigrant would typically maintain his Greek surname, written in the Greek language, within the community of his family and compatriots. Some would also adopt on occasion an English transliteration of this name for use in a broader community setting. Others would abandon this effort altogether and simply adopt more typical American-sounding names as their official surnames, in addition to continuing to use their original Greek surnames within their family or church communities. The 1910 federal census lists nineteen Greek immigrants who had adopted "Brown" as a surname. Many would simultaneously use different English versions of their names, depending on the situation. Vasileios Efthimiou, one of the early leaders of the Greek immigrants, assumed "E. Basil" as the name by which he presented himself to the broader Atlanta community.

Contrary to popular misconception, surnames were not changed by officials upon the immigrant's entry into the country at Ellis Island or other ports. The surnames of arriving immigrants were recorded by officials just as they had been entered on the manifests prepared by the shipping lines. The image of non-comprehending immigration officials arbitrarily assigning American surnames to arriving immigrants is unfounded. The overwhelming majority of later surname changes were the result of voluntary actions by the immigrants.

Compounding the confusion created by the immigrant's own use of different variations of his surname were the multiple spellings provided in the original sources, especially in the newspapers. It is common to see an immigrant's name spelled in two or even three different manners within the same article.

For the purpose of this history, I have chosen to use the surname, and surname spelling, by which the immigrant is most frequently known in the sources. To do otherwise is to risk presuming to know how that immigrant wanted be known at that time.

Regarding the use of quotations, I have chosen to reproduce all quotations exactly as provided in the original source, with no corrections for misspellings or grammatical or punctuation errors. Any misspellings, punctuation or grammatical errors in the text itself are my own.

INTRODUCTION

On December 16, 1887, the *Atlanta Constitution* published a challenge that it stated it had been "authorized" to issue to John Muhler from Greek George, the "world famous" wrestler.[1] George was demanding that Muhler, a fellow Greek professional wrestler, meet him in Atlanta for a match, with $500 or $1,000 to the winner. The *Constitution*, with the flair of a modern promoter, suggested that "if Muhler desires to accept this challenge, he will please call at the office of the *Constitution* this afternoon."[2]

Muhler accepted the challenge at the wager of $250, which was placed in the hands of the *Constitution*'s city editor. The paper predicted that an immense crowd would be present and that "the match between them will be hailed with delight by all of the lovers of scientific wrestling in the city."[3] The *Constitution* stoked the "championship" match with breathless coverage: "No sporting event has occurred in Atlanta in years so exciting as this one."[4] Greek George's arrival in the city was noted in headlines, and he was met by a crowd when he reached the city. Reportedly undefeated in more than five hundred matches, he was described as possessing superhuman strength, able to lift more than nine hundred pounds "with comparative ease" and lift two hundred pounds with one finger.[5] He was the "greatest of all wrestlers," "agile as a cat and strong as a lion."[6] George was one of the foremost of the famous wrestlers of that era and well known to fans throughout the United States.[7]

The match took place two days after Christmas in the packed Concordia Hall.[8] Present were Mayor John Tyler Cooper, publisher Henry Grady and "many prominent citizens," with Mayor Cooper sitting in the front row.[9] For nearly three hours, the wrestlers grappled evenly, with neither man able to prevail decisively. The *Constitution*'s report on the match, titled "The Gritty Greeks," detailed the wrestlers' struggles through three difficult rounds: "The exertions of the men were painful to behold. They worked as if their lives depended on it."[10] Just before midnight, the match was called a draw, and both men agreed to resume the match the following week. The rematch, again attended by a large and eager crowd, was anticlimactic, with Muhler prevailing amid cries from the crowd of a "fixed" match.[11]

Greek George and John Muhler were the first Greeks whom most of these Atlantans, if not all of them, had ever seen. Their visit in Atlanta was brief—its only purpose to entertain. They would not live among the Atlantans viewing their matches and would have no reason to consider or even care about the impression they were making in the city. Nor would the Atlantans pause to judge them. But this most certainly would not be the case with their fellow Greeks arriving in the city to stay within the next two years.

These Greek immigrants cared passionately about others' perceptions of them, always quick to correct what they perceived as unfair or incorrect assessments. They felt no less strongly about their accomplishments in their earliest years in the city, even if Atlantans' publicly stated opinions of the Greeks were decidedly negative. If not exactly hostile, Atlanta's reception of the Greeks was not a welcome one. In a city and state that were aggressively seeking immigrant labor for farms and factories, the Greeks' entrepreneurial inclinations were deemed by business and political leaders to lack value. Their origins in southern Europe counted against them.

Unlike the staged nature of the wrestling matches of Muhler and Greek George, the Greek immigrants' daily struggles on the city's streets were real and the outcomes uncertain, never fixed. Many failed, or failed to adapt, and returned. The history of the Atlanta Greek immigrants is both common and distinctive, possessing the shared experiences of all immigrant groups in America yet also presenting a story that is unique to these immigrants, in this place and at that time.

Chapter 1

THE IMMIGRANT DEPARTS

"We Greeks Love and Protect Our Sisters"

The underlying reasons why young, and sometimes very young, men in the latter decades of the nineteenth century left their families in Greece for the United States were almost always based on financial concerns. The immediate cause of this financial distress at that time was the decline in the price of currants, which had been widely grown throughout Greece to satisfy the French market reeling from a widespread grapevine disease in that country.[12] As the French vineyards recovered, the price of Greek currants plummeted.

Many of these men left with the hope of returning to Greece with money earned in America. Many, however, left their homes knowing that it was unlikely they would ever see their families again. This was not the era of the Greek political émigré. Nor were these men fleeing religious persecution. These Greek immigrants came to the United States to earn the money necessary to deal with the needs of their families. They did not fit neatly into the immigrant image popularized by the Emma Lazarus poem inscribed on the Statue of Liberty. While the vast majority of them were poor, perhaps even desperately so, they could not be described as oppressed men fleeing their native land or as "huddled masses yearning to breathe free." These men had left Greece reluctantly. Many would return at some point in the next two decades to fight, and die, in Greece's various wars. Kinship and village ties to the *patrida* would be maintained. Most had some hope of returning to visit

Greece one day. James Cotsovos in 1911 used the "fortune won in America" since his immigration ten years before to return to Greece to "claim the girl he left behind": "He was returning to his native Greece for his reward after years of labor. He was returning home to a reunion with his family and to claim the girl he had left behind ten years ago."[13]

In many cases, they were saving to provide dowries for their sisters. In an era when large Greek families of five to ten children were the norm, providing dowries for multiple daughters was a major challenge that many fathers and brothers could not meet. Dio Adallis probably spoke for many of these immigrants when he said:

> *This…shows how we Greeks love and protect our sisters, how we work hard and save up to make them happy, and see them contracting happy marriages. We consider it a sin to remain indifferent when the welfare of our sisters is concerned; taking great delight in sacrificing our interests and comforts to make them happy; and it is not a secret that most of us left home and hearth in order to provide for them.*[14]

Between 1891 and 1900, 15,979 Greek immigrants came to the United States.[15] Only a small number of these immigrants would come to the South. Less than 7 percent of Greek immigrants arriving in the United States before 1920 settled in the states of the old Confederacy.[16]

The formation of the community, or *kinotis*, was the initial form of organization of most Greek immigrants. Staying close to your kind is a protective impulse as old as the earliest human migrations. Although assimilating and becoming "good Americans" was as important to these Greeks as it was to immigrants who had preceded and would follow them, maintaining their cultural identity was no less valued. The Atlanta Greeks sought to maintain this identity in the establishment of a Greek Orthodox church and in the organization of village societies. As soon as it was practicable, the main purpose of every Greek *kinotis* became the establishment of a church.[17]

Greeks since antiquity have maintained a strong attachment to place of origin. The mountain and island landscape of Greece creates isolation for most communities, and such isolation has promoted the attachment to one's native place. This attachment was manifested by these early immigrants in the creation of *topika somatia*, or village societies. These societies allowed the immigrants to maintain ties to their village homes in Greece and to preserve dance, musical and religious customs unique to their regions. This, in turn,

Greek emigrants in Patras, Greece, embarking in a small boat for steamers to America, circa 1910. *Courtesy of Library of Congress, Prints and Photographs Division.*

led not only to family kinship clusters in immigration settlement patterns but also to village or island clusters in individual cities.

When Constantine Athanasopoulos, an Atlanta resident and United States citizen, returned to Argos in 1906 to visit his family, he brought back with him to Atlanta five natives of that Greek village, including his brother.[18] As a result of repeated actions of this type, most of the earliest Greek immigrants to Atlanta came from villages in the Peloponnesos, with the largest percentage originating from Argos and Koutsopodi. In the first decade of Greek immigration to Atlanta, more than half of the

Greeks in the city were natives of Argos and the surrounding villages. When the Church Council in 1916 formally recognized a group of donors for church donations, five of the seven donors recognized were from Argos.[19] Even in 1920, after thirty years of Greek immigration, men from Argos and its villages still represented more than one-third of the Greek males in the city.[20]

These Greek immigrants in Atlanta largely settled into well-defined neighborhoods in the downtown area, around Central and Georgia Avenues as well as Pryor, Garnett, Formwalt and Richardson Streets. The concentration of Greeks in these neighborhoods was small compared to that in the country's larger cities and did not lend itself to becoming a well-known, ethnically identifiable neighborhood. There was nothing in the city like the Greek Town of Chicago or Little Italy in New York. Nevertheless, the number was sufficiently large that one former resident of the neighborhood, Cleo Janoulis Edwards, a daughter of two immigrants, described the area as a "Greek village in the city."[21]

We know neither who arrived in the city as the first Greek immigrant nor the exact date of that arrival. The headstone of Angel Sallas in Greenwood Cemetery describes him as "Atlanta's second Greek citizen." Some of Alexander Carolee's contemporaries considered him to be the first Greek immigrant in Atlanta. But Carolee emigrated from Greece in 1893, almost four years after the confirmed presence of Greeks in the city. Charles Brown, a Greek fruit dealer, was operating a fruit stand by August 1889. No earlier published report of Greek settlement in the city is found.[22]

According to the 1896 local census for Atlanta, there were thirty-four Greek immigrants residing in the city, four of whom were women. With the exception of Charles Brown, a review of the 1890 local census does not list any of the other thirty-three Greeks. However, usage of surname variations by these early immigrants was not uncommon. So it cannot be stated conclusively that the inability to match names between these two census listings proves that there were no other immigrants in the city as early as 1890. Nonetheless, it appears likely that most of the earliest Greek immigrants began arriving in Atlanta some time in 1890–91.

Only a small number of Greeks immigrated to the city during the last few years of the nineteenth century. In 1900, the federal census showed forty-three Greek immigrants residing in Atlanta, two of whom were women. Five of the men were married, four of them to American women. The large majority of the men were young. Thirty-five of them listed their occupations as fruit dealers or grocers.

What had been a slow trickle of Greek immigration to the city prior to 1900 became a relative surge after the turn of the century into what was still a small city in the Deep South. By 1906, there were more than two hundred Greek men in the city.[23] However, the number of Greek women remained small. Even as late as 1910, more than twenty years after the first Greek immigrants began arriving in the city, there were only twenty Greek women in a Greek community that then numbered almost four hundred people.[24]

The men spent most of their time working. With very few of them married, they would have socialized primarily with one another. As they acquired their own cafés and restaurants, the socializing would take place in one another's businesses, passing the time conversing and playing tavli, a very popular board game similar to backgammon.

Almost all of these immigrants lived on or near the streets where they peddled their fruits in downtown Atlanta. They shared these neighborhoods with blacks, Jews and other immigrants. By the middle of the first decade of the new century, upper-class whites had begun moving to Peachtree Street and to the planned developments at Inman Park and Ansley Park, several miles away from the downtown neighborhoods.

Many of the men joined American fraternal associations such as the Freemasons and the Odd Fellows. But most of the socializing of these immigrants at this time was with one another. The Grecian Club was founded in 1909 primarily as a social club, and an Atlanta chapter of the Pan-Hellenic Union was also established. While not a local organization, having been founded in New York in 1907 to foster Greek patriotism, the Pan-Hellenic Union became a centralizing force in the immigrant community. It would reach its peak of activism with the start of the Balkan Wars in 1912, when it worked to recruit men and raise funds for Greece's war efforts.[25] By 1915, the Union was riven by internal disputes at the national level that would affect many local chapters, including that in Atlanta, which was dissolved by November of that year.[26]

Apart from the church (and its predecessor organization), however, the most important association established by these early Greek immigrants, in 1908, was the *Panargiakos* Society *Danaos*. Founded by immigrants from Argos, in the Peloponnesos, *Danaos* became the main social outlet for these men and, later, their wives.[27] Photographs of some of the society's picnics are among the earliest of Atlanta's Greek immigrants. Many of the community's leaders were members, including its first president, Constantine Athanasopoulos. The next of these village societies to be established was *Agia Ekaterini*, the St.

Icon, Agios Petros of Argos, patron saint of Argos, donated to the church by Athanasios Bitsaxis. *Courtesy of the Annunciation Greek Orthodox Cathedral of Atlanta.*

Members of *Danaos* celebrating at a Fourth of July picnic, 1912. *Courtesy of the Annunciation Greek Orthodox Cathedral of Atlanta.*

Katherine's Fraternity, founded in 1917 by natives of Megali Anastasova, now Nedousa, a small village in the southern Peloponnesos.[28]

These two organizations, and *Danaos* in particular, developed distinct subcultures within the Atlanta Greek community and provided social opportunities not available in the broader Atlanta community. However, these societies were not established and never served as the more common relief agencies found in other immigrant groups. Instead, both societies served a more important role for these immigrants, allowing them to maintain ties to the villages of their birth through philanthropic works. Monies raised through regular fundraisers were earmarked for various projects in both Nedousa and Argos. These villages benefited from the donations that were made toward the restoration of their respective churches, construction of roads and general assistance for the needy.[29]

These societies assumed identities separate from the church and served different purposes. Unlike more traditional immigrant aid societies, *Danaos* and *Agia Ekaterini* were primarily social organizations for the Greek immigrants sharing the same native villages. The Pan-Hellenic Union developed into the primary voice for these immigrants on issues dealing with Greece. Although representatives of *Danaos* and the Pan-Hellenic Union occasionally were invited by the Church Council to meet with the council on matters of importance, each had distinct roles within the community that were not to be encroached on by the others. Father Petrides would be cautioned by the council in 1915 about his involvement in the work of the Pan Hellenic Association and instructed "to stop speaking in favor" of the association.[30] The number of social organizations and societies would grow to such an extent by 1916 that the Church Council scheduled a dinner for all of the community's groups "in order for us to achieve perfect fraternization among all the Councils and Societies that operate within our Community."[31]

The historical record of the Greek immigrant in Atlanta provides no evidence that these men suffered from the pernicious *padrone* system that plagued their fellow Greeks, and other immigrant groups, in larger urban areas. An exploitative labor system that was an early twentieth-century version of indentured servitude, *padrones* were most common in the shoe shining business, a trade that was a very minor occupation among the Atlanta Greeks.[32] The *padrones*, all fellow Greeks, arranged for the passage of immigrants to the United States from Greece, steered these men to specific cities, established them in shoeshine parlors, demanded a percentage of their earnings and otherwise exploited them.

The fruit stand trade that sustained most of these men during the earliest years of their settlement in Atlanta was a solitary business that was not conducive to the abuses of the *padrone* system. As these Greeks in later years began operating more substantial diners and restaurants, the Greeks employed in these establishments were usually connected to the business owners through kinship or village ties, not through Greek *padrones*.

Whatever were their individual motivations for immigrating and their expectations upon arriving, these Greeks would share common experiences coming to an Atlanta that was still very much scarred by the Civil War. The business and political elite of both the city and state were composed largely of men who were Confederate army veterans and had been active participants in the war. These men were still viewed as heroes to the Atlanta natives. Their contributions to the war effort would regularly be celebrated in public ceremonies and commemorated in statues and paintings that even today bear witness to their participation.

Chapter 2

THE CONFEDERATE LEGACY

"Jefferson Davis Is Dead"

On May 1, 1886, Jefferson Davis, the former president of the Confederate States of America, attended the unveiling of a statue of Benjamin Hill at the intersection of Peachtree and West Peachtree Streets in Atlanta.[33] The old Confederate hero's arrival in the city became the occasion for a large and festive welcoming by the city's populace. Some observers estimated a crowd in excess of fifty thousand in attendance, which included "a grand gathering of veterans in Atlanta from all parts of Georgia."[34] Included among the guests were the former Confederate generals James Longstreet and John Brown Gordon, the latter of whom would soon be Georgia's governor. The reception and ceremonies were planned by the newly organized Confederate Veterans' Association of Fulton County:

> On the day of the unveiling of the statue of Mr. Hill there were thousands of people in the city, to observe the ceremonies of that occasion. School children from every school in the city, white children and colored children, were in line to strew flowers in the pathway of the old hero of the Confederacy. Portions of Pryor Street and Peachtree Street were literally covered with flowers…. Mr. President Davis was conveyed in a carriage decorated with flowers, and drawn by four white horses…. A long procession of Confederate veterans followed that carriage, marching on a pathway of flowers. The scenes and enthusiasm of that day cannot be forgotten.[35]

Confederate army veterans in a reunion parade on Marietta Street in downtown Atlanta, circa 1905. *Courtesy of Georgia Archives, Vanishing Georgia Collection, ful0006.*

When Greek immigrants began arriving in Atlanta less than three years later, only slightly more than twenty-five years separated Atlanta from its burning by General William Tecumseh Sherman in November 1864. The downtown streets and sidewalks that would become the work areas and homes for the Greeks had earlier been scenes of devastation and occupation. The destruction of the city was so complete that Sherman's chief engineer, Captain Orlando Poe, stated that "for military purposes the city of Atlanta has ceased to exist."[36] When Sherman entered the city after its surrender, he established his headquarters in the John Neal mansion at the corner of Washington and Mitchell Streets, three blocks from the street corner that would later become home to the first Greek Orthodox church in the city.[37] The capital had been moved to Atlanta from Milledgeville a few years after the end of the Civil War, in 1868. But the city did not become the permanent capital until 1877, when the move was reaffirmed by a referendum. The capitol building was not completed until 1889.

Atlanta was a city that was rapidly recovering from its destruction in the Civil War and quickly becoming a major mercantile city and the capital of the New South, as proclaimed by Henry Grady. This was just the type of city that would offer economic opportunities to newly arriving immigrants.

However, most of the downtown streets had remained unpaved until the early 1880s. While the city's leadership in 1898 was proudly boasting that Atlanta was the third-largest insurance center in the nation, after New York and Chicago, it also touted the fact that the city was home to the nation's second-largest sales and trading market for mules and horses.[38] It would not be until 1908 that Henry Ford's first Model Ts were traveling the streets.

Atlanta was a small city when these Greek immigrants began arriving. Its population in 1890 was 65,533, less than the population of both Nashville and Richmond and less than half that of Louisville.[39] Even in 1900, its population of approximately 90,000 was exceeded by that of Memphis and tripled by the city of New Orleans' 287,000.[40] About 40 percent of the metro area population was African American, a large percentage of whom had been slaves only a generation before.[41] Atlanta was a city that was strictly segregated, with numerous Jim Crow laws enforcing this separation, its black residents unable to enjoy even the lower rungs of society occupied by the newly arrived immigrants.

The Atlanta that these Greek immigrants had decided to make their home was overwhelmingly a white, Anglo Saxon–dominated city, without the large presence seen in northern cities of the century's earlier arriving Irish and German immigrants.

The dominant white culture in the city was very much a homogeneous population at this time, with a negligible immigrant population present, unlike the more culturally diverse cities outside the South. In 1896, there were only 2,214 foreign-born residents in Atlanta, about 2.7 percent of the total population; there were 620 German, 275 Irish and 38 Italian immigrants among this number.[42] Those few Irish and German immigrants who were in the city had begun arriving in Atlanta about fifty years earlier, by 1840, with the building of the railroads. Irish immigrants were being naturalized at least by 1844. The first Jewish immigrant arrived at about this time also, when the city was named Marthasville.[43]

The number of existing and newly arriving immigrants in the city was so negligible that in neither its 1898 nor 1904 comprehensive city handbooks was there any mention of the growing immigrant presence in the city. The predominance of the Protestant faith at this time was overwhelming.[44] Out of the 112 white and black places of worship in

Governor John Brown Gordon, circa 1890. *Courtesy of Kenan Research Center at the Atlanta History Center.*

1898, 108 were Protestant churches. There were three Roman Catholic churches and one Jewish synagogue.

The Greek immigrants coming to Atlanta were settling in a city and state still strongly tethered to the recent Confederate past. More than forty-seven thousand Confederate army veterans were living in Georgia in 1890, which exceeded the population of every city in the state except that of Atlanta.[45] Former Confederate army officers occupied the highest elective offices in the state and city when these first Greek immigrants began arriving. Georgia's governor in 1890, John Brown Gordon, had been one of Robert E. Lee's most accomplished and renowned generals during the Civil War. He led troops in both the Battle of Antietam and the Battle of Gettysburg. After the war ended, Gordon actively worked to oppose Reconstruction. He was also widely considered at the time to be the head of the Ku Klux Klan in Georgia, although he denied this in testimony before Congress in 1871.

In 1889, Brown became the first commander in chief of the United Confederate Veterans when the organization was formed that year in New Orleans, and he remained in that position until his death in 1904. In that same year, he also helped found the Confederate Survivors' Association, a statewide organization for Georgia Confederate veterans established in Atlanta.[46] Gordon also served as the first commander of this association. Upon the death of Jefferson Davis in December 1889, Gordon, as governor, issued a proclamation in honor of the South's former president:

> *Jefferson Davis is dead! He will be buried on Wednesday, the 11th instant, at noon. The South mourns her hero. His memory will be enshrined in the hearts of her children, and the spotless record of his long and eventful career will be cherished by them to the remotest generation, as their most valued heritage and noblest inspiration. His compatriots, who loved and honored him as the vicarious sufferer for the action of his people, will confidently confide his character and career to the judgment of impartial history.[47]*

In 1893, three and a half years after his death and burial in New Orleans, the body of the old Confederate States president was removed from Metairie Cemetery in that city for the 1,200-mile trip to be reinterred in Richmond. A special funeral train and military escort carried his body. The procession would travel through several of the old Confederate state capitals, including Atlanta, where Davis's body lay in state in the capitol.

Atlanta's city government was no less connected to the Confederate legacy. Both men serving as mayors when these first Greek immigrants began arriving in Atlanta between 1889 and 1893 also had been officers in the Confederate army during the Civil War. Mayor John Thomas Glenn had been a captain and Mayor William Hemphill a colonel. Mayor Livingston Mims, the city's mayor from 1901 to 1903, had also served in the Confederate army as a major under General John Pemberton. General Pemberton's nephew, his namesake, John Pemberton, later invented Coca-Cola in Atlanta.

Thousands of these veterans still lived in the city and its surroundings. Throughout this period, the Georgia General Assembly was annually enacting legislation dealing with pensions for these veterans and their widows. In an article titled "All of Them Heroes: A Day with the Gallant Ex-Confederates at the Capitol," the *Constitution* described how scores of Confederate veterans had thronged the state capitol in 1893 to receive these pensions:

> *The old fellows were fairly bubbling over with good will toward their fellowmen at the prospect of getting in their crisp bills of currency from the big, honest fingers of Uncle Bob Hardeman, the state's treasurer. They were in good humor with the entire world, and it was exceedingly cheerful to see them, maimed and crippled for life as they were, engaging in witty speeches and laughing at the slightest little incident that arose.*[48]

In that same year, the General Assembly enacted legislation authorizing Confederate veterans fifty years of age and older to peddle merchandise anywhere in the state without a license or the payment of any fees.[49] Nine years later, in August 1902, the Confederate Soldiers Home of Georgia was completed on 120 acres of woodland three miles south of the city.[50] However, the reception of the city and the state to the Greek immigrants arriving in these years was much less generous. The state, with its ravaged economy and severe manpower shortages, was welcoming immigrants to its lands, but that welcome did not extend to these Greek immigrants. The skills and initiative they brought with them were not what was being sought.

Chapter 3

THE RECEPTION

"The Scum of Southern Europe"

After the Ottoman capture of Constantinople in 1453 and the conquest of the Byzantine Empire, a long darkness fell on the Greeks and their traditional homelands. With very few western travelers exposed to Greeks in the next two centuries, these descendants of the ancients were shrouded in mystery. The images of Greeks for educated Europeans of this time were the Pericles and Aristotle of their classical educations.

By the second half of the seventeenth century and especially throughout the mid- to late 1700s, upper-class, young European men and women began undertaking "grand tours" of Europe and its capitals. With Greece still under Ottoman occupation, few of these travelers included Greece in their itineraries. But those who did were dismayed at the conditions in which most Greeks lived as a result of three hundred years of Ottoman subjugation. The education of these young men and women had included intensive study of the classics, in particular the history and culture of Classical Greece. In their travels to Greece, they were discovering a Greek people who did not conform to the image of the ancient Hellenes responsible for the glorious Greece of their studies.

Given to recording their impressions, these young adventurers produced diaries, travelogues, letters and observations highly critical of the contemporary Greeks. The Englishman Richard Chandler, traveling to Greece in 1765, was more crestfallen than caustic in his observations after visiting Athens and meeting its people: "By following the lower occupations, they procure, not without difficulty, a pittance of profit to subsist them, to pay their tribute-money, and to purchase garments for the festivals, when they mutually vie in appearing well-clothed, their pride even exceeding their poverty."[51]

These publications became widely distributed. With so very few people actually visiting the Greek mainland, this relatively small number of written sources from these upper-class travelers, which were almost uniformly critical of the modern Greek, became the standard references for contemporary Greek life. They would shape the opinions of the educated elites of Europe and America until the Greek War of Independence beginning in 1821.

Almost fifteen years before he served as the second president of the United States, John Adams had been appointed by Congress as its envoy to the European nations. Writing from Paris in 1783 to Robert Livingston, the United States secretary of foreign affairs, Adams, an avid, lifelong student and scholar of ancient Greek culture, would nevertheless state of contemporary Greeks:

> *The Greeks of this day, although they are said to have imagination and ingenuity, are corrupted in their morals to such a degree as to be a faithless, perfidious race, destitute of courage, as well as of those principles of honor and virtue without which nations can have no confidence in one another, nor be trusted by others.*[52]

However, the start of the Greek revolution in 1821 against the Ottomans produced a transformation in the western world's perception of the Greeks. They were now perceived, especially in England and America, as a courageous people seeking to remove the shackles of their Turkish oppressors. More importantly to these other nations, the Greeks were also seeking to reclaim the heritage of their ancestors, whose democratic, artistic and cultural achievements had so inspired civilization and, in the eloquent words of Thomas Jefferson, "whose merits are still resting, as a heavy debt, on the shoulders of the living, and the future races of men."[53]

President James Monroe's remarks in his message to Congress in December 1822 were typical of the widely held attitudes of many nations' citizenry on Greece and its struggle for independence:

> *The mention of Greece fills the mind with the most exalted sentiments and arouses in our bosoms the best feelings of which our nature is*

susceptible. Superior skill and refinement in the arts, heroic gallantry in action, disinterested patriotism, enthusiastic zeal and devotion in favor of public and personal liberty are associated with our recollections of ancient Greece. That such a country should have been overwhelmed and so long hidden, as it were, from the world under a gloomy despotism has been a cause of unceasing and deep regret to generous minds for ages past. It was natural, therefore, that the reappearance of those people in their original character, contending in favor of their liberties, should produce that great excitement and sympathy in their favor which have been so signally displayed throughout the United States. A strong hope is entertained that these people will recover their independence and resume their equal station among the nations of the earth.

The American people's support for the Greeks' war of independence was widespread. The South Carolina legislature formalized its commitment in a resolution adopted in 1823 and memorialized by being entered into the record of the United States Senate:

Resolved, That the state of South Carolina regards with deep interest the noble and patriotic struggle of the modern Greeks to rescue from the foot of the infidel and the barbarian the hallowed land of Leonidas and Socrates; and would hail with pleasure the recognition, by the American Government, of the Independence of Greece.[54]

Citizen committees in support of the Greek effort were formed in New York, Boston, Philadelphia and other cities. The Philadelphia committee chartered a vessel to ship supplies of food and clothing to the Greek noncombatants.[55] From New York came a letter to Congress urging support:

In the opinion of the meeting, the independence of the Greek nation was a subject of the highest concern to the interests of the human race, and recommended itself to the approbation of every civilized people, by the most powerful considerations that could possibly be addressed, either to the judgment or to the sympathy of mankind.[56]

However, seven decades separated the onset of Greece's independence efforts so fervently supported by the American people and the Greeks' earliest arrivals in significant numbers as immigrants to the United States. Without the emotional immediacy of the Greeks' war of revolution affecting public opinion, the Greek immigrants streaming into the nation's cities, including Atlanta, in the 1890s were viewed no differently than other immigrant groups from southern and eastern Europe. But the Greeks alone among all immigrants of this era, as the ethnic inheritors of their ancestors' renown, were judged as much by who they were not as by the geographic location of their origin. They were not the ancients, and regular, unfavorable contrasts were reminders of that. The Greeks of Atlanta would need almost two decades before they began to enjoy favorable comparisons with their Classical forbears.

The reception of the city to the arrival of these immigrants from southern Europe was not a welcome one. The tone of the reception was set in large part by the daily newspapers: the morning *Atlanta Constitution*, the afternoon *Atlanta Journal* and the evening papers, the *Atlanta Georgian* and the *Atlanta Evening News*. In an era before even the widespread availability of the radio, the tremendous influence of a city's newspapers on the thoughts and actions of its readership is difficult to contemplate in today's environment, where information and a multiplicity of opinions from innumerable sources are disseminated through electronic media. The dailies of this earlier era were both important contributors to the formation of community opinion and behavior and, at the same time, reflective and representative of these common traits of the communities they served.

The impact of the daily Atlanta newspapers on forming community opinions and in inciting action cannot be overstated. In the period covered by this history, from 1890 to 1917, the constant thread and one of the dominant factors throughout this time in how the city treated "the other," whether its black residents or certain classes of less desirable immigrants, was the voice of these papers.

During this period, the two major Atlanta dailies, as well as the evening tabloids, would consistently and almost unremittingly establish a negative tone and attitude toward these southern European and Middle Eastern immigrants. While the editorial positions of the *Atlanta Constitution* and the *Atlanta Journal* on immigration during the early 1890s vacillated between moderate statements of acceptance and extreme nativist calls for resistance to certain immigrants, by the latter part of that decade, the tone had become decidedly more negative, especially for immigrants from southern and eastern Europe. These editorials reflected the national and local emotions attached to the immigration issue.

In 1894, the Immigration Restriction League was founded with the stated purpose of working "for the further judicious restriction or stricter regulation of immigration."[57] However, the overarching goal of the organization was to drastically reduce the number of immigrants from southern and eastern Europe. In 1907, Congress established a bipartisan committee known as the Dillingham Commission to review the effects of immigration. The commission would work until 1911, when it issued its final report, which included a recommendation that immigration from southern and eastern Europe be reduced.[58] Legislation would be introduced in Congress in 1918 and actively supported by the league that would reduce immigration from these areas of Europe by 70 percent. As the league would state in its analysis of the legislation, the effect of the legislation was to "discriminate in favor of immigrants from Northern and Western Europe, thus securing for this country aliens of kindred and homogeneous racial stocks."[59]

Nor was the strong bias against Greeks and other less favored European immigrants unique to Atlanta or the state. In 1907, a customer dispute in a Roanoke, Virginia restaurant owned by a Greek triggered a night of rioting by several hundred of the city's residents that resulted in the complete destruction of all the Greek-owned businesses.[60] In 1909, the killing of a policeman by a Greek immigrant in South Omaha, Nebraska, produced inflammatory stories in the local press. An unsuccessful attempt was made to lynch the Greek perpetrator. The *Omaha Daily News* wrote about the Greeks, "Their quarters have been unsanitary; they have insulted women…. Herded together in lodging houses and living cheaply, Greeks are a menace to the American laboring man—just as Japs, Italians and other similar laborers are." A mass gathering of more than nine hundred men was further inflamed by two state legislators and other speakers who addressed the crowd, "The blood of an American is on the hands of these Greeks and some method should be adopted to avenge his death and rid the city of this class of persons."[61] The inflammatory atmosphere led to a savage riot in the Greek town area of the city. A mob estimated by the *New York Times* as three thousand strong rampaged through Greek town, beating Greek immigrants, looting homes and businesses and burning buildings.[62] One child was killed, and the area was destroyed. After receiving threats to leave the city, the entire Greek population fled South Omaha within a few days of the riot.

This ongoing public discussion of the immigration issue in Atlanta and throughout the state was not occurring in a vacuum. It was being driven by two factors. First, even though the number of immigrants coming to the South was a trickle compared to the numbers being received in other sections of the country, the South was also a participant in the national dialogue generated by the immigration legislation regularly being considered at this time by Congress. The attitudes of Atlantans and Georgians toward immigrants, especially those not from northern Europe, were generally in line with the prevailing views across the country.

The other, and predominant, factor, however, for this continued local debate on the issue was the severe labor shortage plaguing the South. The Civil War had devastated the South's economy. Even two generations after the end of the war, the lack of men to work the region's mills, farms and plants was acute. In losing the war, the South had lost its utilization of its enslaved blacks, who had for generations provided an extremely low-cost labor source that served to enrich thousands of southerners. In waging the war, the South had lost many thousands of its working-class white men, the vast majority of whom had constituted the labor force before the war for their own subsistence farming and for mills and manufacturing facilities. More than 300,000 Confederate soldiers were killed and approximately that same number wounded. The South had lost about one-fourth of its white male population between the ages of twenty and forty to death and disability.

These effects were felt immediately, and government and business leaders throughout the South soon recognized the pressing need not just for increased manpower but also for men with ready cash to purchase the only asset most Georgians possessed that retained any value: their homes and farms. The solution for both the labor and cash shortages was the stream of European immigrants already arriving in the country, but they were destined largely for the major urban areas of the Northeast and Midwest. Prior to the war, the South had little or no need for immigrant labor. Northern cities depended on these immigrants to supply their industrialized workforces, but the South, with its enslaved black population, simply had no motivation to attract foreign workers. As Georgia's agriculture commissioner, Thomas Janes, explained a decade after the end of the war:

> *Peaceful and prosperous until the late civil war consumed her wealth and drenched the land with the blood of her people; with labor abundant, its natural increase unexampled, and its rewards satisfactory, Georgia had no motive to seek immigration from foreign lands.... But the result of the late, long and disastrous war have sadly changed this happy aspect of affairs.*[63]

The devastation wrought by the war on the state's economy produced a fundamental change in the South's attitudes toward immigrants. The war had, as Janes noted, "resulted in the freedom of the negro race and in an entire change in our system of labor," with the result being that "agriculture has not proved profitable under the new system of free black labor."[64] For Janes, as for business and government leaders throughout the region, immigration was the only solution to their problems.

Just little more than one year after the end of the Civil War, the Georgia General Assembly, in December 1866, adopted its first legislation intended to deal with the state's ravaged economy. Owing to "the devastation caused by our late conflict of arms, and the emancipation of our slaves," and recognizing that "the majority of our people are left in destitute circumstances," the legislature's enactment declared its purpose to "facilitate the sale of real estate and to encourage immigration."[65] Three years later, in 1869, the General Assembly adopted legislation creating two new immigration commissionerships, one a domestic commissioner of immigration and the other a foreign commissioner of immigration. The charge to the foreign commissioner was clear and specific: "The Foreign Commissioner shall cooperate with the Domestic Commissioner in encouraging and facilitating immigration into the State, and the sale of lands to immigrants; and, to this end, shall visit Europe and remain there for the period hereinafter designated [one to two years]."[66]

With these commissioners apparently not producing the desired inflow of immigrants, the state legislature almost annually over the next decade passed legislation attempting to increase immigration. In 1871, it established the Southern Immigration and Land Company, with the objective of "procuring and assisting emigrants from foreign countries to settle in the State of Georgia and other Southern States, and to make the wild lands of said States valuable and productive."[67] Then, one year later, it created the European-American Transportation Company for the purpose of maintaining shipping lines to facilitate the immigration of European workers to Georgia.[68]

Despite persistent attempts, the individual efforts of Georgia and the other southern states remained unsuccessful. The region's business and government leaders soon realized that these individual state immigration initiatives should be combined. As early as the meeting of the Southern Immigration Convention in Jackson, Mississippi, in 1868, the southern states began convening immigration conventions for the purpose of developing a coordinated policy for attracting both domestic and foreign immigrants into their borders. But it was not until the organization of the Southern Immigration Association in 1883 that the region's joint efforts came together. Typical of these gatherings designed to redirect the flow of immigrants southward were the meetings of the association in Louisville in 1883 and in Nashville the following year. Attended by representatives from the southern states, the meetings initially were focused on attracting residents from other states to the South, developing, as it was described, "a system, by which will occur the diffusion of the populations of the North and West."[69] The *Constitution* urged the attendees at the Nashville convention to be "bold and practical" in seeking both European and domestic immigrants.[70]

However, notwithstanding the early discussion that centered on domestic immigrants, there was also at these gatherings an expressed realization of the special importance of foreign immigration as a solution to the region's manpower shortage. Among the objectives of the association was the goal of selecting a southern port or ports of entry for the foreign immigrants.[71] Castle Garden in New York Harbor served as the nation's first immigrant processing center, before the opening of Ellis Island in 1892. Southern port cites from Norfolk to Galveston were vying to become the southern version of the New York City center. Delegations from the Georgia cities of Savannah and Brunswick attended the convention in Nashville, openly competing for selection as an immigration center.

Not content to let statewide businessmen take the lead on the immigration issue, municipal leaders from more than thirty major southern cities organized themselves into yet another association, with the goal of increasing foreign immigrants to their cities. Founded in Chattanooga in 1887, the Southern Society of Immigration and Development focused its efforts on convincing the major railroad lines to lower their ticket prices for immigrants coming to the South.[72] Representatives of the society met throughout 1888 with members of various passenger tariff associations in Atlanta, Chicago and New Orleans for this purpose. Chosen to lead the new organization was John Temple Graves, then the editor of the *Rome Tribune*. Graves would later play key roles both in the heated immigration debates in Atlanta and in the events leading up to the 1906 Atlanta race riot.

At its meeting in Montgomery, Alabama, in 1888, the Southern Immigration Association, rechristened as the Southern Interstate Immigration Convention, unambiguously laid bare the states' desperation for immigrants. Reverend M.B. Wharton expressed the desires of all the attendees in his opening prayer to the assembled representatives:

Much of our territory is untenanted and undeveloped. The plow stands still in the field of promise, and briars cumber the garden of beauty. We beseech Thee to send us immigration. Wilt Thou who didst conduct the children of Israel from the taskmasters of Egypt to the land flowing with milk and honey, conduct those who are exposed to the chilling and killing winds of frozen regions to this favored land where summer sings and never dies.[73]

While these early calls for further foreign immigration were devoid of the overt discussion of "desirable" and "undesirable" immigrants that would come to dominate the later public dialogue, it was unmistakable that immigrant farm workers were being sought. As the secretary of the Texas Bureau of Immigration told the delegates to the 1888 convention, "We want good, worthy Immigrants to people our lands and reap the harvests."[74] Four years earlier, Tennessee governor William Bate told those assembled in Nashville that "the man with the pick and those with the saw and hammer were cordially invited to come among us and aid us in developing our vast resources."[75] Although the open denigration of southern European immigrants would not be expressed until the next two decades, these early conventions would already reveal the region's preference for the Irish ("born to the pick, the shovel and the spade"), the Germans ("intelligent farmers") and Scandinavians ("born farmers— farmers from instinct").[76] In his opening remarks to the Montgomery convention, the presiding chairman, Colonel John Roquemore, welcomed this type of immigrant to the South:

> *The movement of men from one place to another, singly and in families, in tribes and in communities, is now recognized as an orderly and constant impulse of the human family, one of the laws of nature…. The movement of emigration is now so well defined and regular, so spontaneous and functional, so independent of the influences of sudden commotion, that it must be regarded as a necessary condition of human advancement—a process of evolution…. The man seeking a home in the South…must be kindly met, and entertained with friendly regard.[77]*

With the impetus provided by the work of the association, the states renewed their own local initiatives for attracting immigrants. The earlier efforts were focused more on immigration of men from the northern states. But the North's own labor shortages caused by the war and the South's lingering resentment toward northerners would soon lead the South's leaders to conclude that foreign immigration provided the only realistic solution to its problems. The legislatures of every state in the region began enacting legislation promoting foreign immigration.

Georgia was one of the most aggressive southern states to act, adopting in 1883 legislation creating the Georgia Investment and Banking Company. Incidental to its main purposes, the corporation was granted by its enabling legislation "the right to establish and maintain bureaus of immigration, and to promote and assist immigration and to colonize and develop any lands, whether belonging to this company or not."[78]

By 1888, the state was publishing the *Southern Empire*, an immigration-themed paper distributed throughout the North.[79] In that same year, Governor Gordon responded positively to the call of the Montgomery convention by promising "to cooperate in any way I can to accomplish the great purposes you have in view."[80] Georgia's counties, under the direction of the state immigration bureau, were publishing guides and handbooks for prospective employers and immigrant workers, promoting their respective virtues. Proclaiming that "our doors are open," Talbot County "proposed to be liberal, and to invite those contemplating a change of residence to come and share with us this fair and prolific domain."[81] In its *Guide to Immigration* published in 1895, Putnam County announced that it was looking for "the immigration of a kindred people" to help in its agricultural development.[82] The county even enlisted the involvement of Putnam County native Joel Chandler Harris, who penned an "Uncle Remus" vignette touting the county's advantages in the *Guide*.[83]

In 1890, the Georgia General Assembly incorporated the South Atlantic Trade and Navigation Company primarily for the purpose of developing increased trade with other states and foreign nations.[84] But the corporation was also specifically empowered "to establish and maintain immigration depots and agencies." Three years later, expressing its interest in securing "choice immigration," the General Assembly took a more aggressive posture in adopting legislation authorizing the governor to appoint an honorary commissioner of direct trade and immigration.[85] The legislature would act even more forcefully the next year with its creation of the bureau of immigration. The bureau considered that "[i]ts purpose will be to disseminate throughout this country, and throughout Europe, reliable intelligence concerning the natural resources of the State."[86]

Under the act, the agriculture commissioner was designated as the ex-officio commissioner of immigration.[87] Among the commissioner's responsibilities was his duty to "correspond with all bureaus, societies, corporations and organizations having for their purposes the development of this State and of the Southern States of these United States, the bringing of capital, home seekers and acceptable immigrants to this and to the said Southern States."

In 1895, Governor William Northen, having just completed his term in office, assumed the leadership of the immigration bureau and would hold this position for several years.[88] He pledged that "the Bureau…will leave nothing undone to bring into the State thousands of immigrants," "people to occupy and till" the lands, without regard to their origin. But the bureau was focused primarily, although not exclusively, on attracting domestic settlers from non-southern states. Northen established contact with prospective settlers from several eastern and midwestern states, with very little success.

With these accumulating official actions, Georgia was now formally welcoming immigrants to the state. These intensified efforts by Georgia and the other southern states inevitably would generate questions from many quarters as to which immigrants were being welcomed. The *Atlanta Constitution* was among the first of the voices heard in the state attempting to answer these questions. Although the paper would later become an advocate for limited immigration from particular European nations, in the last decade of the nineteenth century its opinion was generally negative on the matter: "Society must protect itself from these vicious victims of European tyranny. They represent a class which the wonderful assimilating qualities of our native population can neither redeem nor remodel."[89]

In a nation, and especially in a South, that was still overwhelmingly Protestant, these new waves of arriving immigrants from predominantly Catholic and Orthodox Christian European nations appeared threatening. In 1887, a group of American Protestants formed the American Protective Association, an anti-Catholic and anti-papist secret society. Members pledged in their initiation oaths to use their "utmost power to strike the shackles and chains of blind obedience to the Roman Catholic Church from the hampered and bound consciences of a priest-ridden and church-oppressed people."[90] The association counted members throughout the nation and became active in political races in many states, successful in both electing favored candidates and defeating those considered to be under the control of the Catholic Church. In 1895, the association staged an anti-papist demonstration in Atlanta. In the following year, the organization elected an Atlantan as its president, and the local chapter sponsored a slate of candidates in the city's municipal elections.[91]

As Congress in 1897 was considering legislation that would establish additional educational qualifications for those seeking to enter the United States, the *Constitution* became more specific about those it considered to be desirable immigrants:

Desirable immigrants, those who are industrious and intelligent, will always be welcomed; they will make good citizens. But the pauper and ignorant classes, who have no appreciation of our form of government must not come to be a burden upon the industrious and a menace to American institutions.[92]

Later that year, the paper would comment favorably on the recent decline in immigration to the United States:

There is still room for improvement, however, as the country is not yet free from the contaminating influences of European pauperism and illiteracy.[93]

We are anxious to have foreigners come among us; the better class of immigrants make law-abiding, industrious and patriotic citizens; but we do not want the scum and off-scourings of Europe. If the hard times of the past few years have had a tendency to discourage this element from seeking our shores, they have certainly rendered the country a great service.[94]

The paper would later despair of "the tidal waves of European immigration almost daily washing up on our shores…. Soon we may have schools for Frenchmen, schools for Italians, Polack schools, Russian and Greek schools. But the problem of what may come is too much for us. We give it up!"[95]

By 1900, former governor Northen's views on immigration had also been transformed. Once fully supportive of at least domestic immigration into the state, Northen spoke as a nativist in an address to an audience of young Baptist conventioneers in Hot Springs, Arkansas:

Another class problem you are to meet…is found in foreign immigration. These people, with their destructive ideas of government, order and law, are here nineteen million strong. We have only to read the record of the daily press to see the danger that has arisen against the security of the nation…. The rapid increase of this population is alarming.[96]

The community's exclusionary standards for immigrants at this point, expressed through the editorial voice of its leading daily newspapers, were still general. Only the poor and the illiterate were unwelcome. Finer distinctions regarding the types of immigrants desired were not yet being made by the leading voices in Atlanta. However, this would soon change, as not only the papers but also business and government leaders would begin expressing very clearly that Greeks, Italians and others generally grouped together as southern Europeans were not wanted.

Even before becoming the object of public condemnation as part of the immigration debate, these Greeks and Italians had been regularly subjected to disparagement in their daily encounters with the broader Atlanta community. "Dago" was a common and frequent description for these men by the press, police, court officials and fellow Atlantans. In an encounter with a Greek fruit peddler, Atlanta patrolman Borne was quoted as saying, "I told that dago three times that he must not stop [his fruit wagon] too long in one place."[97]

The papers' negative depictions of southern Europeans escalated in a 1902 column that was published by both the *Constitution* and another daily, the *Sunny South*.[98] The papers had now gone far beyond simply classifying immigrants as either "better" or "lesser" depending largely on their education or financial resources. Now certain immigrants were deemed inherently undesirable and unredeemable based solely on their ethnicity. This column decried the type of immigrants now coming to the United States and made clear that there were several categories of immigrants that were not at all welcome or desirable:

> *In fact there has been a great change in the character of the foreigners who come here in search of fortune. In place of the hearty Irishman…the sturdy German…and the fair-haired Scandinavian, hard working, frugal and a genuine acquisition, we have now an excess of Poles and Slovaks from Austria and Russia, and Italians.*
>
> *It is hardly necessary to say that there is no comparison between the German and Irish immigrant of other years and the Polish, Slovak and Italian immigrants of the present. In physical appearance and vigor the men and women from Northern Europe outmatch the others almost two to one.*

The author complained that the immigrants of "these classes"—the Poles, Slovaks, Italians and Greeks—were only here temporarily, not intending to stay, but merely "draining the country annually of dollars by the millions" that would be taken back to "spend…on their native soil." However, the author reserved his most withering criticism for the Greek and Middle Eastern immigrants:

> *However undesirable from the standpoint of citizenship the Italian, the Slav or the Pole may be, because he doesn't intend to remain in this country, there are two other classes of immigrants now coming here who are undesirable*

because they are nonproductive almost to a man. These are the Assyrian and the Greeks. Men of both of these nationalities prefer commercial life to productive toil. They come here with enough money to insure landing almost invariably, but few of them have trades and they go to peddling or become petty merchants of some sort. The Greeks are almost all fruit dealers, while the Assyrians sell Oriental fabrics.

He went on to describe these immigrants as "non-producing" and "singularly non-progressive." In one final denunciation focusing again on the racial differences:

It goes without saying that the immigrants to be seen in a body at the immigrant station today are by no means equal in appearance to those who were to be seen there daily a decade or two ago. Still there is occasionally a well built, deep chested male specimen, and here and there a woman's face is shown that makes the observer think of a bloom rose or a graceful lily in a garden overgrown with weeds.

The sentiment of this statement was underscored by an accompanying photograph of a young female immigrant from Finland captioned, "A Finnish Bloom."

But the ongoing efforts by Georgia's business and government leaders to use immigration as a tool with which to fix the acute labor shortage in the state would expose much more virulent feelings about these southern Europeans than the casual and frequent use of the "dago" epithet indicated. By 1902, Georgia businessmen were trying to revive the efforts of the 1890s regarding the establishment of an organization that would work to attract the right type of immigrant to the state. What they were looking for specifically were those immigrants who could provide economic value to the operation of their farms, mills and plants: "We at the south have not been sufficiently alive to the fact that the immigrant may have a value outside of the money in his pocket…. We need the immigrant here, especially on our farms, to help us develop our wonderful resources along this line."[99]

The state's business leaders were looking for fruit pickers, not fruit sellers. Those immigrants who worked the farms in the South were welcomed. The Italians and the Greeks, present in the city for more than a decade, were not. The entrepreneurial skills they possessed, which guided them to large urban areas like Atlanta, were not valued by these businessmen. The business interests in the state objected to those types of immigrants such as Jews, Greeks and Middle Easterners who pursued more entrepreneurial vocations, such as dry goods merchants, fruit dealers and rug sellers. These men were looking for immigrants who would fill the labor needs of the farms, railroads and timber operations that would continue to provide profits for them. Those immigrants from southern and eastern Europe generally more inclined to entrepreneurial occupations were not what these men needed or wanted.

In October 1905, Louis Magid, a successful businessman who had developed one of the nation's largest commercial apple orchards in north Georgia, urged the convening of a congress in Atlanta for the purpose of creating an immigration commission. He stated the case for the need to access the relatively cheap source of labor that the immigrants represented.[100] Under his plan, the commission would employ agents to travel to the main ports of entry for immigrants and seek to attract them to Georgia. There was a recognition that these immigrants might serve as a relatively cheap labor pool to substitute for the almost negligible costs of the lost slave labor system. These agents would be charged with finding "the right kind of people."[101]

Another convocation of southern businessmen in Washington, D.C., to study the south's labor shortage provided the final impetus to the reinvigorated immigration effort in Georgia.[102] Other southern states were likewise considering immigration as a solution to the labor shortage, with the South Carolina legislature establishing a state bureau of immigration and Florida considering one.[103] The conferees were urged to take action in their states: "The developers, business men and farmers who so keenly feel the need of additional labor, should exert themselves in every way that promises results."[104]

As Georgia's business leaders were working to reinvigorate their decade-long attempt to organize an association, other southern states were doing the same and committing prominent men to the cause. The president of the Southern Immigration Association in 1907 was the former South Carolina governor, Duncan Heyward.[105] The Georgia efforts were significantly aided by the realization of the state's railroad lines and its newspapers that their own economic interests in the immigration issue were aligned with those of the state's major businesses, some of which were their most dependable customers and advertisers. The railroads would be transporting the anticipated thousands of newly arriving immigrants throughout the state, and the papers would be expected to communicate to the world the state's need for this immigrant labor.[106] The *Atlanta Constitution*, in particular, would quickly become advocate, spokesman and full participant. But success would require more publicity than even the big-city dailies could provide. The South's business leaders would need to reach a broader audience across the nation, and only large national newspapers and magazines could provide this access:

> *As these states and cities reach out for people and for capital they are fast coming to see that the magazines of national circulation and the newspapers are the best means of reaching the millions of people outside of the South and telling them what the South is doing and what opportunity it offers. In absolutely no other way can the South meet this pressing immigration problem so effectively or so economically as by such a broad appeal to the people of the whole country.*[107]

These businessmen were pragmatic and recognized the need to welcome immigrants to the state in order for the local economy to flourish. The labor shortages were significant.[108] The looms of some cotton mills were idle, and many mills were operating at reduced hours because of the lack of qualified loom operators. G. Gunby Jordan, president of Eagle and Phenix Mills, spoke for all industrialists when he said, "The south needs more folks. It will take immigration to make our section blossom as a rose. We want immigrants—immigrants of the right sort, of course—to build up our waste places. We need more labor for the farmers. We need more help for the mills."[109]

The most recent efforts to bring the "right sort" of immigrant to Georgia began to coalesce in May 1905 with the establishment of the Georgia Bureau of Industries and Immigration.[110] Led by Samuel Dunlap, the bureau was largely funded and otherwise supported by the railroads. The goal was clear: to attract to the state the type of immigrant who would "produce wealth" for Georgia's businesses. "Within our state there are millions of unused acres of land. What we need is the labor to till them."[111]

The prime movers behind the bureau were two railroad companies, the Atlantic Coast Line and the Louisville & Nashville Railroad. Initial goals called for locating mills and manufacturing facilities along existing railroad lines throughout the state. The railroads would then transport to these facilities immigrants "of a desirable character" to serve as the new workforce.[112]

Although this particular plan foundered, they continued to realize their goals. The organizers met in Augusta in the summer of 1906 as the reincarnated Georgia Immigration Association.[113] The meeting was attended by business leaders from throughout the state, including Atlanta, who once again committed themselves to an organization dedicated to attracting a "desirable class of immigrants."[114] They again urged the state legislature to reestablish a bureau of immigration to address their labor needs.[115]

Finally, the efforts of the previous ten years came to fruition in an October meeting of the association in Savannah and a subsequent meeting in February 1907 in Macon. These meetings were well attended by representatives from throughout the state, which included W.G. Cooper, secretary of the Atlanta Chamber of Commerce. John A. Betjeman, a native of Columbus and president of the Albany & Gulf Navigation Company, an inland shipping company, was selected as chairman of the association's executive committee. G. Gunby Jordan, elected president of the association, again persuasively stated the businessman's case for increased immigration to Georgia in a speech to the Georgia Bankers' Association in June 1907. Although the immigration association's contemporaneous comments and attitudes toward certain classes of immigrants were more negative and discriminatory, this speech was notable for its positive characterization of immigrants and its urging of a welcoming reception:

> [I]t is known and recognized that there is a peculiar psychological self-conceit upon the part of most men—who imagine that they are better than others, and that their own race and their own nation is the best in the world. It is to talk about this and to discuss this seeming misanthropy, that I have the honor of addressing you today upon the subject of "Immigration." Let us try not to despise foreigners…. Immigrants as a rule, my friends, are an enterprising people. They are people who think and plan; they are people who will toil; they are people who are willing to go away from home, to sever ties that have grown around them and move to a foreign shore. First, that they might better their own financial condition; second, that they might breathe the free air of Heaven and know what liberty is; and, third, that they might own their own home, and with it obtain and retain all the magic influences and comforts which that name ever signifies.
>
> If the nervous activity of this Nation is phenomenal, we owe much of it to the spirit of enterprise and to the brain and nervous activity of the people that Europe has sent to us in the past; for in the wise discrimination of the law of our land, we keep the desirable immigrants, and send those back to their own shores who would spread disease or otherwise infect our people. The law forbids their entering and the law is powerful, and the law is doing that today as it has in the past.[116]

Jordan also appealed to these bankers' deepest fears and prejudices by making the case for immigration as an antidote to the perceived threats of "Negro enfranchisement." In remarks that he subtitled "Population Is Power," he reminded them:

> *It is immigration that has given political power to other sections, which was even only partially and horribly offset by the enfranchisement of the negroes in the South. It is to immigration that we must look if we are to solve the race problem. Georgia should have and must have enough white people to insure just and peaceful control forever to the white man in every county and in every nook and corner of her domain. The negro is so numerous that immigration is the only means of doing this within our life time. When that condition is brought about we shall have a better country to live in, better politics, better schools, better roads and greater security in the remote agricultural districts. This will be best for the negro himself, best for the white man, and best, for Georgia's future.*[117]

Just as he had offered immigration as a counterpoint to the specter of black domination, Jordan also sought to reassure his broader audience that the immigrants to Georgia would not be classed with the "Negro" population of the state:

> *They have an idea that the negro is put on an absolute equality with every immigrant that comes, and he must work side by side with him…. Far from wishing immigrants to associate with negroes, the white people of the South discourage equality of any kind between white and colored people!*[118]

Jordan's Macon speech is noteworthy both for his openness in welcoming immigrants to Georgia and his unqualified acknowledgement that a partial source of that openness is his realization that immigration can help offset the political and social gains of the state's black population. Whatever his motivations, he concluded his remarks by challenging the audience to be "broadminded" about immigration and to "look for the best in others and give to others the best that we have."[119]

The focus of the earlier, organizational meeting in Savannah was a report by a committee that had traveled to Charleston, South Carolina, to observe the arrival of 420 immigrants from Belgium and neighboring countries. These immigrants had been brought to Charleston under the auspices of leading South Carolina businessmen to provide labor primarily in the state's cotton mills.[120] The committee commented favorably on the arriving immigrants, noting that "it was an excellent lot of people, very far above average of those who land at Ellis Island."[121]

The plan of action adopted at this meeting included a commitment to raising $50,000 from the business community to assist the state in establishing a bureau of immigration. Atlanta businesses were critical to the effort to underwrite the expenses involved in shipping the immigrants to Georgia, with almost $5,000 raised in the initial solicitation.[122] With these underwriting funds, however, would come strict control of the process by these men. Their money would be given to the state "with the understanding that the commissioner of immigration will send competent agents abroad to select from Northern Europe a good class of immigrants and bring them to Georgia."[123]

What was finally about to be realized was a new model for immigration first proposed at the meetings of the Southern Immigration Association twenty-five years earlier. The state was not interested in the masses arriving through Ellis Island, most of whom it considered undesirable. Although Betjeman and the state agriculture commissioner visited Ellis Island to review the immigrants' entry through that port, the association's stated purpose was to "bring immigrants to Georgia direct through Georgia ports."[124] Its first steps would be to send its representatives to selected European nations, identify desirable immigrants and then ship them directly to the state through the Port of Savannah.[125]

Initially, at least six immigration agents were directed to their destinations.[126] Before these agents had even left Georgia, Betjeman claimed that twenty-seven German families were en route to rural Georgia farms.[127] Unlike the earlier efforts, detailed plans were being developed to attract the type of immigrants they desired. The steamship lines were being encouraged to begin transporting these immigrants to Georgia along with imported goods. The heart of the plan, however, entailed ensuring that the shipping companies delivered these immigrants directly to the state through the Savannah port, "thereby avoiding contamination resultant upon any stay in New York city."[128] Significant effort was being made to convince steamship lines to begin these direct transits. Contact was initiated with the companies' executives, and the Georgians guaranteed to underwrite the shipping lines' expenses on those transports in which costs exceeded their revenues.[129]

Optimistic plans were made for direct shipping of immigrants from a German port to Savannah, with a scheduled departure once every three weeks. This was anticipated to begin within three months, and it was expected "that in a very short time the tide of immigration will set in to Georgia from all parts of Europe in such numbers as will make a real and practical showing in the solving of the present scarcity of labor and the development of thousands of acres of land which now lie idle and unoccupied."[130]

An intervening meeting was held in the office of the Atlanta Chamber of Commerce.[131] The agriculture commissioner, T.G. Hudson, was now serving as the ex-officio Georgia immigration commissioner, in accordance with the General Assembly's actions creating the position in 1894.[132] He reassured those gathered that he would assume full control of this immigration initiative and would direct his efforts toward immigrants from England, Scotland, Ireland, Norway, Sweden and Germany.[133] The *Constitution* urged the legislature to go further by establishing a completely autonomous Department of Immigration, independent of the agriculture department, with its own commissioner, "an official who will go after that class of immigrants that Georgia wants and needs."[134]

Shortly after the Macon convention, Betjeman presented a report on the association's activities. There were positive reports on the immigrants who had already arrived and many requests for immigrants from farmer and timber interests throughout rural Georgia.[135] The association reported that by June 1907 it had received more than seven thousand such requests.[136] It was also reported that about seventy immigrants had been brought into Georgia since the association's Macon convention less than a month before.[137] The first of the association's agents were also being sent to Europe at this time, with a group leaving soon for Sweden and Denmark, accompanied by a delegation from the agriculture department.[138] Even as the association was being formed, the Southern Development Company of Columbus, Georgia, concluded arrangements with the Southern Immigration Association to settle "thrifty Swedish and German families" on 1,365 acres in north Georgia.[139]

The targeted date for the inaugural arrival of the selected immigrants was changed again, to September 1907.[140] In the interim, the association was developing a detailed plan for the distribution of these immigrants throughout the state wherever they were being sought. County immigration associations were being formed, and tenant housing was being identified.[141] Statewide, the association was also appointing district directors in the state's Congressional districts to assist in the execution of the plans.[142] Betjeman and Governor Smith were part of a delegation that visited immigration officials in Washington for advice and then traveled to Europe for a "close investigation of the farming and laboring classes with a view to determining what inducements are necessary in order to move these people into Georgia."[143] The delegation visited Germany, Austria, Denmark, Sweden, Belgium, France, England and Scotland. A formal screening process was established to ensure the arrival into the state of "only such as are desirable." Betjeman cautioned against the use of New York immigration agencies, which would not "hesitate to flood the south with the riffraff from the streets and slums of New York."[144]

Five months later, in an August interview with the *Constitution*, Betjeman gave a progress report outlining further accomplishments, in particular the establishment of several communities of immigrants throughout the state. There were groups of Germans in Bremen and in Sparta; Swedes in Rome and Savannah; Swiss at Mount Airy; Austrians in Valdosta and in Pinia in rural Dooly County; Hungarians in the small, established community of Budapest; and several other communities of Germans, Scotch and Belgians.[145] A large contingent of 138 Austrians arrived in Savannah in December. All except 3 passed their health inspections and were distributed to farms in nine rural counties that had made applications for these men.[146] In February, the association announced the imminent arrival of several hundred Scottish and Swedish immigrants "to relieve the urgent demand for help."[147]

Sixty Scotchmen already en route to the state in May were openly welcomed to join the Scots immigrants who had arrived earlier: "A large number of Scotchmen…have already arrived in Georgia and have proved useful citizens from the very first. Not only have they proved entirely satisfactory to their employers as mill operators and in other positions, but many of them have gone on Georgia farms and are helping in the development of the agricultural interests and resources of the state."[148]

This welcome, and others like it for the northern Europeans, was not extended to southern Europeans and to other less favored immigrants and stood in sharp contrast to an almost contemporaneous sentiment expressed by John Betjeman about the Greeks in Atlanta. For with the reorganized immigration effort would also come the beginning of a different and sharper-edged public dialogue between these business leaders and the press regarding immigrants and a decidedly more negative opinion of the Greeks and other non-northern Europeans.

Betjeman cautioned that unless they acted to regulate the flow of immigrants into Georgia, many undesirable immigrants would continue to flock to the state:

> *Very few in the state are aware of the fact that certain people operating out of New York are systematically sending in to us Greeks, Hebrews and Italians.… How well the Greek society had done its work is fairly*

illustrated by the fact that nearly 700 Greeks now reside in Atlanta alone. A casual investigation by any one interested will disclose that fact that about one-half of the eating places in Atlanta are operated by Greeks. They are thrifty, energetic and are, perhaps, making good citizens, but WE ARE NOT DIRECTING THEIR MIGRATION TO GEORGIA.[149]

No matter their positive qualities, the Greek immigrants in Atlanta—inclined to entrepreneurial opportunities of their own and unwilling to work in factories and fields of these industrialists—were not wanted. Their skills offered no economic value to these men. The association's plan was that

the best way to aid ourselves, not merely in developing more of our property, but in sustaining that which has already been developed, is to take hold of this subject at this critical juncture and by selecting desirable people from Europe and elsewhere, bring in a great enough number to offset the influx through the organizations above referred to, and at the same time keep the power within the hands of good, industrious white citizens.[150]

These immigrants who were being settled in the state under the association's guidance well represented its ideal of "selected, able-bodied, pure-blooded, white people."[151] Betjeman left no uncertainty as to what he was looking for: "The Immigration Association is bringing in pure-blooded Celts and Teutons, whose blood flows in the veins of every pure-blooded Georgian."[152]

These organizing efforts were providing others the opportunity to comment on immigration, the most influential of which would be the editorial voices of Atlanta's dailies. In two lengthy editorials published one week apart in June 1906, the *Atlanta Georgian and News* would join the issues of race and immigration by blaming the "idleness and profligacy of the negro laborer" for the arrival of "the scum of southern Europe."[153]

Forty years after the emancipation of the slaves and the end of the Civil War, the South was still struggling to adjust to an economic model that was no longer based on enslaved labor:

Immigration looms large now upon the horizon of the south's future as one of the great problems which we must grapple and utilize to the development and prosperity of this country…

[T]he South is confronted with great and menacing scarcity of labor. In the factories, in the fields, on the farms and in domestic employment the cry goes up for more and better labor than we have today…

It is nothing less than true and honest to say that the present lack of labor is due in large part first to the idleness and profligacy of the negro laborer.... Now, to supply this need of labor caused by the defection and demoralization of the negro, the cry is going up from every section of the South for immigration, and that immigration is being sought from the countries across the sea...

Time was when most of our immigrants came to the country from England, Scotland and Ireland...

Now the sorrow of the situation is that while the influx from the wholesome, helpful and homogeneous countries is falling off it is leaping marvelously forward from the undesirable countries of Europe...

The menace in this situation lies in the fact that the class of foreigners who come to our country from these stormy, revolutionary countries of southern Europe are so full of anarchy, riot and lawlessness of the countries from which they came, that their presence becomes a menace and entails another mighty problem upon the civilization which must amalgamate and absorb into citizenship these alien and almost unassimilable races who have no conception of our government and no sympathy with our institutions, and whose creeds and records are reeking with the lawlessness which has made Chicago and Pittsburgh and other cities centers of revolution and anarchy. The amalgamation of these foreigners who represent almost the scum of southern Europe, is one of the tremendous problems of our civilization. Fortunately for us, few of them have come to the South.[154]

The editorial then called on the southern gentry to press their congressmen to restrict these types of immigrants:

Southern business men should vigorously impress upon their representatives in congress the necessity of such restriction of foreign immigration as will exclude from our shores the scum of Europe and the undesirable and lawless representatives of these southern countries...

We need such people of the better class. The negro has already drifted almost out of our industrial life. We must supply his place with that class of immigrants who will be assimilable to ourselves—Germans, Englishmen, Irishmen, Danes, Norwegians, Swedes and Frenchmen.[155]

This was the blueprint that was followed by Georgia's business leaders in the formation of the immigration association. They recognized the need for a continuing influx of immigrants to supply their factories and farms but welcomed only those immigrants predisposed to this type of work. For some, their negative opinions of these southern Europeans, who were so visibly represented in Atlanta in the Greek fruit dealers, were formed by more than just the low economic value they attached to the Greeks' entrepreneurial endeavors. Instead, their characterizations of these immigrants would sometimes assume a racial tone:

> We have the finest and purest population in the world in these Southern states. If we are going to bring any foreign people here to share it we should make it a rigorous prerequisite that they shall be of the best and highest class of foreigners that can be brought to our American shores. If we can not get this class of people we can richly afford to do without any…. We are seriously opposed to any amalgamation of these great Caucasian races in the South with any people who will bring with them the infernal jargon of the foreign tongues.[156]

The railroads and others with personal stakes in increased immigration were reminded that some types of immigrants posed a danger to the South's "great and homogeneous future."[157] In contrast to these negative portrayals of southern Europeans at this time, a settlement of thirty German immigrants in rural Hancock County would personify the idealized northern European immigrant often portrayed by the papers and offer support for the self-congratulatory narrative being developed by the association. Brought to farmland near the small town of Sparta, these six families were depicted as having adapted well to the move and productively working this land:

> The rich, virgin soil of old Hancock, the dense forests of valuable hardwoods…are now yielding prolific harvests to two score emigrants, not one of whom has been in the state long enough to cast a legal vote, but each of whom is most pronouncedly and satisfactorily demonstrating that Georgia fields can be made to produce rich and abundant crops of all sorts, as urged by Governor Hoke Smith, and the committee that accompanied him when they went to Europe to tell the tale of the inducements offered immigrants by the south.[158]

However, working farmers would continue to oppose even this limited form of immigration for northern Europeans that the state's industrialists had worked so long to develop. A resolution opposing immigration adopted by the Barrow County chapter of the Farmers' Union was typical of their sentiments: "We…do not believe that foreign immigration is now or ever can be conducive of any good results to this country…. We have enough to contend with in the negro, and those foreigners in all probability would be much worse than the negro."[159]

The opposition of the state's many farmers was significant. Farmers throughout the South and Midwest had by this time organized themselves into a potent national force. The national Farmers' Union had been established in 1902 but only became a viable and well-organized association under the leadership of Charles S. Barrett in 1905. A native Georgian, he led the association for twenty-two years and established its headquarters in Union City, a small town near Atlanta. The association was dominated by southerners and was represented by local chapters throughout the state. The organization was at the peak of its influence just as the work of Betjeman and the Georgia Immigration Association was beginning. Barrett's opinions on immigration set the tone for Georgia farmers. He decried the immigration into the United States of "some of the rankest human products of European and Asiatic institutions," whom he said were leaving "a slimy trail of decay and disruption over the entire fabric of our ideals and our aspirations."[160]

Governor Hoke Smith had been publicly supportive of the industrialists' pragmatic approach to limited immigration during the campaign prior to his election in 1907.[161] But he began to withdraw and further qualify that support after his inauguration as a result of the overwhelming opposition of the Georgia Farmers' Union, which had adopted several resolutions to that effect. The *Nashville (GA) Herald* condemned both the immigration association and Smith for their efforts "at bringing over the dagoes."[162] When the state House of Representatives invited him to address them on the issue, Smith refused to respond.[163] In addressing charges two years later that he had traveled to Europe with representatives of the immigration association to attract immigrants to the state, he described that simply as a "private pleasure trip."[164] A disturbance by Italian immigrant miners at the Durham mines in Pittsburgh, Georgia, produced charges that Smith had been responsible for their presence in the state during his previous term as governor. He denied responsibility for the Italians, saying that "Germans and those from northern Europe" were the type of immigrants that Georgia should seek.[165] This opposition forced Governor Smith to retreat on the issue and served as a warning to all elected officials in the state of the perils of supporting immigration in any manner. Smith had "shut up like an oyster and was not heard from any further along that line."[166]

But the *Constitution* had by this time become the leading advocate for the industrialists' position on immigration. Whether motivated by enlightenment or by self-interest, the paper was prepared to accept "immigrants of the right sort," so long as they could be certain "that the flotsam and jetsam of Europe is not going to be dumped on our shores."[167] The issue remained important to the city's business leaders, and the *Constitution*'s publisher, Clark Howell, became an active participant in support of their interests. By 1912, the Atlanta Chamber of Commerce had formed an immigration committee, and Howell served on that committee. Each of the other four members on the committee was connected to the railroad industry.[168]

Notwithstanding the continued advocacy of the *Constitution* and the best efforts of the Atlanta Chamber of Commerce, the vocal opposition of the working farmers appears to have stalled and eventually stopped the initiatives of the association after Smith's inauguration in 1908. Without strong support from the office of the governor and the legislature, the businessmen's efforts withered. The Georgia Immigration Association simply faded away. Although Atlanta businessmen led another effort in 1909 to revive a unified southern initiative with the creation of the Southern Immigration and Publicity Bureau, by that time the momentum had been lost.[169]

If the negative portrayals, casual discrimination and daily condescension experienced by the Greeks during these earliest years in Atlanta made their lives occasionally unpleasant and difficult, the experience was nothing in comparison to the often brutal existence of the area's black residents. The Atlanta race riot of 1906, one of the nation's most notorious in the first half of the twentieth century, and the ongoing lynching of black residents throughout the state made it clear that the Greeks and other less favored immigrants nevertheless occupied a higher and safer place in the city's pecking order than blacks.

Chapter 4

THE ATLANTA RACE RIOT

"Comes the Deluge"

In 1904, as the growing city entered the new century with a confidence matching its full recovery from the effects of the Civil War, the Atlanta Chamber of Commerce published a tract, *Atlanta: A Twentieth Century City*, touting the city's attractiveness for investments. Atlanta's business leaders took seriously the city's role as the leader of the "New South," as proclaimed by Henry Grady two decades before. The chamber boasted about the cordial relationship between the city's white and black populations, especially pointing out the absence in Atlanta of the lynchings and race riots that had plagued other cities. This situation would change dramatically within two years.[170]

The newspapers' editorials about immigration in 1906 and its news stories on the efforts of the state's business leaders to form an immigration association were a mere sideshow to their feverish coverage that year of the state's gubernatorial campaign. The focus was actually on the extremely contentious contest in the Democratic primary, where Clark Howell, the editor of the *Atlanta Constitution*, and Hoke Smith, the former publisher of the *Atlanta Journal*, were the leading contestants. The primary was dominated by debates about excluding black residents from participating in elections.

Smith, the eventual winner, conducted an especially virulent campaign, openly supporting a platform of black disenfranchisement: "If we study the true character of the negro, we are forced to the conclusion that

Left: Governor Hoke Smith. *Courtesy of Library of Congress, Prints and Photographs Division.*

Right: Clark Howell, circa 1919. *Courtesy of Kenan Research Center at the Atlanta History Center.*

the best progress the negroes, as a whole, ever made was through the institution of slavery."[171]

The newspapers, especially the *Journal* and the *Georgian*, provided incendiary coverage throughout. In a debate with Clark Howell, Smith declared, "I advocate legislation which will disenfranchise 95 percent of the negroes of Georgia…. I believe the wise course is to plant ourselves squarely upon the proposition in Georgia that the negro is in no respect the equal of the white man."[172]

When introducing Hoke Smith at the Democratic convention in Macon following his primary victory, James Anderson, Smith's campaign manager and a prominent Atlanta lawyer:

> *The election of Mr. Smith…means that the black and sickening cloud of negro insolence, which has darkened our beautiful land these forty years, and caused the heart of man to wither, must pass away, and God's blessed sunshine will fall upon us and make all nature green and beautiful. It means that the white man will again govern his own country, and govern it forever,*

without suggestion from the negro or his designing allies. It means that the negro will no longer think of equality with the white man—political or social; that our homes and our wives, and our daughters, will no longer be threatened with his insolence; his heart will no longer be filled with malice toward the white man—with murder, rape and arson—but he will again become the humble "marster" loving negro of antebellum days. It means the solution of the "negro problem."

No, the negro for ages—perhaps for always—must be the servant of the white man; he has no other place in a white man's country. He shall not aspire to equality with the white man. We must nullify—yes, repeal—this odious fifteenth amendment, else, my friends—miserable thought—the educated negro is justified in his claim of social equality with the white man and in his attentions to the white man's daughter.[173]

Smith then accepted the Democratic nomination for governor by declaring:

I accept the nomination for the office of governor charged with the ordinary duties of the position and with certain specific obligations created by the canvas. Let me state briefly the specific obligations:

The white voters of Georgia are to be given the fullest opportunity to rule the state and to express their wishes at the ballot box…. As a step toward solving the race problem in Georgia, a constitutional amendment must be passed by the legislature and submitted to the people for ratification providing for the protection of the ballot box, so far as it can be done, against ignorant and purchasable negro votes.[174]

The highly charged campaigns had intended to reassert complete white supremacy in the state and to roll back the limited gains achieved during Reconstruction. Added to the racially polarized governor's race as a backdrop that summer were the newspapers' combustible and sensationalistic accounts of alleged but unsubstantiated attacks by black men on white women. Prior to his move to Atlanta, John Temple Graves, the editor of the Hearst paper, the *Atlanta Georgian*, had defended lynching as a solution to the perceived attacks: "The mob answers it with the rope, the bullet, and sometimes, God save us! with the torch. And the mob is practical; its theory is effective to a large degree. The mob is to-day the sternest, the strongest, and the most effective restraint that the age holds for the control of rape."[175]

Lynching had become an accepted, if not encouraged, method of dispensing justice to blacks. During this first decade that marked the arrival of the Greek immigrants in Atlanta, between 1890 and 1900, more than 115 black residents had been lynched in Georgia, more than in any other state.[176] These lynchings were marked by savagery and staggering brutality. The lynching of Sam Hose in April 1899 was typical. Hose was a black field worker for a planter, Alfred Cranford, in Newnan, Georgia, a small town about thirty miles southwest of Atlanta. During a dispute with Cranford in which the planter drew a pistol and threatened to kill him, Hose defended himself with an axe, killing Cranford. He pleaded self-defense, to no avail,

John Temple Graves. *Courtesy of Library of Congress, Prints and Photographs Division.*

even though in a later investigation Cranford's wife would support his story. Newspapers quickly reported that Cranford had been murdered by Hose and that Cranford's wife had been raped. Hose was seized by a mob, and his upcoming execution well publicized. On the day of its occasion, more than two thousand white Georgians, some of whom had arrived from Atlanta on a special excursion train, gathered in Newnan to witness the event.[177]

Hose was stripped of his clothes and chained to a tree. Stacks of kerosene-soaked wood were placed around him. Before dousing Hose with oil and lighting the flame, some in the crowd cut off his ears, fingers and genitals and skinned his face. Others stabbed his body with knives. With Hose still alive, the stacked wood and his body were lit, and the crowd watched as his body contorted in the flames. Once dead, his body was further mutilated. His heart and liver were removed and cut into several pieces, and bones removed from his body were crushed into small pieces as souvenirs. One of the participants reportedly left for the state capitol in Atlanta, hoping to deliver a slice of Hose's heart to Governor Allen Chandler.[178]

But three years after his public statements praising the practice as effectual, Graves would despair of the effectiveness of lynching in the summer of 1906 and call for even more extreme measures in an August editorial titled, "The Reign of Terror for Southern Women."[179] With rumors of black men assaulting white women sweeping through the streets of Atlanta, Temple declared, "The mere suggestion of the slightest familiarity on the part of a black and filthy negro with a refined and gentle woman of the Caucasian race is enough to stir the blood to fever heat."[180]

Temple then asked, "Does lynching prevent rape…. It would seem not."[181] Temple suggested that another remedy be found to deal with the "ebony devils." Because, he said, "killing, shooting, burning" had not served as deterrents, new forms of punishment were needed.[182] He advocated "personal mutilation" and "some new and mysterious mode of punishment—the passing over a slender bridge into a dark chamber where in utter darkness and in utter mystery the assailant of women's virtue would meet a fate which his friends would never know and which he himself would never come back to make them understand." He concluded with this foreshadowing: "[I]f all other expedients fail, as they are failing, the time may come when the dominant and triumphant civilization of the South will rid itself of this awful terror in a more radical and a more revolutionary way. Patience is growing frazzled in Caucasian hearts. And after patience comes the deluge."[183]

These stories, and the accompanying editorials, further incited the city's white residents in the months and weeks before and after the nomination was secured by Smith. The *Georgian's* readers responded to these editorials with calls for the resurrection of the Ku Klux Klan and the support of "lynch law" as a solution to the "black peril."[184]

And the deluge finally did come on the evening of Saturday, September 22. Based on inaccurate and incomplete facts, inflammatory articles about alleged sexual assaults on white women were the proximate cause of the rampage of white mobs that began in the streets of downtown Atlanta on the Saturday evening of September 22.

On that day, the papers reported four separate assaults by black men on white women, with suggestions that lynching the accused, when found, would be in the natural course of events. As Temple had earlier suggested, protestations about lynching would go unheeded: "But as long as they continue to howl resolution against lynching and orate against lawlessness while they are shamefully silent toward the crimes which produce the mob, then the back of our hand is against them and all they represent."[185]

With the backdrop of the papers' inflammatory reporting of these rumors, the city exploded that evening as more than five thousand whites began roaming the downtown streets of Atlanta and indiscriminately attacking blacks. The rioting continued over the next three days, leaving more than twenty-five black residents—men, women and children—dead and scores injured.

Black residents were dragged from streetcars and beaten by mobs of white rioters. Several were beaten to death. The rioting swept onto the streets and sidewalks, where most of the Greek fruit peddlers maintained their stands.[186] They became mute witnesses to the carnage. During the peak of the riot, one victim fled into the fruit stand of a Greek fruit dealer, Jim Brown, seeking refuge. The "Greeks attempted to defend themselves and their property, and picked up stools and chairs to drive the crowd back." The Greek's futile efforts to defend his property further incited the attackers, who proceeded to destroy his stand but failed to claim another victim.[187] A man was dragged from a trolley and stabbed to death, "cut to ribbons," while another man was likewise dragged from a trolley, badly beaten and allowed to escape to provide a chase for the crowd. He was again caught, pleading with the mob, according to the paper, "For God's sake have mercy on me, white folks," before collapsing.[188] Two black barbers were shot in their shop near Marietta Street. Their bodies were dragged to the statue of Henry Grady and then disrobed and mutilated.[189]

The response of the papers the following day was to place the blame for the riot on the lawlessness of the black victims and on the alleged assaults on white women. In response the next day as to how he would deal with the tense situation, Mayor Woodward said, "The only remedy is to remove the cause. As long as black brutes attempt rape upon our white women, just so long will they be unceremoniously dealt with."[190]

The passions created by the racial demagoguery of the 1906 gubernatorial race had been further stoked that summer by the press's accounts of unverified attacks on white women. Hoke Smith, John Temple Graves and Clark Howell, in their roles as political candidates and newspaper editors, were in varying degrees responsible for creating this atmosphere. While the city's dailies, ever sensitive to Atlanta's image, did not linger on what had transpired in the city, others did. Reaction to the riot was swift and harsh, and damage to that image had been done. The story was featured in front-page newspaper accounts across the nation and even internationally.[191] The *New York Times* condemned both the mayor and Governor Terrell for their passive responses to the violence of the white mob. The Parisian daily *Le Petit Journal* featured the riot on its front page with the headline, "The Lynchings of the United States of America—The Massacre of Negroes in Atlanta."

A 1906 cover of *Le Petit Journal,* headlined, "The Lynchings in the United States—The Massacre of Negroes in Atlanta." *Courtesy of* Le Petit Journal.

With fault being placed on the city's dailies for stoking white passions, even before the riot's end, the *Georgian* was quick to absolve itself of any responsibility. In a large header in its Monday, September 24 edition, titled "In Justice to Itself," the paper's publisher declared that "the *Georgian* feels bound to say that it is free from any of the responsibility of inflaming the mob on Saturday night."[192]

Local and national black leaders condemned the mob violence and the killings in strong language. Just two weeks after the riot, Reverend Francis Grimke, the pastor of Atlanta's black Fifteenth Street Presbyterian Church, published a discourse on the riot, accusing Smith, Graves and Howell of doing "everything in their power to fan the flames of race hatred." He lamented that "we are in constant peril; no one is safe for a moment. We are liable at any time to be shot down, to be brutally murdered. Character, wealth, intelligence count for nothing."[193]

Graves, in particular, was held accountable for his and the *Georgian's* role in fomenting the unrest. Less than three months after the riot, Dr. Kelly Miller, a professor at Howard University, penned an open letter to Graves excoriating him for his published remarks and his paper's coverage leading up to the September events: "The world has read with horror of the Atlanta massacre and of the part you played during that awful hour. The outbreak is but the fruit of the seeds of race wrath which you and others have been assiduously sowing. They who sow the wind may expect to reap the whirlwind."[194]

W.E.B. DuBois captured the rage and the anguish of the black community in his poem "A Litany of Atlanta, Done at Atlanta, in the Day of Death, 1906," written and published less than two weeks after the riot:

> *Bewildered we are, and passion-tost, mad with the madness of a mobbed and mocked and murdered people; straining at the armposts of Thy Throne, we raise our shackled hands and charge Thee, God, by the bones of our stolen fathers, by the tears of our dead mothers, by the very blood of Thy crucified Christ:* What meaneth this? *Tell us the Plan; give us the Sign!* Keep not thou silence, O God!...*Thy will, O lord, be done!* Kyrie Eleison.[195]

The business leaders of the city were appalled by the negative publicity. A committee was formed to investigate the riot and to dispense financial aid to the victims of the mob violence. A report issued two months later concluded that "every one of the negroes killed was innocent.... The toughs have crucified Atlanta in the eyes of the world and shocked the moral sense of our own people."[196] In the aftermath of the riot, former governor Northen became a passionate advocate of the rule of law and a vocal opponent of the lynching of blacks. He worked for several years to establish committees or "civic leagues" in each county of the state dedicated to countering mob violence and to the eradication of this crime. His stated goal for every county was ambitious: "Why not have the coming year, 1912, absolutely free from criminal outrage and the savage barbarism of lynching and burning human beings?"[197]

Two of these civic leagues were established in Atlanta by the leading white residents of the city. Whatever their motives, they were moved to denounce the violence of the race riot as "so deplorable an outrage against our Christian civilization."[198]

The Greek whose fruit stand was destroyed in the riot was just one of scores of Greeks who maintained their places in the city's economy through the operation of these simple stands. Derided though they were for this type of work by the state's business leaders, the Greeks persisted in this trade to the dismay of the city's councilmen, who made numerous attempts to strictly regulate the business. By the time the city council finally put an end to their operations, the fruit stands had made many Greeks prosperous and had put them in a position to assume more substantial livelihoods.

Chapter 5

FRUIT STAND MEN

"Merchants of Foreign Extraction"

Until the establishment of the church in 1905, what would most clearly bind these Greek immigrants together over the first two decades of their presence in the city and would most frequently bring them to the attention of their fellow Atlantans was the fruit stand business. When Charles Brown began operating his fruit and vegetable stand some time in 1889 on Whitehall Street as one of the first Greek fruit dealers, he and his fellow Greeks who were doing the same were unknowingly beginning a twenty-year struggle with the Atlanta City Council over the small patches of downtown sidewalks needed for their stands.

The Greeks were not the first to open these businesses. The Italian immigrants who had preceded them in Atlanta by a few years had first developed the trade. But the Greeks would soon overtake the Italian presence and come to dominate this business.[199] As a business that required little operating capital and minimal English language skills, it presented an ideal opportunity for these immigrants to begin their lives in Atlanta. By 1892, the Greek immigrants had developed the street fruit stand business to such an extent that they had already become closely identified with this trade.[200] Fruit stands were being set up on streets throughout the heart of the downtown area, on Decatur, Peters, Auburn, Edgewood, Whitehall, Pryor, Marietta and Forsyth Streets. By 1895, several Greek immigrants had moved to Perry in rural Houston County to operate a produce farm for the purpose of supplying their brother's fruit and vegetable business.[201]

Just as these Greek immigrants were first arriving in Atlanta, Georgia's farmers were committing thousands of acres of farmland, once used for cotton production, to the planting of fruits and vegetables.[202] All types of fruit were grown throughout the state and had become after the war some of the state's most important agricultural commodities. "The growing of fruit has been so profitable in the State, the variety is so great, and the soil and climate is so admirably adapted to the successful raising of fruit" that the state's bureau of immigration in 1894 featured the "fruit culture" in its prospective guide for future immigrants.[203]

Cotton, the chief agricultural crop of Georgia, had declined significantly in value since the end of the Civil War. Bringing one dollar per pound in 1865, cotton by the 1890s was selling for about 7 cents per pound.[204] Even though cotton production would still represent more than fifty percent of all of Georgia's agricultural crop production until 1909, the market prices for cotton had fallen so sharply by the last decade of the nineteenth century that it was difficult for most farmers to earn a profit from it.[205]

In 1890, Georgia farmers established the Fruit and Vegetable Growers' Association to help them market their product.[206] Georgia farmers would continue these efforts over the next two decades, which culminated in 1908 in the organization of the Georgia Fruit Exchange.[207] This represented a more aggressive effort than the earlier association to efficiently regulate market prices. The exchange was established by leading business and government leaders, and Atlanta mayor Robert Maddox served as treasurer of the organization.[208] The overarching goal was to control the wholesale distribution of both locally grown and out-of-state fruits and vegetables so as to avoid oversupply in any one market, thereby depressing prices.[209] The immigrant fruit dealers were unintended beneficiaries of these developments, which not only ensured ready availability of produce for their stands but also helped to set higher market prices.

As the number of fruit stands on downtown streets increased with the continuing arrival of the Greek and Italian immigrants, the *Constitution* attempted to explain these "foreign fruit vendors" to its readers:

> *The average fruit vendor's stand offers, seemingly, very few temptations as a business enterprise. The stock of fruit always seems to be hopelessly out of proportion to the chance of getting rid of it and decay and ruin apparently stare the unhappy proprietor in the face.*

Fruit vendor at the corner of Alabama and Broad Streets in downtown Atlanta, circa 1900. *Courtesy of Kenan Research Center at the Atlanta History Center.*

But, gentle readers, do not waste any sympathy upon him. In spite of his old coat and dejected mien, the chances are at least two to one that he is making more money than you are and will be comfortably well off inside the next few years.[210]

The article claimed that the most successful of these dealers sold about $75 worth of fruits and vegetables per day. (Undoubtedly an exaggeration, as this would be equivalent today to daily sales of about $2,000.)

These men were creating a trade that had never before existed. The appearance of these simple fruit stands and plainly dressed immigrant dealers belied a more sophisticated operation and shrewder business acumen than was realized. One fruit importer described his impressions of them: "Yes, we do a great deal of business with the fruit-stand men…they are the sharpest traders in the world and one must look sharp in dealing with them not to be worsted. They know values to the cent and there is not a trick of the trade that they are not experts in."[211]

They purchased their product unripe in bulk quantities from commission houses or directly from importers at inexpensive prices, allowed the fruit to ripen in rented cellars behind their stands and marked the ripened fruit for sale at retail prices. Any fruit and vegetables that went unsold were used for their personal consumption.[212] The small profits realized on each sale added up. "The proprietor of one of these establishments is a melancholy eyed gentleman from Greece, who wears a suit that would disgrace a scarecrow, and can draw a check for $30,000."[213] Whatever the exact profit margins were, they were sufficient to propel most of these men within a decade into ownership of more substantial businesses.

There were difficulties and dangers inherent in operating these sidewalk fruit stands, where work began before dawn and continued late into the evening. Robberies and assaults were not uncommon, with the dealers often suffering serious bodily injury.[214] Many of these men also slept in the rear of the shops that rented them space, further exposing them to crime.[215]

The earliest known Greek immigrant fruit dealer, Charles Brown, comes to our attention in the historical record as the victim of an assault and battery at his downtown stand in 1889.[216] In May 1909, the press reported on a string of assaults on Greek fruit dealers that left one of their number dead. A few days after this murder, Jake Krantz, another Greek dealer, was the victim of an attempted murder in his home. The police suspected that the assailant was targeting the immigrant fruit dealers.[217]

Throughout these years, the Greek dealers competed ferociously with one another and the Italians for prime locations on the downtown sidewalks. Unwilling to cede the best locations to their competitors, they often located their stands very near to one another.[218] Inevitable disputes were the result, often leading to civil litigation between the dealers.[219] The court appearances involving them became so frequent that Greek interpreters were regularly employed so that the litigants could be understood by court personnel.[220]

Much more frequently, the disputes between them led to physical altercations on the streets that usually produced criminal charges.[221] The worst of these altercations would often develop into violent mêlées between rival factions of the fruit dealers involving multiple participants, resulting in arrests and leaving some of them "bathed in blood."[222] In one incident, the bitter competition between two factions in the fruit business who were "in close proximity to each other" initially led the dealers to begin selling their produce at or below cost. This eventually escalated into a mêlée involving ten of the Greeks. "For a few minutes the air was filled with bananas, cantaloupes, apples, pineapples and other delicious fruit, which were hurled by the fighters." Nine of the dealers were arrested.[223]

With their livelihoods at risk and the economic stakes so high, the disputes were very often intense and violent. Whatever solidarity these Greek immigrants shared in their limited social lives or in their intense loyalty to the land of their births did not extend to these sidewalks.

Constant inspections and relatively petty or selective enforcement actions by the police also challenged these fruit dealers. In one case, civil fines were imposed for violations of the city's "garbage can" ordinance, with all of the offenders being Greek and described in the press as "foreigners."[224] Minor complaints could result in their arrest on the weakest of charges. Pano Carolee was arrested after a customer complained that he had not given the customer the correct change after a purchase.[225] Operating licenses for fruit stands approved by the city council could be vetoed without comment or explanation by the mayor.[226] In the arrest of eleven fruit dealers and dry good merchants for illegally opening on Sunday, the men were described in press reports as "either dagoes or Russian Jews" and as "merchants of foreign extraction."[227] The newly elected police chief, John Ball, issued a warning to others: "This is but a start. I wish to warn every person that from now on the police will be instructed to arrest all who break the laws respecting the legal observance of Sunday."[228]

This warning signaled the beginning of the city's far more aggressive campaign to rid the streets and sidewalks of these stands. The city council would continue to ratchet up the pressure on the fruit dealers until the ordinances it adopted forced the closure of the stands.

Chapter 6

ATLANTA SHUTS DOWN THE STANDS

"An Active and Relentless Crusade Will Be Waged Against the Greeks and Italians Conducting These Businesses"

From the earliest years of the 1890s, concerns were being expressed about these fruit stands operating on the sidewalks of the city. They were novel, as this fruit stand trade had simply not existed before the arrival of the Italians and then the Greeks. They were highly visible, necessarily being located on streets with the most pedestrian traffic. They were also mobile. The stands could be quickly moved to other locations when circumstances demanded. Charles Brown was operating his stand in August 1889 on Whitehall Street and had moved it to Pryor Street by October of that year.[229] Perhaps most significantly, they posed to the more traditional brick-and-mortar grocers a type of competition never before experienced.

The fruit peddlers would pay street-front merchants for the privilege of setting up their stands in front of the merchants' stores. Apart from the cost of their produce, these rental payments and the modest licensing fees paid to the city, the dealers had very few other operating expenses. As a result, their fruits and vegetables could be priced to sell at lower retail prices than those charged by traditional grocers. It was inevitable that these grocers would soon complain to their elected officials, who were quickly persuaded to take action to deal with these "foreigners." What began as simply enhanced police enforcement of various city code provisions, as previously described, would transform into a focused effort on the part of the city, almost a preoccupation, to control the fruit trade. Eventually, it became a self-declared "war."

From its first attempts at regulatory control in October 1896 to its final actions almost fourteen years later in May 1910, the city would spend considerable efforts and devote a great deal of discussion to the matter. On October 5, 1896, a resolution was presented by the Street Committee of the city council directing the police chief "to remove all fruit stands in the city occupying the sidewalks which projected more than two feet onto the sidewalks or more than two feet from the wall of the building which the stand is supposed to attach to."[230] The full council adopted this resolution the following month.[231]

In March 1897, an attempt was made by some of the aldermen to codify this "two foot" standard. The council submitted a resolution to the council's tax committee that would have affirmatively formalized the use of two feet of sidewalk space by the fruit dealers for their stands.[232] The committee rejected the proposal the following month.[233] Nonetheless, the two-foot restriction established by the council in 1896 became the operating standard for these fruit stands and was accepted by the dealers as well as the police.

But strict enforcement of this and other code provisions would continue: "Patrolman Childs has declared war against those fruit dealers who persist in selling their wares on Sunday. He says that it is unfair to the Americans who close up their stores on Sunday to allow the Italians and Greeks to supply the Sunday demand."[234]

This was not the first and would not be the last time that the matter would be cast as a "war" against these immigrants. On another occasion in 1899, the *Constitution* reported on the denial by the tax committee of a license application for a fruit stand on the corner of Whitehall and Alabama Streets. The committee determined that this was "no place for a fruit stand," and the paper declared that the "[f]ruit stand war is waging again."[235]

When the city council next addressed the fruit stand issue about two years later, it was to consider a proposed increase in the license fee for the stands.[236] The fruit vendors submitted a petition in opposition to this proposal, a significant development in their ongoing struggle with the city.[237] This marked the first collective action of the Greek fruit vendors to protect their interests. All previous efforts were those of individual dealers seeking to respond to challenges to their own businesses. However, this limited group response to the city's ongoing "war" on their trade was inadequate. Nor would this pattern change in the future. Another eight years would pass before these dealers would act collectively again on their own behalf, but by then it would be too late. In contrast to the limited nature of the collective response of the Atlanta Greeks, their Chicago compatriots, also in the fruit business, would respond much more forcefully to similar challenges. When the Chicago Grocers' Association tried to stop the operation of sidewalk fruit stands because of the competition they presented, the Greek dealers organized themselves into the Fruit Dealers Association and successfully rebuffed the attempt.[238]

However, the Atlanta City Council's actions to date had not produced the desired results, and it determined that further action was necessary. The *Constitution* announced that the city was again prepared to "wage war" on the fruit stands, predicting that

> *steps may be taken at once to put an end to this particular branch of business...*
> *that the death knell of the small sidewalk stand has been sounded...*
>
> *[I]t is only a matter of a comparatively short time when an active and relentless crusade will be waged against the Greeks and Italians conducting these businesses.*[239]

The issue reached a climax in August 1902 when a resolution by Alderman Walsh was adopted by the council creating a special task force to review the fruit dealer "problem."[240] Consisting of the chairmen of the council's tax, ordinance and street committees, as well as the city engineer and the city attorney, the task force was charged with the responsibility of reviewing the licenses and operations of each of the city's fruit stands to assess compliance with the city's ordinances.[241] The task force was empowered to take action against violators and was instructed to submit a report at the following meeting of the council.

It is worth reproducing the language of the resolution here rather than in the notes:

> *Be it resolved by the Mayor and General Council that:*
>
> *Whereas, it has been stated that different persons are conducting fruit stands and other businesses on the side-walks of the city without having registered and obtained license as required by law, and otherwise in violation of city ordinances, and.,*
>
> *Whereas, such persons seem to enjoy immunity from proper operation of the City Ordinances, and from the penalties for violating the same, therefore.*

Be it resolved, that a special committee consisting of the Chairman of the Ordinance Committee, the Chairman of the Tax Committee, the Chairman of the Street Committee, and the City Attorney and City Engineer be appointed whose duty it shall be,

To investigate and ascertain what persons, firms or corporations are doing business of such character in which they are required under the laws of the City to register and pay a license therefor, and who have failed to so register and pay said license, and that said Committee shall make cases in the Recorder's Court against any or all such persons so violating the City ordinances,

Such Committee shall ascertain if any persons, firms or corporations are doing business on the side-walks of the City of Atlanta otherwise in violation of the City ordinances, and if so they shall make cases in the Recorder's Court against all such persons.

That, should said Committee find persons doing such business, who can show that in good faith they believe they have proper legal authority for the same, and as a matter of fact they have not, the Committee will notify such parties promptly that their failure to comply with all the laws and requirements of the City Ordinances said Committee shall make cases against each and all of said parties in the Recorder's Court for such violations.

Said Committee is herein instructed to report in detail its findings and doings to the next meeting of the General Council.[242]

At least one fruit stand was closed as a result of the task force's work, with its license revoked and its "obstructions removed."[243] The report of the task force was also referred to the ordinance committee, as was a proposed ordinance further regulating fruit stands.[244] Unfortunately, there is no record regarding the contents of the report. Nonetheless, the fruit stands were allowed to continue operating within the established restrictions. On the same day that the task force's report was received, the application by Jim Brown to operate a new fruit stand was approved.[245] The council continued to wrestle with the issue as additional licenses were sought: "The fruit stands of the city and the sons of Greece who run them occupied the time of the city fathers for two hours yesterday afternoon."[246]

Sporadic action by the city council would continue over the next several years. An ordinance was proposed that would prohibit the operation of fruit stands on the sidewalks while continuing to allow the outdoor display of fruit for those grocers who operated regular street front businesses.[247] No action was taken on this. There were also proposals to prohibit the stands from encroaching on the sidewalks, to further license the dealers, to regulate their operation on Sundays and to restrict their location near churches.[248]

But the stands remained. However, this situation would change dramatically in May 1910. Whether motivated by the complaints of their grocer constituents, frustration with overcrowding on the sidewalks, impatience with the seemingly endless licensing and enforcement issues they were forced to contend with or the simple enmity that they felt toward these Greeks and Italians (most likely due to all of these), the council on May 16, 1910, finally put an end to the fruit stand trade in the city.[249]

In the years since the turn of the century, the population of Greeks in Atlanta had increased almost tenfold. While many of these later arrivals were entering different occupations, the fruit stand business would continue to attract many more; the council would be forced to continue dealing with all of the matters associated with the trade. In addition, many of the fruit dealers had begun offering their produce in hand-pulled or horse-drawn carts or wagons by this time. This had become an effective way in which the immigrants could continue their livelihoods while avoiding the increasing restrictions being adopted by the city on sidewalk stands. But to the pedestrian congestion resulting from sidewalk sales was now added the street congestion produced by the stopped wagons.

The city's leaders had lost all patience. So, on a motion by Councilmen Harrison and Chosewood, the council adopted a resolution "repealing the existing ordinance providing for the maintenance of fruit stands and restricting the use of the sidewalks for such" and a separate resolution effectively ending the sale of fruit and vegetables in carts and wagons on the streets:

> *Whereas, the licenses now granted for peddlers in wagons only permit such wagons to stop for purpose of sale, and they are not permitted to stand said wagons on the street for the purpose of waiting for customers, and*
>
> *Whereas, the holders of such licenses frequently use such licenses to stand their wagons for great lengths of time, and obstruct the street, and compete with others, doing similar business and renting store rooms for that purpose,*
>
> *Therefore, be it resolved by the Mayor and General Council that the Chief of Police instruct the members of the Department of Police to enforce the ordinances against the obstructing the streets and especially to keep those*

peddling in wagons moving, and only permitting them to stop on the streets for the purpose of making sales only.[250]

The city's long campaign against the "sons of Greece" operating these stands was over. Obviously, reactions to the council's decision varied. The Greek fruit dealers most directly affected by this accepted the decision with resignation but no visible anger.

Paul Varles, one of the dealers, said, "I will have to move, I guess. Will have to do what the law says." Likewise, George Poulos remarked, "Must move if they make me. Don't make any difference to me. Don't want to move, but have to if they tell me." Gust Ellin would wonder at the logic of the decision, "I got fine place here in front of new city hall and new post office. Ain't in anybody's way. Don't want to move, but have to if they tell me. Try to find another place somewhere."[251] The dealers remained powerless in the face of the council's decision.

Atlanta mayor Robert Maddox with members of the 1910 city council. *Photo by Francis Price. Courtesy of Kenan Research Center at the Atlanta History Center.*

Alderman Hancock viewed the action of the council as necessary to address a public safety concern: "The sidewalks are too crowded in this growing city of ours."[252]

The *Constitution* responded with equanimity: "Under an ordinance adopted by the general council yesterday afternoon all the fruit stands on the sidewalks in the city will be abolished.... There is a large number of fruit stands in the city owned principally by foreigners...and frequently they and their customers block the sidewalks."[253]

Several days later, a petition was submitted to Mayor Maddox by a large group of fruit dealers asking that the effective date of the new ordinance adopted on May 16 be deferred until November 1.[254] The action of the council had not been expected, and the dealers sought a reprieve that would give them time to dispose of their produce and otherwise make the necessary transition to other livelihoods. Two weeks later, the fruit dealers submitted a similar petition to the council.[255] The petition to the mayor went unanswered, and the petition to the council was referred to the ordinance committee and never addressed. No reprieve was granted. A livelihood that had sustained many in the Greek community for more than twenty years was finished.

Memis Moundreas in his downtown grocery store, circa 1915. *Courtesy of the Annunciation Greek Orthodox Cathedral of Atlanta.*

Not one time since the community had begun in 1906 keeping detailed meeting minutes of its Church Council and general assembly proceedings were these difficulties with the city ever referenced in these written records. While this group of men would spend several meetings discussing matters as trivial as the lottery of one of the church's pianos, they apparently never saw fit to discuss in any of these gatherings how to respond to the actions of the city council that threatened the livelihoods of a sizeable portion of their community.[256]

But the Greeks had been able to operate these fruit stands long enough to accumulate savings that enabled them to open the diners, restaurants, cafés, grocery stores and other substantial businesses that would begin to earn them the respect long withheld by the broader Atlanta community.

Chapter 7

IMMIGRANT AS ENTREPRENEUR

"A Man's Lunch at a Child's Price"

The action of the city council in ending the selling of fruits and vegetables in sidewalk stands and in wagons presented significant difficulties for these men whose livelihoods had depended on this business. This foothold in the American economy for these immigrants was gone. The effect was immediate. Many would struggle to maintain even the simple lifestyles that the fruit business had afforded them. Others would transition directly into a more traditional grocery business. Christ Gyfteas's fruit stand at the corner of Broad and Marietta Streets had been one of those closed by the council's action.[257] Within months, he had opened the California Fruit Company, a grocery on Edgewood Avenue.

But the council's action in 1910 would have no direct impact on those later arriving men who had never been engaged in the fruit business. Nor would it seriously threaten the financial security of most of those Greek men who had come to Atlanta during the decade of the 1890s. They had already before this date begun using the savings generated in the fruit business to establish themselves as proprietors in other occupations, with employees of their own. Commenting on the frugality of one of these immigrants, Athanasios Bitsaktzes, Dio Adallis noted approvingly that "the man has ample means, but in a safety vault."[258]

It is also worth noting here that the poverty widely evident in other cities and associated with other immigrant groups never manifested itself in Atlanta with the Greeks. Among the years-long complaints published in the city's dailies about how the Greeks conducted the fruit trade, there were no comments or criticisms about Greek poverty. The immigrant slums and shantytowns of other cities did not exist in Atlanta. Nor, as noted earlier, did the Greeks themselves ever establish the types of relief agencies so common among other ethnic groups. Negative depictions of how the Greeks actually lived were nonexistent. There would be no characterizations of Greek housing similar to that made about Irish and German immigrant tenements in New York, as "dim, undrained courts oozing with pollution, dark narrow stairways, decayed with age, reeking with filth, overrun with vermin, rotted floors, stuffed with rags...[inhabited by] gaunt, shivering forms and ghastly faces."[259]

This transition from itinerant Greek fruit peddlers to owners and operators of much more substantial businesses was noted in 1912 by the publication of Dio Adallis's *Greek Merchants' Reference Guide*.[260] The book was intended as a Dun and Bradstreet–style guide and rating of the many Greek businessmen in Georgia, South Carolina and Alabama. It claimed to list more than 650 of them.[261] But it also achieved other purposes. It served as a directory of potential customers for the guide's advertisers and the broader Atlanta business community, and it also provided useful and practical advertising for these Greek business owners in their local communities.

But more importantly, the guide's publication served to informally announce that the Greek immigrants were substantial contributors to the city's prosperity, businessmen worthy of the respect that they had been largely denied since their first arrival. These men were no longer, the guide was saying, the same Greek immigrants who pushed fruit carts around the downtown streets but rather substantial businessmen with solid roots in the city. The Atlanta Greeks recognized the benefits they would receive from this publication. In his earlier presentation to the Church Council regarding his plans for the book, Adallis had claimed that the book "would greatly benefit the Greek reputation in the American Community." With this understanding, the council unanimously approved his proposal.[262] These men were now being presented to the Atlanta community like debutantes at a society ball. As Adallis said:

> *The Greeks who come to this country are not going to make a pile of money and return to Greece to live in idleness. They may want to do that now, and some of them used to do it, but they get so used to American customs, ways and freedom here that they are unhappy when they go home.*

Nick Chotas (center), later to become the first Supreme President of AHEPA, 1908. *Courtesy of the Annunciation Greek Orthodox Cathedral of Atlanta.*

It's safe to say that the Hellene who comes to America today will stay here for good and become in time a naturalized citizen of the United States and in the end die here. That is what should appeal to the native-born population, the fact that their Greek neighbors are not making money to carry back to the old country, but are making money to spend here in their later years and to leave to their children here.[263]

Adallis had swept away almost every charge that had been leveled against the Greek immigrants. They were now going to earn and spend their money in Atlanta, reside in the city permanently, become naturalized citizens, die and be buried here and, most importantly, raise their children as Americans.

By 1911, about 150 Greek men, nearly 40 percent of the Greek immigrants in Atlanta, had become proprietors or partners in a variety of businesses, with many of them having ownership interests in multiple businesses.[264] The large majority of these were cafés, restaurants, soda fountains and groceries. But there were others who were successful hotel owners, grocery wholesalers and confectioners. Vasileios Efthimiou, proprietor of Child's Café, placed regular advertisements in the city directories and the daily newspapers, urging Atlantans to try "A Man's Lunch at a Child's Price."

They were not only providing for their families in Atlanta but also making regular remittances to Greece to assist family members left behind. By this time, the community was also financially able to assist the poor among their fellow immigrants with funds gathered from special collection trays for their benefit.[265]

Typically, most, if not all, of the employees of these Greek business owners were fellow Greek immigrants. The Bon-Ton Café, on Peachtree Street downtown, owned by the Pefines family, employed eight other Greeks as cooks and waiters.[266] The Arcade restaurant, also on Peachtree Street, employed ten Greeks. Eleven Greeks were employed by the Manhattan Café, and the Peachtree Café employed eight Greeks.[267]

For the most part, Adallis's *Greek Merchants' Reference Guide* served to introduce these Greek men to the broader community as the successful businessmen they had become, oftentimes in florid prose:

> *The soul of business, salesmanship incarnate, the essence of attention, alert to a superlative degree, tactful, watchful, always found in the attitude of a domesticated feline specie, ready to jump upon the rodent the instant it should issue out of the aperture*—this is Mr. Pete Verge...[268]
>
> [Leonidas] *is a very industrious business man, who night and day (almost) is found at his post, superintending his two places, and finds no time to rest.*[269]

The number of businesses and properties that some of these men had acquired in a brief period of time was impressive: "If praise is due, certainly George Moore deserves all the credit. He owns a confectionary, an ice cream and candy factory, valuable real estate property and five large houses in town."[270]

But there were other purposes as well. In some instances, the guide simply commented on their personal qualities: "Mr. Nick is a good-hearted 'old man', and many are the soft spots upon which one can easily 'touch'"; "We all liked Jim for his good character, his quiet manners and for his meek and genial disposition. Fine boy, Jim"; "Andrew says he can run twenty-five miles without stopping"; and "John seldom indulges in the frivolous practice of smiling."[271]

The economic success of the Greeks remained puzzling to some, explainable not by innate skills and much hard work but as the product of some centralized national scheme that assisted Greeks throughout the country. The *Constitution* gave voice to this myth of some "central bureau" in New York that not only financed Greeks seeking to establish businesses but also guided the immigrants to various cities that were experiencing shortages of "cheap lunch counters and fruit stands." This explained, according to the author, that "the reason the Greeks in this country succeed so well in business is because they know what cities to go for the carrying on of certain lines of trades."[272]

Nonetheless, with their establishment of these businesses and after two decades of presence in the city, the Greeks were finally being extended a measure of respect for their economic achievements, at least by the *Atlanta Constitution*, the most progressive of the city's dailies. These former operators of sidewalk fruit stands and fruit wagons were becoming business proprietors, and they were eager to portray themselves to the Atlanta community in a manner befitting their improved economic status. The Adallis guide served to reintroduce the immigrant Greeks to Atlanta. The text accompanying a photograph of Nicholas Matrangos, dressed in a three-piece suit and sitting comfortably in a carved wooden chair, with legs crossed and arms carefully placed on the armrests, captured the desired image: "In this picture he sits like a lord and surveys the world after full periods of hard work and hard times…one of the richest men and philanthropists of Atlanta."[273]

In several articles over the course of 1912–13, the *Constitution* expressed the type of favorable opinions about these southern European immigrants rarely shown before. In one of these articles, titled "Our Greeks," the paper would say:

> *No small part of the credit for the remarkable growth of Atlanta during the past two decades is due to the Greeks. Coming here in large numbers in recent years, they have taken a prominent part in the building up of the smaller trades of the city, and giving a cosmopolitan spirit which would otherwise have been impossible.*
>
> *Atlanta has no more loyal citizens than the Greeks, and the sooner that they are recognized for their true worth, just so soon will the city realize their further importance and benefit.*[274]

Again, several months later:

> *Among what might be called the "welcome invaders" of Atlanta, the Greeks who have established themselves in this community are rapidly proving themselves a valuable asset.*[275]

There was even some recognition that the Greeks had not been welcomed when they had first arrived and over the course of their presence in Atlanta:

> [T]*he Greeks have not been treated with absolute fairness, but they have progressed withal. The average American looks upon them with supreme indifference and condescension. They think that the Greeks have trespassed on their grounds and transgressed on their desires. But the sentiment is changing. The Greek is no longer an interloper. He is being held in highest regard, respect and esteem in the social world, and business men are regarding him as one of the great factors in the industrial growth of Atlanta.*[276]

The author further gave the Greeks singular credit for the growth of the restaurant business in the city:

> *There were few restaurants in Atlanta before the advent of the Greek. It was considered a luxury by one to dine or sup in a restaurant, as the prices were high, the service bad and the waiter insolent.*[277]

The growing size and importance of the Greek presence in Atlanta led to the Greek government establishing a consulate in the city by March 1913, with Dimitri Vafeiades serving as its first consul.[278]

Chapter 8

IMMIGRANT SELF-IDENTITY AND SELF-IMAGE

"We Are Honest; We Are Thrifty"

The image and identity of the Greek immigrants as created by their American neighbors was almost exclusively a function of their socioeconomic status. When the Greeks worked on Atlanta's streets as fruit peddlers, their occupation was viewed derisively. The Greeks were described as being noncontributors to the city's and state's prosperity, "undesirable" and "nonproductive almost to a man." As they later became proprietors of their own businesses, the city belatedly showed its pride in their success and praised their accomplishments.

How the Greek immigrant saw himself was more complicated. While he undoubtedly felt the usual immigrant pride in his economic success and enjoyed the community's recognition of his progress, his self-image and self-identity were more significantly based on factors not perceived by the American community.

The story of how the Greek immigrants identified themselves (i.e., their self-image) is a story most often revealed indirectly and interpretively. Whereas the image of these Greeks created by others was usually expressed directly through spoken and written characterizations, their self-identity was most often inferred through their actions. Their self-identity is a story of the continual pulling of and responses to dual allegiances or loyalties. These dual forces were, first, their ongoing desire to become fully American and, more importantly, their being accepted by their fellow citizens as true

Americans, and secondly, the importance in maintaining loyalties to their native country and in perpetuating their Hellenic traditions, customs and Orthodox Christian faith. The individual, internal responses to these forces would lead to sometimes seemingly contradictory behavior. Men who would casually anglicize their names, strive to become naturalized citizens and generally adopt assimilating behaviors would also on almost an actual day's notice repatriate to Greece to risk their lives fighting in the Balkan Wars for their native land. How the immigrants constantly responded to these dual forces is the story of this chapter.

Dio Adallis's advice to Pano Kourogiannopoulos, a recent young immigrant to Atlanta, was representative of the thinking of these early immigrants: "Pano, in time, may see fit to curtail his name, also other little differences he may have brought from the old country;—and he may want to assimilate himself and be a valuable citizen of this glorious land of our adoption."[279]

This advice—to anglicize their names, to deemphasize the customs of their native land, to fully assimilate and to become naturalized citizens—would to a certain extent serve as their civil creed, which they would repeat often, in various ways, in many of their public utterances.

The record does not reveal whether Pano followed this advice, but most of the other Greek immigrants did. Anglicization of names was a simple but important way in which the immigrant was able to proclaim his mutual identity with his fellow Americans. Georgios Papageorgakopoulos officially changed his name to George Moore, noting that his name was "foreign and confusing."[280] Nikolaos Papademetropoulos became Nick Pope, and Vasilios Efthimiou adopted E. Basil as the name by which he was known to the Atlanta community.

Both the 1896 local Atlanta census and the 1900 and 1910 federal census show the vast majority of these Greek immigrants using either anglicized versions of their Greek names or adopting new, American-sounding names entirely. Carter, Mitchell, Akers, Fort, Williams and Thomas were just some of the surnames chosen by these men. Nineteen Greek immigrants listed in the 1910 census had selected Brown as their official surname. Among those Atlanta Greeks adopting the Brown surname were three sets of brothers, George and Panos Grammatikopoulos, Athanasios and Theodoros Bitsaxis and Petro and Victor Kakouriotis.

But anglicization of names, while publicly very symbolic of the immigrant's commitment to his new country, was also a relatively easy step to take. These men continued to maintain their original names within the Greek community. Not one anglicized name—no Browns, Mitchells or Moores—is listed in the registry of the church treasury from 1905 to 1907. The immigrants' strong allegiances to both their new land and their old could be kept without conflict, at least with respect to their names. The usage of both their Greek and American names allowed them to maintain dual identities without compromising either their commitment to becoming fully realized Americans or their preservation of their Hellenic identity.

However, the ultimate litmus test for determining the immigrants' total commitment to their new country was citizenship. In the many disparaging remarks made about these Greeks during this early period of their presence in Atlanta, it was often remarked that they lacked the will and intent to become citizens of the nation that was now their home. Without this commitment, they were viewed as interlopers simply earning enough money to allow them to return to Greece in an improved financial condition. So for these Greeks, ever sensitive to the image of their community in the eyes of the Americans, obtaining that citizenship became the principal means by which to establish their credentials as true Americans.

By 1907, sixteen of these Greek immigrants had filed declarations of intention and petitions for naturalization in the Fulton County Superior Court. The first of these was Vasseleios Foufas, who submitted his petition on August 9, 1894.[281]

An *Atlanta Constitution* article in 1908 demonstrates the importance attached to citizenship by both the immigrants and the broader American community. Discussing the activities of the Evangelismos Society, established in 1902 as a precursor to the establishment of a church, the paper applauded the work of the group and its goals of "educating the Greeks regarding our laws, customs and institutions, to have them become naturalized and voters." The paper noted with approval that thirty-two of the seventy-two current members of the society had already become naturalized citizens and that the remaining forty members were in the process of doing so.[282] These same Greek immigrants, so recently vilified in the pages of the paper, were now praised lavishly for their commitment to American ideals: "The great purpose [of the society] is for the upliftment of those who reside in this country, to make the Americans appreciate them more and more, to regard them not as fortune-hunters, but as a people who wish to live here, and share the country with its other citizens."[283]

The Adallis guide, which had served to proclaim the business successes of the Greek immigrants, also reflected these men's hopes for acceptance from the American community. It provided assurances, almost pleadingly, to its American audience that these men shared their understanding of the importance of citizenship to the immigrants' complete acceptance by society:

George [Economy] *has declared his intention to become a good citizen, and for this act, we laud him, pointing to him as an example for others to follow. We should be good citizens of our adopted country, thankful of the blessings we enjoy here undisturbed. George is very appreciative of this.*[284]

[Andrew Berry] *is a full citizen…. He shows marks of progress, and in time, we have no doubt whatever, that he will be thoroughly assimilated with our ways and institutions.*[285]

[Jim Manos] *declared his intentions for citizenship.*[286]

[George Caltis] *is a full American citizen.*[287]

[Pete Potagos] *married an American lady and declared at the same time to Uncle Sam his infallible intention to become an American citizen.*[288]

[Constantinos Charalambides] *is a full citizen of America.*[289]

[Phil Pappas] *is a full American citizen.*[290]

[Angel Smerles] *is ambitious, intending to become a citizen and vote for the ticket which may appeal to him as sane.*[291]

[Argyr Pheles] *is a full citizen.*[292]

[Andrew Dagress] *became a full-fledged American citizen.*[293]

Charles Keramidas has already given himself up to the Melting Pot, and is getting gradually assimilated.[294]

[Athan Prattes is] *a Full American Citizen.*[295]

Paul Varellas…is a full citizen with voting power.[296]

While most Greeks employed fellow Greek immigrants, the employment of Americans in their establishments was also highlighted. In one of the advertisements placed in the guide by E. Basil for the Child's Hotel, he emphasizes that he has not employed just his fellow Greeks in his business: "American help employed also in all departments."[297] Nicholas Kutres highlighted the Adallis listing of his wholesale fruit and produce business by noting, "Nine American help employed."[298]

Not only, then, were these Greek immigrants anxious to become naturalized citizens, but they were also keen to show their worthiness as Americans by their willingness to marry American women and maintain good relationships:

> [Pete Potagos] *married an American lady and declared at the same time to Uncle Sam his infallible intention to become an American citizen.*[299]
>
> *Mr. and Mrs. Potagos are a matched couple…. His wife is an accomplished and congenial American lady. They are happy. We have quite a number of Greeks who have intermarried and who are making ideal husbands. The prevalent idea of some that intermarriage of races proves a failure is a bugaboo, and can be taken with a pinch of salt.*[300]

Eli Chotas was held up as the ideal representative of the best of the Greek immigrants. He was portrayed not only as the embodiment of hard work and perseverance but also as a symbol of the ideal father, husband and family man that these Greek immigrants had and would become. Adallis was telling his American readers that this was what the Greek immigrant was capable of, given the opportunity:

> *Eli Chotas has four children, Dionisia, Nicko, Matthew and a boy child, yet to be named. He is an ideal and affectionate father, loves his children and his home….* [His family] *belongs to the most amiable, the most generous-hearted, the most liberal hearted sympathetic, good and true, typical Christian Greek of our community—ELI CHOTAS. If there is one who has capacity to feel for humanity, who is sincere and true to oneself and his fellow-men, it is ELI CHOTAS.*[301]

If Eli Chotas was the embodiment of the finest qualities that the Greek immigrants wanted to project to Atlanta, then it was important for them to vigorously defend this image, as it was central to their community's self-identity. Expressing themselves through the only medium then available,

Atlanta's daily press, they were sensitive to negative portrayals and quickly responsive to articles or remarks that cast them in a negative manner.

A reporter for the *Atlanta Constitution* in 1906, in preparing an article on the economic success of the Greeks, expressed his wariness in speaking with E. Basil, one of the leaders of the Greek community, because of an incident in court a few days earlier. The reporter had observed Basil's reaction in the courtroom when a Greek witness in the case was referred to as a "dago": "I saw a flush on the face of the Greek as he hung his head…. Remembering the deeds of valor that made his countrymen illustrious, this Greek of Atlanta hung his head in shame when he heard the word 'dago' applied to him and his race."[302]

Basil's defense of his fellow immigrants was passionate; it was that of a man intent on informing the broader community of the worthiness of these Greeks. He described his fellow immigrants as "thrifty, industrious and honest," who "want their children to become thoroughly Americanized" and who "never engage in objectionable businesses" and "rarely ever fail in business."[303] Responding to all slights, real or imagined, he concluded:

> *We are honest; we are thrifty; we attend to our own business; we keep out of debt; we do not fill the jails and chain gangs; we try to be decent and respectable, and I do pray that the name of "dago" will not be applied to us. We are proud of being Greeks, for our people have a noble name in history, but we are equally as proud of being citizens of this grand country.*[304]

Responding to an *Atlanta Constitution* article resurrecting the old charge that a central booking office in New York was guiding Greek immigrants to certain cities, one of these immigrants, P. Stephens, addressed a letter to the editor, protesting that the offending remarks "cast discredit upon the Greeks as a whole" and that the characterization of the Greeks as "foreigners"[305] was offensive: "At least 75 percent of us are naturalized American citizens, and have been such for the past ten years or more. We are married here and our children are born in this country. We do not hoard our money and send it back to the old country! No, on the contrary, we spend it right here."[306]

Reverend J.W. Ham, the assistant pastor of the downtown Baptist Tabernacle, sermonized in 1911 that Greek soda fountains, "under the roof of a foreign nationality who are noted for secrecy and attention," were used as meeting places between young girls and "libertines" for "immoral purposes" that served as "the gateway to hell." George Themelis, a Greek businessman, responded in a letter to the editor with a confidence and assertiveness that the Greeks had not shown a decade before:

> *I have read with feelings of regret and indignation the extracts you published from the sermon, if it could be called such, delivered by Rev. J.W. Ham on last Sunday night at the Baptist Tabernacle. Rev. Ham, by his sweeping indictment of the Greeks in this city, has shown himself so ignorant of the real facts, or else so prejudiced, that I feel it impossible to let such an insult pass unchallenged…. I again repeat that Rev. Ham showed his ignorance or his prejudice…and this making of an accusation against all as a class is wholly improper for a minister, whose creed should be fairness and justice to man…. And I further take this opportunity of telling Rev. Ham that if he was not aware of these facts, he is not fulfilling his duty as a minister when he indicts as a whole a class of citizens which is one of the best in Atlanta. And if he was aware of these facts, then to so indict a class shows more of the demagogue who tries to bring strife and discord into his community than the minister who tries to further its moral welfare.*[307]

This was no ordinary defense offered in response to one of the more typical insults casually directed at these immigrants but rather a well-reasoned and direct broadside and rebuke to an institution that was a pillar of the white Protestant establishment of the city. The membership of the Tabernacle alone at this time was substantially greater than the entire Greek immigrant population of Atlanta. Less than six months after Reverend Ham's sermon, the congregation would move into a new building that would seat more than three thousand people.[308] That a Greek immigrant would publicly chastise a man of this stature underscored the self-image transformation of a community that had once been defined largely as street peddlers but now prided itself on its role in the economic progress of the city.

The immigrants had become very protective of the image they portrayed to the broader Atlanta community. Maintaining this image remained important to the Greeks throughout these early years. In 1913, the community faced the possibility of either making a delinquent payment to former governor Joseph Brown for property purchased from him for expansion or seeking an extension for repayment. In rejecting both options and resolving to raise the necessary funds, the community carefully considered that neither "of these solutions would be particularly dignified for the prestige of our Church, or the prestige of our Community: to appear, that is…in the eyes of a former

Governor that the Church is not in a position of fulfilling its obligations, on time, and with mathematical precision."[309]

Similarly, in 1917, as the community debated whether to proceed with the production of a play that would be open to the American public, the primary concern was not the financial success of this fundraising endeavor but the reception by their American neighbors. The possible negative impact on the image of the Greeks in the event of a poorly produced play weighed heavily on the council's deliberations. The council was urged "to be very careful, because…it is possible for something which is actually good to lead to something bad in the Community, and in case of failure, to lead to the defamation of the Greek name. We should primarily be careful about that, and not necessarily about the material outcome of this event."[310]

Sustaining this positive image, hard won over the years, was critical to the Greeks in their quest for full acceptance by society, and the deep pride they shared in their economic achievements provided them with the self-confidence to publicly respond to any portrayal they felt posed a threat to their identity as a community. Defensive responses were evoked equally by trivial slights as well as by more significant disparaging remarks. As the community matured, its sensitivity to negative portrayals of any type increased. Slurs on the community's character were no less aggressively dealt with when the source of the insult was also a Greek immigrant. Responding to a perceived, published insult by a fellow Greek, the Church Council threatened to prosecute him:

> *Due to the fact that the despicable individual…throwing off all restraint, has insulted in an astonishing way, the Priest, the Church Council, and the Community, by means of his worthless rag, where he accumulated tens of thousands of imaginary false accusations, it was decided that for the sake of the dignity of all the accused, and for the sake of justice and the truth, that was shamelessly violated, the Church Council will undertake the criminal prosecution of this charlatan, without spending a single penny of the Church's money.*[311]

When Angel Sallas, as a result of a personal dispute with fellow Greeks, charged that the "Black Hand" society had threatened him, the response from his community was swift. The leading members rejected the existence of such an organization among the Greeks and sought to differentiate themselves from Italian and other non-Greek immigrants: "There is no such thing as a Greek Black Hand Society. Such an idea is ridiculous. The

Black Hand Society is composed of Italians and other classes of foreigners. The Greeks have the greatest respect for the law, and don't countenance any infringement."[312]

Similar sentiments would be expressed in response to one of the frequent characterization of the Greeks as "dagos": "My countrymen now living in Atlanta and adopting this city as their future home do not wish to be referred to in a slighting manner, and classed with people unworthy of Greece."[313]

During the investigation into the highly publicized murder of Mary Phagan, detectives identified a Greek restaurant employee as a possible suspect and commented that she had been murdered in the "Mediterranean style."[314] One hundred members of the enraged community gathered to protest these remarks. The Greek consul, Dimitri Vafeiades, replied, "We protest most vigorously against such use of the word Greek in flaring headlines." The president of the community, Gerasimos Algers, declared:

> *If a Greek had committed this crime he would never get out of Atlanta alive. The Greeks would have lynched him. And we protest most vigorously against such treatment as we received today in the newspapers. We are industrious and law-abiding and the majority of us are prominent property holders in Atlanta. We do not wish to have the public turned against us. If a Greek should ever be arrested, say Mr. Petros as you would say Mr. Smith.*[315]

The Greeks' resentment spurred the *Constitution* to editorialize that "[t]he Atlanta Greeks, especially, are justified in their protest."[316] Soon after this incident, the Greek vice-consul from Wilmington, North Carolina, D. Einetitajial, donated twenty-five dollars to a fund established to aid in the case. In the letter accompanying the check, he said, "Dear Sir: The Greeks of Atlanta wish to see the mystery surrounding the tragic death of Mary Phagan solved and the reputation of their good city of Atlanta untarnished."[317]

The community understandably wanted to completely disassociate itself from what remains one of the most notorious murder cases in the city's history. Vafeiades would respond just as quickly a year later when the *Constitution* incorrectly reported that a Greek had been arrested for a minor matter involving the mayor. Addressing his complaints to the paper's editor, he chastised him for the indiscriminate use of "Greek" to describe certain suspects:

> *Having read the dramatic story in this morning's issue of the arrest, by Honorable Mayor Woodward, of a Greek, I called at police headquarters, to investigate the matter, and I found that the man is a Hungarian. I must confess that I did not take the trouble to see about this matter but for… the slight abuse of the word "Greek", which is very often applied to every dark-haired, strange-looking foreigner who happens to commit something. I am sure that there ought to be some remedy to this state of affairs, and the simplest way would be to call each individual by his own name.*[318]

These comments are revealing of the positive self-image that the Greeks possessed by the first decade of the twentieth century. Regardless of the fact that society at large could barely distinguish any differences between its Italian and Greek immigrant residents, the Greeks perceived themselves to be made of finer mettle than their fellow southern Europeans. The Greeks may have shared the same downtown sidewalks and streets in selling fruits and vegetables, but only the Greeks were inheritors of a classical civilization so highly esteemed by contemporary society. Apart from their own accomplishments, the Greeks could, and would, draw frequently on the deeds of the ancients to counter unfavorable depictions.

Nevertheless, despite the evident economic and social progress of the Greek immigrants, and their resulting pride in their own accomplishments, the early depiction of their condition by Greece's official representatives in the United States was negative and unflattering. Lambros Koromilas, Greece's first envoy to the United States, came to the position well qualified. Educated in Greece and France, then earning a doctorate in physics and mathematics from the University of Tubingen, he had most recently served as the consul general in Thessaloniki.[319]

Upon his arrival, he quickly developed a condescending and caustic impression of the Greeks he found in America, and he communicated this portrayal to his superiors in Athens: "Do not expect me to encourage the patriotic and religious thoughts of the Greeks in America…. I inform you that the Greeks here are so coarse, and so simple that there does not exist any danger of losing either their religion or their patriotism."[320]

Koromilas's depiction of the life of the Greek immigrants as being one of misery and poverty was criticized even by George Horton, head of the American legation in Athens.[321] Theodore Saloutos, in his history *The Greeks in the United States*, described Koromilas's feelings as "a manifestation of the contempt that members of the educated, professional, and government classes of Greece had for the immigrants," "the peasants of yesterday," whom they "despised as a horde of crude illiterates who had to be driven like cattle."[322] Koromilas would be gone within two years, and the later assessments of subsequent Greek diplomats were markedly different, as the immigrants began achieving economic progress and receiving measured social approval.

The economic progress of the Greeks undoubtedly contributed to the group's self-esteem. It emboldened them in their aggressive defense to any perceived slights to their community and contributed to the identity they were fashioning for themselves in their new Atlanta homes. But how these Greeks perceived themselves depended more significantly on other matters, and nothing could more clearly reveal the Greek immigrant's struggle for his self-identity than his responses to his motherland's call for help in its armed crises.

Chapter 9

THE *PATRIDA*

Dual Allegiances

"We Have Sold Our Fruits and Are Going Home"

Over the course of over two decades from 1890 to 1913, Greece would engage in several wars with the Ottoman Turks and the Bulgarians. More frequent during this period were the ongoing guerrilla actions between Greeks, Bulgarians and Slavs over lands of the Ottoman Empire as it was disintegrating in the early years of the 1900s. Almost from the time Greece had gained its independence from the Ottomans in 1832, its foreign policy had been based on the concept of the Megali Idea, an irredentist concept that called for liberating ethnic Greeks sill living in lands that were under the rule of the Ottomans. With the Ottoman Empire in its last stages, Greeks were anxious to reclaim these lands to realize the vision of reinstating the glories of the Byzantine Empire. The vision stoked the passions of Greeks everywhere. The Bulgarians and Slavs were just as anxious to claim these territories to satisfy their own nationalistic desires.

This passion was especially strong in the many thousands of Greek men who had immigrated to America. Throughout the Unites States, Greek immigrants would respond to the call for help from their native land by forming units in their communities and repatriating to Greece to fight in its armies.

Nothing could better manifest the conflicting dual allegiances that these immigrants would often deal with than their ready willingness to risk their lives for their native country while still maintaining the strong desire to become citizens of their new land. Their oft-stated expressions of their plans to become naturalized citizens were passionate and sincere, as were the strong feelings of attachment they had developed for America and the cities they called home.

When Pete Pappas and Nick Speropoulos departed the city in 1912 for a visit with their families in Greece, they painted "Atlanta, Best Town in America" on their travel baggage and printed several hundred cards providing information about the city: "We will tell them all about Atlanta and her people, and are sure that it will cause many to want to return with us."[323]

Still, notwithstanding their commitment to their new lives in America, these immigrants would return home to risk their lives in Greece's wars. The Greco-Turkish War of 1897 began when the Ottoman province of Crete declared its desire for independence and union with Greece. The reaction of the Ottomans was swift, and the need by Greece for troops was immediate. Almost the entire small community of Atlanta Greeks gathered to discuss the war and their plans.[324] King George had issued a call to all Greek reserves to return to Greece to fight.[325] Soon after these initial meetings, eleven Greek immigrants, about a quarter of those residing in Atlanta, departed to return to Greece to engage the Turks.[326] "Their worldly goods were left in the hands of their friends, farewells were spoken and those who were members of the reserve, with the exception of a few, returned to their native land."[327] Nicholas Konts was one of those who sold all of his belongings prior to his departure for Greece for what the *Constitution* described as a "more than probable death on the battlefield":[328]

> *The war cloud had reached Atlanta. It had settled over the fruit stands and had clouded the Greek colony in the city…. The dark-faced Greek lost interest in his occupation. The selling of fruits and the bartering of vegetables was abandoned…. At noon these eleven patriots were at the carshed. They carried in their hands long, green tickets, and they anxiously waited for the Seaboard train to puff out of the station. They were on their way to New York, and tomorrow they will sail for the war.*
>
> *"We are going to fight," said one of the number in broken English. "We can't stay in Atlanta while our countrymen are up in arms in our native land. We have sold our fruits and are going home."*[329]

One member of the community's leaders, C. Constantine, predicted that, within a few days, all of Atlanta's Greeks would return to fight and "that there will be no Greeks in the city."[330] His passion for support of

C. Constantine, one of the early leaders of the Atlanta Greek immigrants, 1897. *Courtesy of the* Atlanta Journal-Constitution.

Greece was shared by almost all of the men of the community. For those half dozen men who failed to attend a meeting to gather volunteers for their native land, Constantine was clear in his feelings:

We began an investigation to know if they were going to contribute and give their life, if necessary, for the cause of humanity. We learned that they would not assist us in any way and we did not hesitate in calling them traitors. I have not the power to choke them or I would take great pleasure in doing so…. We intend to take the name of Greek from them and call them only dogs.[331]

Later, in 1902, as hostilities with the Bulgarians were threatened over the fate of Macedonia, the Greeks of Atlanta came together and prepared to depart as a group for this latest war effort. Bulgarians and Greeks were engaged in brutal fighting, village by village. A British traveler in the region, John Foster Fraser, described the intensity of the hostilities: "Both races believe they are engaged in a high patriotic mission. They will not listen to reason. They regard the others as vermin deserving only extermination. So the burning of houses, the murder of partisans, is proceeding apace in a more flagrant manner than during the times of Turkish atrocities."[332]

It was into this bloodshed that the Greek immigrants were willingly returning, leaving behind the ordered, if difficult, lives they were creating for themselves in America. Led by Victor Canares, who was selected by the community as captain, 150 of the approximately 173 Greek immigrants in the city formed themselves into a company prepared to depart for Greece if necessary.[333] As the *Constitution* colorfully described the scene:

Animated groups stood in front of nearly every fruit stand and copies of the well known Greek papers published in New York, The Atlantis, *were being read in feverish haste. At times, the sale of fruit was forgotten, for the modern Greek is still a warrior in spite of ages of commercialism. Deep down in his Latin soul the price of fruit is as nothing to his love of country.*[334]

Greeks departing from Port of New York for Greece and fighting in Balkan War, 1912. *Courtesy of Library of Congress, Prints and Photographs Division.*

A decade later, in 1912, the outbreak of the First Balkan War would again challenge the allegiances of the Greek immigrants. With the Ottoman Empire now almost at its end, the eastern European states that were formerly subjects of the Ottomans—Greece, Serbia, Montenegro and Bulgaria— sought to release their ethnic populations remaining in the empire. The irredentist claims of these nations were strong, and they unleashed powerful emotions in their respective diasporas, especially among the Greeks in America. The Greeks in Atlanta were no exception to this. Committed as they were to establishing permanent homes in the city and becoming citizens, the emotional tug of their homeland was strong.

However, by this date, as we have seen, many have them were far removed from the simple occupation of a street vendor and had acquired a measure of economic success and financial security that could not as easily be left behind in a return to Greece. Moreover, as will be discussed later, the community now had a church around which its members' lives revolved. Many of these men were also now married with families. All of these should have been mitigating factors against the same types of patriotic responses produced by the conflicts of 1897 and 1902, but this rush to defend the *patrida* by Greek immigrants throughout the United States was the same.

As the *Constitution* reported, five hundred Greek men of the city had again assembled to discuss their plans, gathered together "from the reek of the kitchen and the counter of the corner soda fountain to wage war upon the terrible Turk."[335] Their priest, Father Demetrios Petrides, challenged them, "What are you going to do? Will you fight for your country?"[336] The *Constitution* reported that one hundred of the men responded by volunteering to enter the war, that $10,000 was pledged to support the volunteers' families during their absence and that fifty-five Greeks had left Atlanta for the fighting.[337]

Whatever the actual number of men who left the city for Greece, it was sufficiently large that the treasurer of the church's council informed the council at its meeting in January 1913 "that owing to the departure of a good number of Church members, due to the war, the number of members had been noticeably reduced, therefore, the income was reduced, too."[338] When, in the following month, a resignation from the Church Council created a vacancy, none of the runners-up from the earlier council elections was available to fill the position, "due to the fact that they had left, to go and fight the war."[339]

On the day before their departure, the men were honored by a parade down Peachtree Street, cheered by "thousands" watching and accompanied by the Georgia National Guard's Fifth Regimental Band, a police guard and an honor guard of five hundred of their compatriots staying behind.[340] Many of those departing were veterans of the 1897 engagement in Crete, including their officers, Dr. S.J.B Vryonis and J. Philaretos.[341]

A photograph accompanying one of the *Constitution*'s articles that captured the assembly of these Greeks provides graphic testimony to the dual and sometimes conflicting loyalties of these immigrants. They are shown "standing between the Stars and Stripes on the one side as a token of their good will toward America and the blue banner of Greece on the other as a pledge of their allegiance to their own country."[342]

Greece would profit immensely from its victories over, first, the Ottomans and then the Bulgarians in the two Balkan wars, increasing both its territory and population by more than 60 percent. The euphoria in Greece and in the Greek-American communities in the United States occasioned by these conflicts fueled dreams of finally realizing the long-held irredentist goals of liberating all Greeks still living in Ottoman lands. For the Greeks, the reestablishment of the Byzantine Empire throughout the old Ottoman lands had become a very real possibility with its decisive victories.

George Nikas, one of the first of the Atlanta Greek immigrants to return to Greece as a volunteer in the Greek army, 1912. *Courtesy of Vickie Klemis and Mary Ann Hiett.*

In Atlanta, the president of the community, Gerasimos Algers, and Father Petrides cast these wars as the biblical fulfillment of the visions of the Prophet Daniel and the prophecies of Revelation, and they predicted not only "doom" for the Turks but also the recapture of past glory:

> *The defeat of the Turks and their expulsion from Europe; the recapture of Constantinople; the driving back of the Moslem into Asia Minor, and the resurgence of the old Byzantine empire have been looked forward to with the deepest religious convictions.... Some day in 1913 Christian rule will be re-established in Constantinople. The Turks will be driven back into Asia Minor, where they belong.... For four centuries the Grecian race was under the unbearable yoke of the terrible Turk. But true to his religion, and having in mind the Word of God, the nation has patiently waited for the fulfillment of the time which God set for their salvation.*[343]

The subject nations achieved early and significant successes against the Ottomans in the First Balkan War. The territorial conquests of Greece realized long-held dreams of uniting traditional Greek lands. These victories were celebrated by the Atlanta Greeks as "the big and glorious events that took place in our motherland."[344] At a regularly scheduled general assembly meeting, the community decided to forego the deliberation of official church matters and instead opted to "keep the festive character of the day intact."[345] Father Petrides, in his remarks, "glorified the Almighty God for the successful outcome of the war and the enlargement of our own country."[346] The pride felt by these men in the Greek army's victory in the First Balkan War's Battle of Bizani prompted them to distribute twenty copies of the history of this important engagement to libraries and schools throughout the Atlanta area.[347]

Less than six months after the start of the war, however, the Greeks were mourning the death of King George I of Greece, who had been assassinated in Thessaloniki. The man to whom each of the Greek naturalized citizens had disavowed any loyalty in their petitions for citizenship was honored with a large memorial service. Five days after the king's assassination, the community came together in an "extraordinary" general assembly to make plans "for the expression of our mourning over the death of His Majesty our King George the First."[348] Dimitri Vafeiades, the Greek consul, attended the meeting and emphasized the importance of a solemn, public memorial for the king that all of Atlanta's Greeks would support.[349] All Greek-owned shops would be closed, and photographs of the king would be prominently

Funeral procession of King George I of Greece in Athens on March 20, 1913. *Drawing by Sotiris Christidis. Courtesy of Wikipedia.*

displayed. Vafeiades expressed the opinion that "the Americans will be the first ones to congratulate us on the closing of our shops."[350] A committee was appointed to notify the Greek businesses about the plans for the memorial.

On the day of the public mourning, the community gathered at the offices of the Pan-Hellenic Union and processed several blocks to the church for the memorial service. All Greek-owned businesses would be closed from 2:00 p.m. to 5:00 p.m. the following Sunday, and the Greeks would observe their mourning by wearing black armbands for ten days. Cablegrams were sent by members of the community to the widowed Queen Olga and her son Constantine expressing their condolences: "Greek community of Atlanta expresses condolences for national calamity, and wishes to your majesty a glorious reign."[351]

However sincere their mourning for their former king and however committed to their homeland these Greek immigrants had remained, the community and its self-identity had been transformed in its two decade presence in the city. No longer fully Greek, as the settlers of a "Greek colony," and perhaps still not yet completely accepted as "pure Americans," the community occupied a middle ground as Greek-

Americans where it had become a "they" for their Atlanta neighbors as well as their compatriots in Greece.

In a visit to Atlanta in 1911, Greece's vice-consul from Nashville, Seraphim Canoutas, according to the *Constitution*, put words to this transformation in comments he made praising the progress of the city's Greeks:

> *Mr. Canoutas is extremely enthusiastic over the future of the Greek-Americans. Thousands of them are becoming naturalized he says, are coming to look upon the United States as their home, and are proving themselves to be most excellent citizens. And, in Mr. Canoutas' opinion, the Greek-Americans will, at no distant date, come to be a prominent factor in the progress and development of the country.*[352]

With the conclusion of the Second Balkan War in July 1913, the community undertook efforts to financially assist the families of those men killed in the conflicts and to honor those returning from the wars. Father Petrides "emphasized that the war, which glorified the Greek arms so much, and became the reason for the praise of our dear native country, had its painful and sad aspects, too, which can be seen in the death of the heroes, who fell honorably in the fields of honor, and in the widows and orphans, who were left behind, unprotected, and they can rightfully claim the protection of the Greek expatriates, wherever they may be."[353] A special committee was formed to solicit donations, with the money collected to be sent directly to King Constantine.[354] Many of those men returning to Atlanta from the Balkan Wars had been awarded medals for valor in battle, and the Atlanta community hosted a ceremony for these men in recognition of their war efforts.[355]

That these immigrants had also by this decade committed themselves fully to their civic obligations as Americans was underscored later by their actions when the United States entered World War I as a combatant. The nation had maintained strict neutrality since the start of the war in July 1914, only declaring war on Germany on April 6, 1917, after the latest in a series of submarine attacks on its merchant ships. Almost exactly two months later, these Greeks marched down Peachtree Street to the state capitol, "parading for Uncle Sam" in a noisy demonstration of their commitment to the war effort:

> *Downtown Peachtree gave way to a brand-new war thrill yesterday afternoon when a great body of patriotic Greeks, many of them veterans of the Bulgarian war, paraded behind the flags of Greece and America carried at the head of a band combining Greek national airs with "Dixie" and other*

*American anthems. The parade concluded a grand patriotic demonstration
held on Central Avenue by the Greek colony of the city. It also followed
a stirring address delivered on the capitol steps by Governor Nat Harris,
whither the Greeks had marched at the invitation of the governor.*[356]

It was reported that scores of the Greeks had registered for the draft
before the start of the parade. The president of the community, Gerasimos
Algers, boasted "that not a member of his nationality in Atlanta of eligible
age had failed to register."[357] Leading the parade down Peachtree Street was
the community's priest, Father Demetrios Petrides.[358] He pledged to the
governor "the allegiance of Atlanta Greeks," many of whom carried signs
proclaiming, "We are ready, Uncle Sam."

What is especially interesting about this very public commitment by
Atlanta's Greeks to the war effort was its timing on June 5. Like the United
States, Greece had maintained its neutrality in the conflict despite strong
pressure by the Allies to join their efforts. The Greek prime minister,
Eleftherios Venizelos, favored Greece's entry into the war on behalf of the
Triple Entente—Great Britain, France and Russia. But King Constantine,
the brother-in-law of the German emperor Kaiser Wilhelm II, supported
neutrality. This dispute played out over several months until Greece finally
declared war on the Central powers on June 30, more than three weeks
after the Greeks of Atlanta, almost all of whom were Greek natives and still
very fond of their king, had already declared their support for the American
effort against Germany.

Even as early as August 1915, the Greeks of Atlanta were expressing the
hope that Greece should commit to the war effort on behalf of the Triple
Entente. Animated more by concern for their fellow Greeks living under
Ottoman rule than by the type of more clearly patriotic sentiments shown
in 1917, the community had sent a telegram to the recently resigned prime
minister Venizelos, urging his continuing involvement in Greece's foreign
policy. Believing "that the present is the logical time for Greece to strike for
the freedom of large numbers of the race who are now living under the
domination of Turkey," the telegram urged:

*We, the Greeks of Atlanta, ask you, the liberator of the old and new Greece,
to continue your work of emancipation, and to remain in politics until the
remaining of our nationality is free from foreign yoke.*

THE GREEKS OF ATLANTA[359]

These differences between the king and Venizelos on the conduct of Greece's war effort foreshadowed even more serious future disagreements between the men and altercations between their followers. The long-simmering divisions in Greece between the Royalists and the Venizelists, further inflamed by the actions leading to Greece's entry into the war, would roil Greece's politics and Greek communities throughout the United States for the next decade. The Atlanta Greeks would not be spared. Open disputes between the Royalist and Venizelist factions first appeared several months before Greece's entry into the war in June 1917 and increasingly plagued the community throughout the 1920s. Traces of these old divisions were still present in the community to some extent more than a decade after Greece abolished the monarchy in 1974.

The Greek immigrant's answering of Greece's many calls to arms laid bare the dual allegiances to Greece and America that he felt. Likewise, his unwavering commitment to his Orthodox Christian faith in the face of America's religious pluralism just as clearly revealed his close and enduring identification with the faith of his fathers. His Orthodox Christianity, however irregularly he might have practiced it, was an inseparable part of his self-identity.

Chapter 10

FAITH

"Εις το όνομα της Αγίας και Ομοουσίου και Αδιαιρέτου Τριάδος"

I n the name of the Holy and Consubstantial and Indivisible Trinity." So begins the Greek constitution, which then goes on to provide that "the prevailing religion in Greece is that of the Eastern Orthodox Church of Christ." There has been no separation of church and state in Greece since its modern founding, nor was the Eastern Orthodox Church ever shaken, as was western Christianity, by the Protestant Reformation of the sixteenth century. Orthodox Christianity was, and still is, the official religion of the nation. The Greek Orthodox faith was an inseparable part of the identity of both the Greek nation and its citizens, including those who had decided to leave their homeland for better economic opportunities. Greece was an overwhelmingly Orthodox Christian nation. The 1920 Greek census reveals that 99.7 percent of the population of the Peloponnesos, from which most of the Atlanta Greeks emigrated, was Orthodox Christian.[360]

Unlike the French Revolution, which precipitated the de-Christianization of the French state, the Greek War of Independence witnessed the active participation of the church in the initial liberating event of the war and in the foundation of the modern Greek state. According to tradition, on March 25, 1821, Bishop Germanos blessed a Greek flag at the monastery of Agia Lavra and proclaimed the beginning of the revolt against the Ottoman Empire. That date is celebrated today as Greek Independence Day and is a national holiday. It is also the date of the celebration of the feast day of the Annunciation, one of the twelve major feast days of the Orthodox Church.

With the exception of the Holy Trinity Church in New Orleans, there were no Greek Orthodox churches, clergy or hierarchs when most of the earliest Greek immigrants began arriving in the United States in the last two decades of the nineteenth century. Like their countrymen everywhere, these men coming to Atlanta had brought with them their faith but had no way to receive the church's sacraments or to participate in the liturgical life of the church without ordained clergy.

The record is relatively silent about how these men were able to regularly practice their faith prior to the arrival of Father Christos Angelopoulos in 1903 as the interim priest. We don't know exactly how, when or if the immigrants worshipped in the last decade of the nineteenth century, whether there were gatherings of these Orthodox men to share their faith with each other or simply private devotion within their homes. Nor do we know whether they worshipped on occasion in the churches of other Christian denominations or were individually targeted for evangelization. In at least some instances, these men indicated that the absence of any Orthodox priests forced them to turn to ministers of other Christian denominations to sanctify their marriages and to assist in the interment of their deceased.[361]

In 1913, Reverend S.L. Morris of Atlanta, the secretary of the home mission board of the Southern Presbyterian Church, urged the need for evangelical efforts among the immigrants coming to the United States.[362] But by this time, Orthodox churches had been established in scores of communities, and the sacramental needs of the immigrants were being met in the churches of their fathers. But in the almost fifteen-year period between their earliest immigrations and the arrival of Father Angelopoulos in 1903, the Greeks in Atlanta were largely detached from the active practice of their native Orthodox faith. As mainly unmarried men, they were especially vulnerable to any proselytizing efforts directed toward them. The missionary efforts aimed at the Greeks were very real, both in the native country they had left behind and in some of the American cities and towns that were becoming their new homes.

During the decades in which the early Greek immigrants to Atlanta were arriving, Protestant missions were present in Greece and eastern Europe and throughout Asia Minor. The traditional Orthodox nations of eastern Europe, recently freed from Ottoman occupation, and the Orthodox Christian subjects essentially defenseless in Asia Minor were seen as an especially fertile field for missionary work. Missionaries were working in all of the larger Greek cities and were particularly active in the Ottoman lands as that empire slowly disintegrated. As Moslems were not allowed to profess Christianity openly, the missionaries directed most of their efforts in Turkey toward the Greek, Armenian and Syrian Christians who were Ottoman subjects. The American Board of Commissioners for Foreign Missions, the largest and oldest of the Protestant missionary organizations, was especially active in Turkey, with scores of active missionaries, grade schools and seminaries.[363]

The targeting of these Orthodox Christians for Protestant proselytizing at this time was in sharp contrast to the attitude of the missionaries toward Roman Catholics in Europe. At its 1898 annual meeting, the American Board of Commissioners for Foreign Missions considered abandoning its missionary activities for Catholics "in Papal Lands" as an unproductive endeavor:

> *Your Committee are well aware of the fact that to many of the most intelligent supporters of the Board Papal Lands seem a doubtful field for foreign missionary work. Devout Protestant scholars cherish the hope that the next reformation may be a peaceable one, wrought by the Spirit from within the Roman Catholic Church; and they think that the present attitude of Protestantism toward that great communion of believers should be one of expectant waiting upon Providence rather than of missionary propagandism.*[364]

Nonetheless, the Protestant efforts to establish churches in Greece were almost universally unsuccessful, as "Greek Protestants are looked down upon as unpatriotic and sneered at, if not openly persecuted."[365] A Protestant church in Piraeus was attacked and burned in 1888, and the church's minister, Reverend Kalopothakes, "escaped lynching or stoning with great difficulty."[366] Although a few small churches were created, and Greek-born Protestant ministers were leading these churches, the overall result was dismal. As described by a Greek Protestant minister, "The direct result of the whole movement to organize a separate Protestant body is rather small and discouraging."[367]

However, the situation was different in Ottoman Turkey. With the Ottoman rulers unconcerned about the proselytizing activity among its Christian subjects, gains were made there at the expense of the Greek Orthodox and Armenian Apostolic Churches. The Protestant seminaries, such as the one in Marsovan, educated Greek and Armenian men and produced Protestant ministers. One of these was Reverend J.P. Xenides, who was born in Asia Minor to Greek parents and later taught at the seminary.

Protestant missionary organizations began to focus their efforts on Greek and other southern and eastern European immigrants as they began arriving in America in the 1890s. Taking the lead in this initiative was the Home Missions Council of America, an interdenominational mission agency organized by twenty-three Protestant denominations. Among its stated objectives was mission work among the nation's immigrants. Xenides and other Greek Protestant ministers trained in the seminaries of Asia Minor would become the leaders of the effort to establish Protestant churches among the Greek immigrants in America. Although small Protestant Greek-immigrant churches were established in Lowell, Massachusetts; Boston; and Chicago, the overall results were meager. Xenides recognized that "there is little effective work being done by the Protestant churches exclusively among the Greeks."[368] He could only lament that there were no "men of the type of Luther" to get the job done.[369]

Most likely because of the relatively small number of Greek immigrants in Atlanta, there is no record whatsoever of any organized Protestant missionary activity among these men. The Episcopal and Presbyterian communities that made their churches available to the Greeks for marriages and other services seemed motivated by nothing more than neighborly charity. Nor does the record reveal any noticeable conversions to other faiths, although there were undoubtedly individual exceptions. Instead, it seems clear that these men remained committed to their Orthodox faith in spite of the absence of priests and other challenges that were presented in the fifteen years before the arrival of their first priest.

By the turn of the century, these immigrant men had begun to gather together on Sunday in a rented hall at 120½ Decatur Street, reading the Divine Liturgy and the Psalms and chanting the liturgical hymns.[370] In order to receive the sacraments, however, the community was forced to wait for the infrequent and irregular visits of Orthodox priests, who were few in number in the United States at this time and much in demand by Greek communities everywhere.

The first recorded Orthodox sacraments were the baptisms of Sappho and Antigone Constantine on June 25, 1900. The rites were performed by Archimandrite Dorotheos Bakaliaros. Without a church structure within which to worship at this time, the baptisms took place in the home of Alexander Carolee, a fellow Greek immigrant. Sappho was five and Antigone three, much older than the traditional age of children baptized

ARCHIMANDRITE DOROTHEO OF GREEK CHURCH BAPTIZES TWO CHILDREN HERE

Archimandrite Dorotheos Bakaliaros celebrating the baptisms of Sappho and Antigone Constantine, the first Greek Orthodox baptisms in Atlanta on June 25, 1900. *Courtesy of the Atlanta Journal-Constitution.*

in the Orthodox Church, where infant baptisms are the norm. The lack of access to Orthodox priests had forced the Constantine family to endure a long wait for the arrival of a visiting priest to baptize its daughters.[371]

Well educated and multilingual, Father Dorotheos served Greek communities throughout the United States by traveling to celebrate the sacraments for the faithful in those cities that lacked a full-time priest. The Atlanta and Birmingham communities shared the responsibility of underwriting the expenses of bringing Father Dorotheos to the South.[372] He was one of the earliest Orthodox hierarchs sent to the United States by Ecumenical Patriarch Constantine V to tend to the spiritual needs of the growing Greek communities.[373] The *Constitution* noted the significance of this event with a lengthy article providing a detailed description of the ceremony: "The service began by Father Dorotheo blowing into the faces of the children and making the sign of the cross upon their breasts."[374]

By the end of the ceremony, the girls had become the first native Atlantans to be baptized into the Orthodox faith. The community was hopeful that the visit by Father Dorotheo would be "instrumental" in the establishment of a church in Atlanta.

About eighteen months later, in December 1901, John Nekas died, and with his death the city witnessed the first Orthodox funeral in Atlanta. Still without a priest, the community brought Father Kallinikos Kanellas from Savannah to conduct the funeral service, which was held at Patterson's Funeral Home.[375] Father Kallinikos was one of the first Greek Orthodox priests to serve in America, helping Greek communities as early as 1893.[376] He was among a small group of priests that traveled around the country conducting baptisms, weddings and funerals and otherwise ministering to the needs of various Orthodox communities.[377]

By at least autumn of 1902, the Greeks had made arrangements with St. Luke's Episcopal Church to use that community's sanctuary for funerals, baptisms and weddings. The small hall on Decatur Street would continue to serve their needs for Sunday gatherings but was not suitable for these sacramental services attracting a larger gathering. The use of St. Luke's would continue until at least April 1904.[378] The funeral service for James Pagonas was held that month in St. Luke's, officiated by a "priest of the Greek church in Birmingham."[379]

Depending on the occasional visits of Orthodox priests for their spiritual needs and the kindness of other church communities for the use of their sanctuaries had sufficed for the Atlanta Greeks in the past. But the rapidly growing community now needed its own church to adequately serve its people.

Chapter 11

ESTABLISHMENT OF THE CHURCH

"And Bring Us Back to Our Dear Orthodox Church"

A s Greek immigrants continued to arrive in Atlanta after the turn of the century, the pressure to organize an Orthodox church increased with the sacramental needs of the expanding community. Only a church and a permanent priest could serve these needs as well as become the centralizing entity around which the community could coalesce. This immigrant group of largely Greek men, whose fruit stand livelihoods had been continually challenged by the city's elected leadership for more than a decade and who had also during this time competed fiercely with one another on the downtown sidewalks, was at last beginning to work collectively for the establishment of a church.

The result of this initial collaborative effort was the formation of the *Evangelismos* Society in October 1902.[380] The incorporators were Gerasimos Algers, Constantine Boutos, Constantine Athanasopoulos, Alexander Carolee, George Carolee, Constantine Charalambides, Christos Kotsakos, Nicholas Kouloukis, John Stavropoulos, S. Pergantis, Angelo Demopoulos, V. Petropoulos and Panayiotis Vergiotis. The primary purpose of the organization was to lead to the establishment of a church for the community.[381] The name *Evangelismos*, or the "Annunciation of the Mother of God," was adopted by the society as the formal name of the parish and the future place of worship. With the formation of the society, the community rented another hall at 113½ Whitehall Street, which would be converted in 1905 to a small chapel and serve as the first Greek Orthodox church of the city.[382]

Later, in 1908, after the establishment of the church, many in the community believed that the society should be disbanded. They felt that its origination had "aimed only at the erection of a Church" and that "once this goal, the establishment of a Church, was accomplished…it had no reason to exist."[383] However, the society was revived, still under the name of "*O Evangelismos*," much to the consternation of some. By that time, it had been transformed into a social and cultural club, and its primary goal was assisting its members in securing their citizenship.

With the formation of the *Evangelismos* Society in 1902 and the availability of the spare hall on Whitehall Street as a small sanctuary, the community now only needed a priest to fulfill its liturgical and sacramental needs. That priest was Father Christos Angelopoulos, who would serve the Atlanta community for a brief period of time. Accompanied by his seventeen-year-old daughter, Olga, he arrived in New York from Greece on May 24, 1903,

The top floor of building on the left (with decorative roof detail) became in 1905 the first space used for liturgical services. *Courtesy of Kenan Research Center at the Atlanta History Center.*

destined for Atlanta and the home of his brother-in-law, George Carolee.[384] Born on February 12, 1867, he served as a parish priest in Argos from 1897 to 1907.[385] He was married in 1886 to Ekaterina Pita, also a native of Argos.[386] They had six children, although only four survived to adulthood. He was a graduate of the Theological School of Halki in Constantinople and also a graduate of the Teacher Training College in Tripolis, holding the church offices of archimandrite and confessor.[387]

However, Father Angelopoulos was never formally assigned to the Atlanta community by the Ecumenical Patriarch.[388] In a biographical statement that he prepared for Archbishop Athenagoras in 1931, he did not even list Atlanta as one of the communities he had served in America in his long ministry in this country. According to his statement, he first assumed his priestly duties in America for the Memphis community in 1907. With his still active service as a priest in Argos, he had almost certainly come to Atlanta in an informal capacity. He most likely came to Atlanta, a city that was then home to many of his fellow Argos natives, as a personal favor to his brother-in-law to assist the community for an interim period. The extensive list of liturgical items and vestments purchased after Father Hadjidemetriou's later arrival in 1905 and the obvious absence of these items prior to his arrival also strongly suggest that Father Angelopoulos came to Atlanta only in a temporary capacity.

Father Christos Angelopoulos, the Atlanta Greek community's first priest. *Courtesy of the Greek Orthodox Archdiocese of the United States.*

While it is uncertain exactly how long Father Angelopoulos served the Atlanta community, he did so at least from late May through mid-September of 1903. He officiated at the wedding of Gerasimos Algers and Hariklia Seretis on September 13, 1903, which was just the second Greek wedding in Atlanta.[389] With many of the Greek men now having achieved a certain level of financial success, their desire to marry and begin families would provide additional impetus for the establishment of the community's church. However, Father Christos may have already departed from Atlanta within a year, as Father Kallinikos Kanellas was again summoned to the city to perform the funeral service for James Pagonas in April 1904.[390]

By July 1905, the community was in contact with Ecumenical Patriarch Joachim III in Constantinople seeking the assignment of a full-time priest to the community in order to establish a church.[391] In a September letter to the Patriarch, the Church Council extended to the new priest an offer of a salary of $1,000 per year, with the opportunity for additional income to be derived from marriages, christenings and funerals.[392] The council also committed to allow the priest to provide pastoral care to Greeks outside Atlanta so that he could supplement the small income it would pay him.[393] This last provision of their proposal would later become a matter of some dispute within the community.

As they expressed in their letter to the Patriarch, these men were keenly aware of the effects on their community of not having the permanent presence of a Greek Orthodox priest in Atlanta:

> *Ever since they arrived at Atlanta, these Greeks did not have the chance to attend Divine Liturgy, due to the lack of a Priest. For that reason, they are obliged to perform their marriages with Ministers of other religions, and they do likewise for the interment of their dead.... For all these reasons, we implore your Divine Holiness to send us an appropriate Priest, who will guide us worthily, and bring us back to our dear Orthodox Church. Because, as we have earlier mentioned, we fear that we will be de-touched from our Holy Orthodox Church, for not having a Priest in our community.*[394]

It appears unlikely that the immigrant Greeks drifted toward other faiths in these early years. But certainly this letter to the Patriarch revealed their fears of the effects of their long separation from their church and of losing their connections to the "Holy Orthodox Church" without a priest in their midst.

After assuring the Patriarch of their accumulated savings earmarked for the construction of a church on property that they were negotiating to purchase, the council concluded: "We are, therefore, addressing your Divine Holiness our fervent supplications, asking that you seriously consider all the things mentioned in this letter, find the right Priest for us, and send him over here on time. This way, by his presence and advice, we will be able to construct our Church in short time."[395]

Soon after this request, the Patriarch appointed Father Constas Hadjidemetriou as the priest for the Atlanta community. The council cabled

Patriarch Joachim III, Ecumenical Patriarch of Constantinople, circa 1878. Photograph by Vasili Kargopoulo. *Courtesy of the Ecumenical Patriarchate and Father Nephon Tsimalis.*

$147.30 to Constantinople for Father Constas's ship fare.[396] In the meantime, the community had submitted on July 22 a petition to the Fulton County Superior Court for a legal charter creating the Greek Orthodox Church of Atlanta.[397] The petition was granted on September 5, and the church was officially founded.[398] With its incorporation, the Annunciation Greek Orthodox Church of Atlanta became only the sixteenth Greek Orthodox parish in the United States. Composing the initial board of the church were Nick Pope, Leon Campbell, George Moore, Constantine Athanasopoulos, Steve Gialelis, Evangelos Botsaris and Dionis Fotou.[399] Constantine Athanasopoulos was elected as the first president of the community.

Father Constas was born in 1872 in the small village of Pyrgos on the island of Samos, one of five children of George and Kalomira (Maniates) Hadjidemetriou.[400] Both of his grandfathers had been priests.[401] At the time of his birth, Samos was not yet a part of Greece but rather was a semi-independent tributary of the Ottoman Empire. Atlanta would be one of eleven parishes that he would serve in his ministry in the United States.[402] He was married to Maria Travlos in Constantinople, and they would eventually have five children.[403] He spoke several languages fluently and had earned a Doctor of Divinity degree.[404] An erudite and committed church man, he was capable of both energetically participating in the mundane tasks of the church, such as fundraising, while also challenging his parishioners with thoughtful sermons. On the Sunday celebration of the Annunciation feast day and Greek Independence Day in 1908, he delivered a sermon on the "Refutation of Pantheism and Its Results on Society."[405] Father Constas would later publish in 1929 a catechism of the Eastern Orthodox Church and be awarded Greece's oldest and highest decoration, the Order of the Redeemer.

He arrived in Atlanta by October 1905 and began serving the community that month.[406] The council executed an order for vestments, necessary liturgical items and icons, all of which were to be shipped from Constantinople.[407] Nine icons were also ordered, and two additional icons were donated to the community by the Patriarch.

The first regular liturgies celebrated by Father Hadjidemetriou and Atlanta's Greeks took place in the chapel on Whitehall Street, the converted hall being rented at that time by the community. Its small size and temporary nature notwithstanding, the community was intent that it not lack all of the appointments and liturgical items expected in any Orthodox Christian church. In addition to the icons, oil was purchased for the votive lamps, as was wax for the candles, which were handmade by the sacristans; a *stavromenos*, a cross and "a crucified body of Christ," in preparation for Easter; a wooden stand for the candles; a reading stand for the Gospel; and, most importantly, a Holy Funeral Shroud, or *epitaphios*, for Holy Friday and the midnight Easter Liturgy.[408] Mr. Theofanis Gounaris served as the church's first chanter.[409]

Seventeen years after the confirmed presence of Greek immigrants in the city, the community, now several hundred in number, began celebrating regular church services in the small chapel on Whitehall Street at least by the feast day of St. Nicholas on December 6, 1905.[410] In the weeks leading up to their first Easter service the following April, the Greek immigrants also celebrated the March 25 Annunciation feast day and Greek Independence Day with a special ceremony. The ceremony was held on the afternoon of Sunday the twenty-sixth in order to allow the men working on Saturday to attend. A fortepiano was brought into the church hall, and a musician from New York was hired to play the Greek and American national anthems, as well as other music.[411]

In its letter to Patriarch Joachim, the Church Council had committed to him its intent to build a church to serve the rapidly growing community. The rented hall on Whitehall and the small converted chapel there were no longer sufficient. Negotiations were completed in September for the purchase of a lot directly across from the state capitol at the corner of Piedmont Avenue and Hunter Street.[412] The church was listed in the 1906 city directory as the Hellenic Orthodox Greek Christian Church, with a street address of 8 Capitol Avenue. Plans were made to construct a Byzantine-style edifice based on Hagia Sophia in Constantinople.[413] However, Father Demetry, as he became known to the Atlanta community, expressed early concerns about the small size of the property.[414]

The strong preference of the community was to construct this Byzantine-style church on the Capitol Avenue site, but the lot was not large enough. The purchase of an adjoining strip of property would be required.[415] The additional costs involved in this, as well as the construction costs for a new church building with this architectural style, forced the consideration of other options. By March 1906, a Presbyterian church at the corner of Garnett Street and Central Avenue became available and was offered to the Greek community by the board of trustees of the Associate Reformed Presbyterian Synod of the South, based in Abbeville, South Carolina.[416] Although the community made clear that "no one was really happy with the thought of having a Presbyterian style Church," the economic advantages of purchasing this building dictated the community's final decision in favor of this option.[417] Notwithstanding these reservations, within three years the community demonstrated its pride in the new sanctuary by ordering five thousand postcards depicting the interior of the church, as well as six enlarged photographs of the church's interior, three of which were presented as gifts to the priest, Patriarch Joachim and Archbishop Theoklitos I of Greece.[418]

The purchase of the Presbyterian church, executed on July 9 at a cost of $9,000, was formally announced at a meeting of the church's general assembly on July 15.[419] Father Hadjidemetriou reminded those gathered of "the joy that every Greek heart should be filled with, for having acquired a Church so fast."[420] The church structure that the Greek community was acquiring was relatively new, no more than ten years old. The Presbyterian Synod had purchased the property in May 1895 for $3,750 and had constructed the building some time after that.[421] Although still a relatively new building, attending services there would have reminded the immigrants in some respects of the much older churches they had left behind in Greece. Electric fans for the church were not purchased and installed until 1915, so the "excessive heat" of Atlanta's summers was simply endured during church services for the first decade of its use; in winter, the church was inadequately heated with small charcoal and gas heaters.[422]

The first liturgy in the new church was celebrated on Sunday, July 15.[423] Although the acquisition of the building also included the furnishings of the church—such as pews, an organ and a gas stove—several additions were needed to transform the interior into a sanctuary appropriate for Orthodox worship.[424] The Church Council decided to extend an invitation to an artisan from Greece, Angelis Kalovedouris, to prepare a proposal for the construction of an icon screen.[425] Most important for these Orthodox Christians was the installation of the icons themselves. Rather than burden the church's budget with the purchase of these, donors were solicited for each of the icons necessary for the icon screen, with their gifts being recognized as having been made in dedication to their patron, or namesake, saints.[426] These icons, as well as the votive lamps and additional priest vestments, were purchased in Greece by Constantine Athanasopoulos while on a visit there, with funds sent to him by the council in Atlanta.[427]

Even as final plans were being made to acquire the church, a feeling still persisted that this arrangement was only a temporary one and that once the community had risen "to the level of financial freedom that would allow the building of another Church, then, we could always demolish this one, or alter it so as to look like our own, the Byzantine style."[428]

With their establishment of the first Greek Orthodox church of Atlanta, these immigrants were introducing a form of Christianity radically different

Icon of the Annunciation from the original 1907 Iconostasion of the Garnett Street church. *Courtesy of the Annunciation Greek Orthodox Cathedral of Atlanta.*

from the overwhelmingly Protestant culture of the city. The elaborate rituals, Greek-language liturgy, bearded priests, Byzantine chanting, candle stands, iconography and incense-filled church presented a stark contrast to the far more spare Protestant expressions of the Christian faith. The Greeks were aware of the widespread unfamiliarity in Atlanta with the Greek Orthodox faith and were intent on ensuring that their American neighbors understood that they were, in fact, Christians. As a result, the community adopted the Hellenic Orthodox Greek Christian Church as its rather unwieldy formal name. Atlanta's annual city directories would list the church as such for the next decade.

The only accommodation that the Greek Orthodox Christians made to the prevailing worship culture was the introduction of the organ and choirs into their liturgical services. Although we don't know when these began to be used, each would become and remain a fixed part of Orthodox worship. However, there would be no accommodation from the Greek immigrants in the matter of the church calendar. The Orthodox Church had not adopted the calendar reforms of Pope Gregory in 1582 but rather had maintained until this time the older Julian calendar. With a difference of thirteen days between the Julian and Gregorian calendars, the liturgical calendar of Orthodox Christians was thirteen days later than the western calendar. The Greeks in Atlanta did utilize the Gregorian calendar in at least some civil capacities. Payments for Father Hadjidemetriou's housing rent were made according to the western calendar.[429] For a period of about three years, the dates of the Church Council and the general assembly meetings were recorded in the official records of the church according to both the Julian and Gregorian calendars.

Atlanta's first Greek Orthodox church at the corner of Garnett Street and Central Avenue, circa 1917. *Courtesy of the Annunciation Greek Orthodox Cathedral of Atlanta.*

The present-day Atlanta Municipal Court Complex on the former site of the Greek Orthodox church. *Photo by Stephen Georgeson.*

For example, the initial cash receipt entry in the church's accounting book is listed as "October 1/14, 1905." By 1909, all records were being kept according to the Gregorian calendar.[430]

But there would be no deviation from the Julian calendar in the immigrants' observances of the church's cycle of feast days. This would be most notable around Christmas, when the city's newspapers would invariably comment on the delayed observance of Christmas by the Greeks on January 7.[431] Not only was Christmas celebrated thirteen days later, but the Nativity services also did not begin until 1:00 a.m. and extended for about three hours.[432] On almost every occasion, Father Hadjidemetriou would provide a detailed explanation in the city's dailies of the differences in the two calendars.[433]

Even in the face of assimilationist expectations to fully adopt the local customs, the community would continue to adhere to the old Julian calendar and maintain the necessary preparation for one of its holiest days. The *Atlanta Georgian and News* commented approvingly:

> *For the Orthodox Greek approaches the sacred holidays not like the modern American—with much jollification, shooting of firecrackers, loud and bibulous conversation and other external evidences of physical and mental exhilaration—but with due preparation for the proper celebration of the most memorable event in the history of man…. The Greek recognizes no Santa Claus.*[434]

One of the immigrants, Peter Louis, explained their attitude to the American celebration of Christmas on December 25: "[W]e have no celebration whatever on that day. My people celebrate Christmas thirteen days after the Americans, and while we may give presents to our American friends on that day, it means nothing to us as a race."[435]

Chapter 12

ORGANIZATION OF THE CHURCH

*"Those Who Are Not Members of the Church Have No Right to Criticize,
Blame or Express Disapproval of the Priest"*

Raising the funds necessary for the establishment of its church was difficult for a community still dependent to a certain extent on incomes generated from the fruit stand business. Furthermore, these men had emigrated from a nation where Orthodoxy, as the official state religion, was financially supported by public funds. So the difficulty of producing church revenue from the earnings of these fruit dealers was compounded by the challenge of transforming the mindset of men who were not accustomed to the need for the independent financial support of the church. While the sacristan's responsibilities included the collection of the Sunday offerings and the donations pledged to the church by its members, the major responsibility for generating sustained pledges fell to the priest, with some assistance from the Church Council.[436] In addition to traditional donations, the church raised funds through the issuance of notes, or bills, which were loans extended to the church by certain of its members.[437]

Father Hadjidemetriou, Constantine Athanasopoulos and Kyriakos Kyriakopoulos traveled to cities throughout the Southeast and even as far as Brownsville, Texas, where there were Greek immigrants, to raise funds for the church.[438] In some of these cities, they were simply soliciting donations; in others, Father Constas led liturgical services and administered the sacraments, gathering collections in his ministerial activities. In less than five months after Father Hadjidemetriou's arrival, they had visited fifteen cities and collected $1,772, which represented almost one-third of the church's revenues by the end of 1906.[439] The funds that were donated for candles and in the collection plates during the services he performed in these cities were also donated to the church, even though the Church Council had earlier promised these donations to him as a supplement to his salary.

The church's financial condition had become acute, and having already collected donations from Greeks in other cities, the Atlanta congregation could look only to its own parishioners for further assistance. As pointed out by Father Hadjidemetriou, "Although he recognized that presently our fellow patriots living in the Atlanta area may not be going through happy times, yet the dire necessity we find ourselves in indicates that the only anchor of salvation left to us is the additional contribution."[440] The council struggled with ways to increase the church's revenues. For those Greeks unable to make cash donations to the church, the council and Father Hadjidemetriou devised a system that allowed these men to issue promissory notes to the church that, in theory, guaranteed a reliable stream of future income.[441]

But this would still not be sufficient. Father Hadjidemetriou also expressed the concern that their present method of making the church's collections "is no different than plain beggary," which could deter volunteer service on the council itself. More troubling to him was that this "beggary" would eventually result in diminished respect for himself as a clergyman. "It is imperative that the respect for the Priest remains undiminished for a great many matters."[442] He then proposed a plan that he had recommended to the community in Savannah with success. This called for every Greek shopkeeper to sign a promissory note to the church by which he would be committing that, as long as he resided in Atlanta, he would make regular quarterly payments of his annual pledge to the church, as well as a quarterly contribution of $1.50 for each of his employees. The shopkeeper would maintain the responsibility of withholding this amount from the employees' salaries.[443] Father Hadjidemetriou's plan was adopted by the council.

Practical as the plan seemed, actual implementation proved difficult, as the shopkeepers were sometimes reluctant to withhold the church dues from the salaries of their employees who claimed financial hardship.[444] Two members of the council assumed the responsibility of the monthly collection of the contributions to the church and "were given the right to use a carriage whenever they might need to go to far away places."[445] Eventually, the cooperation of both the shopkeepers and their employees was secured, and the council determined that "the new system was proven even more successful than we had hoped for."[446] In just a few months, more than two hundred men signed promissory notes on behalf of the church.[447]

The still vacant lot across from the capitol also continued to place financial pressure on the community, as it had incurred a debt in its purchase that had become an unsustainable burden once the Presbyterian church had been purchased. In May 1907, the council first broached the idea of disposing of the property through a lottery or raffle.[448] Advised by an attorney that the lottery would violate federal law, the council next rejected both a public auction and a sale of the property to a group of parishioners as ways of selling it.[449] Finally, a buyer for the lot was found. With this sale, the community's dream of constructing a Byzantine-style church would not be realized. The church at the corner of Garnett Street and Central Avenue would remain its home until 1930, and it would be sixty years after the sale of the property before the community would be able to worship in a Byzantine-style church, when it completed construction of the present sanctuary on Clairmont Road in 1967.

In spite of the ongoing struggles of the Greeks to adequately fund their new church, other important work was being completed by the council in 1908. Under the chairmanship of Stephanos Psychalinos, the Church Council acted to adopt the church's first regulations or bylaws that would provide a formal framework for its operation. Prior to this time, the church's minutes disclose several references to a "Regulation" as guidance in conducting the meetings of the community. Lacking at that time any bylaws of its own, the Church Council was almost certainly utilizing some type of parliamentary publication such as *Robert's Rules of Order*.

The church was now prepared to adopt its own guidelines for the conduct of its affairs. On April 6, 1908, the council presented to the general assembly for its approval twenty-nine articles for the "Regulation of the Greek Religious Association '*O Evangelismos*.'"[450] Each of the articles was presented and approved individually by the members gathered.

The document is a remarkable product for these men at this particular time. They were continually dealing with the threats of the Atlanta City Council to the existence of the fruit stands that many of them still depended on for their livelihoods. At the same time they were struggling for the very existence of the church. The regulations are a combination of thoughtful, legalistic controls designed for the long-term administration of the church and more specific, personalized provisions dealing with issues of the moment facing the community.

Constantine Athanasopoulos (standing) with family, friends and Father Basil Lambrides, circa 1910. *Courtesy of the Annunciation Greek Orthodox Cathedral of Atlanta.*

What is most striking about these regulations, at least from an Orthodox perspective, is the almost total autonomy that the Church Council and the general assembly ceded to themselves in the operation of the church. The Archdiocese of North and South America would not come into existence until 1921. Without the presence of any bishops or other church hierarchs in the country when these regulations were drafted, there was little explicit recognition of any hierarchical authority or supervision, either pertaining to theological or spiritual matters or in the administration of the church's affairs, in accordance with Orthodox canonical practice. The concept of lay church councils or boards with full governing authority over church affairs is completely foreign to Orthodox ecclesiology and tradition and was unknown in the Orthodox world until its introduction into the Greek Orthodox churches established in the United States by these Greek immigrants. We can only speculate as to the actual motivation of these men. Were they simply adapting to a church environment in this country that was without the presence of the traditional hierarchical structure of clergy that existed in the old lands, or did they knowingly assume the governing models and lay authority that were prevalent in the ubiquitous Protestant communities?

The only limited exception to the self-autonomy created by these regulations pertained to the church's priest. He was to be "recommended by the Ecumenical Patriarchate or by the Synod of the Church of Greece," but the council reserved for itself the final decision to "choose and recommend the Priest of the Church."[451] Likewise, although the regulations provided for addressing any disputes with the priest to "the Higher Church Authority, which is the only appropriate body to judge and decide as for the fairness of the submitted case," the regulations made clear that the council and the church's general membership nonetheless retained the ultimate authority to dismiss the priest.[452] Reserving for themselves pastoral and ministerial responsibilities that Orthodox canon law properly delegated to the church's bishops and hierarchs, these men had crafted rules for the church's operation that adhered closer to a Protestant model of an independent, self-governing church body. The regulations nonetheless provided a solid foundation for the operation of the church and commonsensical solutions to problems faced by the church community. Even with these significant assertions of lay control over the administration of the church's affairs, the ultimate spiritual authority of the Ecumenical Patriarchate in Constantinople and the Synod of Bishops in Athens was recognized. There was no effort by the Greek immigrants in these early years to disconnect themselves from the church's hierarchs in the old countries or to create a new native hierarchy in America.

Included within the very first article of the proposed bylaws was an expression of the community's plans for a school "which will serve the children of Greek expatriates." This was to be an alternative Greek community school, but not just a school for the instruction of the Greek language. These first-generation immigrants, still very much fluent in the Greek language, were nevertheless concerned about maintaining proper Greek fluency in their children. The Greeks were also intent on maintaining cultural cohesion for future generations through the formal education of their children by instruction in Greek. Their plans were for a school offering the youth a rigorous curriculum, "providing them with an education befitting a Greek."[453]

Although the exact nature of the curriculum is not detailed at the school's inception, it was broad enough a decade later that a member of the Church Council would suggest that "we should recommend to the parents and guardians of our students not to send their children to American schools" because he believed "that it was not possible for the children to learn both languages well."[454] With the adoption of this article, the community was soon planning for the conversion of certain areas within the existing church building into the school rooms necessary for instruction.[455]

This article also provided that church services were to be conducted "exclusively in the Greek language" by a priest who "should possess a Degree from a renowned Theological Seminary of the Nation [Greece]." Although the vast majority of these immigrants had come to America from small villages in the Peloponnesos, they would not be satisfied with village priests in their new communities.

Whoever ultimately became a priest in the Atlanta congregation would be protected as much as possible from undue criticism. The regulations provided that "those who are not members of the Church have no right to criticize, blame or express disapproval of the Priest."[456] Nor did nonmembers "have the right to express judgments, or to get actively involved in community affairs, regarding ecclesiastic matters."[457] These provisions were directed at those men in the Greek community in Atlanta who were not members of the church and had its genesis in recent criticisms of the Church Council and Father Hadjidemetriou by a disgruntled Greek. Similarly, any church members who had grievances or complaints about the priest did not have "the right to defame the Priest by involving his name here and there. Instead, they ought to address themselves to the Church Council, so that necessary explanations can be provided."[458] Furthermore, if a member of the church was accused of "'sowing discord' to the disadvantage of community interests, then, based on the decision of a community meeting, this member will be crossed off the Register of the community members, for improper behavior."[459] The same underlying desire of these immigrants to present a positive image to the broader Atlanta community, seen in their other dealings with the press, no doubt motivated the drafting of these particular articles.

Membership in the church was open to "any person of Greek descent, and of Orthodox Christian faith."[460] The regulations balanced strict dues payment requirements, the violation of which could result in loss of church membership, with obligations placed on the priest to offer his sacramental services "to poor Greek expatriates free of charge."[461] However, the priest was "not allowed to offer his services to those who, although they prosper, refuse to pay their membership fee to the Church," with exceptions in the case of death, christening and sickness.[462] Violation of this article by the priest could result in a charge against his salary. There was apparently no realization of the significance of an article that potentially denied the

Eucharist to Orthodox Christians. In assuming ecclesiastical responsibilities for themselves in the absence of church hierarchs, these men were creating authority as laymen that was contrary to Orthodox church law, which reserves all decisions about the administration of the church's sacraments to the clergy and the bishops.

The twenty-eighth article of the regulations included an interesting provision expressing the "wish" to transfer in the future the property of the church to the "Greek State," once the debt had been eliminated, "for reason of insuring entirely this property, against the case that the Church would cease meeting the purpose that it was established for."[463] Under traditional Orthodox canon law, the property of any dissolved parish should devolve to the appropriate bishop. The absence of any church hierarchs in America at this time left these men without any local bishop to whom the property could be entrusted upon the parish's dissolution.

With the community desiring, then, to codify a contingency plan for the church's property in the eventuality that the church was ever dissolved, it sought the assistance of the Greek ambassador, Lambros Koromilas, to redraft this article. The severe financial problems facing the church at this time most likely influenced the decision to include such a provision in the church's new bylaws.[464]

However, the article as revised by Koromilas and adopted by the general assembly on May 20, 1909, went further than originally drafted by the Atlanta Greeks. It's not known if the revised provision accurately expressed the intent of the Church Council or merely reflected the ambassador's lack of confidence in the community's survival. Nonetheless, the article now provided that all of the Atlanta church's property was to be donated to the National University of Greece in Athens, with the church maintaining free tenancy of the property for as long as the church existed:

> *The Church and all of its property, as well as its future property, are here forward donated, on behalf of the whole Community, to the National University of Greece, in Athens. This donation gives to the Greek Community of Atlanta free tenancy, for as long as the community is in existence. The University can sell the Church, and dispose of the property of the community, only after the community is dissolved. The University has the obligation to use the resulting sum of money for the purpose of supporting education, especially among the groups of the enslaved Greek populations, with the approval of the Greek Government.*[465]

In spite of this expression of intent in its bylaws, the community must have developed reservations about making such a donation to the university. No such transfer was ever legally effectuated, and the Garnett Street property would eventually be sold by the community when the church moved to its Pryor Street location twenty years later.

One of the other articles of the regulations was specific to the understanding that the Church Council had reached with Father Hadjidemetriou concerning his salary. His annual salary had been set at $1,000, but the council had provided that he could retain whatever donations and gratuities he received in administering sacraments and celebrating the liturgy for Greeks in other cities in order to supplement his compensation. The sixth article adopted represented an attempt to formalize that understanding:

> *When the need arises for the services of the Priest, to those members living outside* [the city], *on a week day, the Priest has to notify the Church Council about it. Exception is made when the Priest is called urgently for some religious ceremony, and there is no time for the regular procedure. With regard to Sundays: the Priest is granted 12 Sundays in a year, which he can use either for the benefit of the Church and of the Greek expatriates, "Omogeneis," who, live around, or for his own benefit. In order for him to use these particular Sundays, he needs to make arrangements and come to agreement with the Church Council.*[466]

Chapter 13

THE CHURCH GROWS AND A
SCHOOL OPENS

"Our Fathers Have Preserved Them with Fire and Sword"

Despite the best intentions of the council and Father Hadjidemetriou to clarify and properly formalize their understanding, disagreements would soon arise that would present a serious challenge to the young church. Four months after the adoption of these regulations, a group of parishioners petitioned the Church Council to revise the provision allowing the priest to minister to the needs of Greeks in other cities on twelve Sundays during the year, claiming that his absence harmed the financial interests of the church.[467] Also in order to reduce expenses, the petitioners called on the council to "do away with" the *epitaphion* flowers on Good Friday and to discontinue the "blessings" of the Greeks' businesses on the feast day of Epiphany because "it appears to offend the dignity of the shop keepers."[468] The council was strongly supportive of allowing Father Hadjidemetriou to make these trips, as it fulfilled the commitment made to him and the Patriarch when Father Hadjidemetriou first came to Atlanta:

> *The Council will emphasize that it is not fair for the priest to be deprived of his rights without any compensation. In this case, though, that compensation is an impossibility, then, things should remain as they are, for it is not in our interest to let the priest go, on any account; because, this will be the next thing to happen, if the Community insists in cutting back his rights. Besides, those rights are the obligations that the community took on by its letter to the*

> *Patriarchate. Furthermore, the priest has made such a conscientious and,*
> *also, brilliant use of his rights, that until now, he was able to bring to the*
> *Church of Atlanta, from the neighboring communities, practically as much*
> *money as he was given as salary over the last three years.*[469]

Father Hadjidemetriou was invited to offer his response to this petition at the next general assembly meeting. This he would do in a lengthy and passionate statement that not only served as a vigorous defense to the complaints that had been made by some about him personally but also stood as an eloquent declaration on the dignity of the priesthood and the sanctity of the teachings and traditions of the church.

Father Hadjidemetriou's main defense was presented in an extended written statement that he read to the members of the general assembly on August 27, 1908. It is a remarkable document, preserved in its entirety in the minutes of the general assembly and deserving of extensive quotation. With its formal structure, dramatic rhetorical flourishes and interrogatory approach, the statement resembles a classical *apologia*, and his defense has some of the tone of Plato's *Apology of Socrates*: "It has been said, Gentlemen, that I have the magical ability to read prayers over those who come to serve on the Church Council, and turn them into unquestioning supporters."[470]

In response to the petition that he no longer liturgize on twelve Sundays during the year for the benefit of Greeks in other cities, Father Hadjidemetriou referenced both the community's original letter to Patriarch Joachim and the adoption of the regulation just four months earlier specifically granting him these privileges. He reminded them that his trips had not only allowed him to supplement his inadequate income but had also benefited the church:

> *Time, however, Mr. Chairman, has shown that the Greeks in America go*
> *to the Divine Liturgy only on Sundays. Even here, in this Church, during*
> *the feast days of our Lord the Christ, or the Mother of Our Lord, or the*
> *Saints, when they fall on week days, is it not true that there is just one,*
> *or not even one churchgoer attending? In such days, am I not obliged to*
> *address the chairs, for lack of any human presence, and pronounce "let us*
> *love one another…" or "bow your heads onto the Lord"? Yes, I am. So, it*
> *became necessary to have 12 Sundays in a year granted to me, in accordance*
> *with the existing Regulation. As you well know, I made an intelligent and*
> *advantageous use of those Sundays, managing not only to bring in the*
> *amount of money, in excess of my salary, which I need as a family man*
> *and as a priest, but also to bring in, from the neighboring communities,*

*both money and offerings for the Church that are equal in value to the total
amount of money that I have received as salary, to this day. One could
say that for the past three years, the community was not burdened with the
payment of a priest's salary.*[471]

Father Hadjidemetriou further pointed out that his ministrations to the
Greeks in these other cities had been directly responsible for the establishment
of churches there also:

*These people are not foreigners, after all, and I am well aware that they
have organized themselves considerably, in every respect, ever since I have
started calling on them, as they, themselves, would declare, too. I am asking,
then, Mr. Chairman: Who helped the community of Savannah form,
and provide its members with a Church? Who provided the motive for the
community of Memphis to form...? The Greeks in that community were
not even willing to go to the Liturgy, at first, because they did not know each
other. Who organized the community of Augusta...? Who helped with the
formation of the numerous neighboring communities...? None other, Mr.
Chairman, than your priest, with all his homilies addressed to the Greeks
in the surrounding areas. Those homilies, though, would have never been
heard by Orthodox Christians, if they had not been preached on Sundays.*[472]

Nevertheless, he was prepared to accept whatever decision the
community made:

*If, on the other hand, in spite of the fact that you are not in a position to
increase my salary, you still insist in taking away from me the Sundays in
question, this will only mean that, actually, it is not pleasing to you to have
me as your priest. If this is so, there is no need for excuses; the community
can say it overtly, and you can rest assured that I will not attempt to stay
by force. I will seek a position elsewhere in America.... In this case I can
only wish you to find a successor who will be better than me, so that you
will never need to remember me; and even from far away, I will not stop
to wish the best for your community, as I do for all the communities that I
have served until now.*[473]

The second and third items in the petition to the Church Council would
lead Father Hadjidemetriou to admonish the men of the community on
the importance of faithfully maintaining the traditions and beliefs of the

Orthodox Church and on the proper role of the church hierarchs in all matters pertaining to the expression of the faith. Although he remained willing to compromise on the matters pertaining to his compensation and to discuss alternative solutions, he was unyielding in his insistence on maintaining the customs and traditions of the church:

> So, Mr. Chairman, as far as the financial aspect of this matter is concerned, I will accept any arrangement that will allow me to have a more dignified way of life, but as for the religious aspect of it, I can not accept any annulment or reform, because it is part of my duty to preserve everything that was entrusted to me by my Church.[474]

The second item of the petition recommended that the flowers traditionally used to decorate the *epitaphion* on Good Friday be eliminated. The third item sought to stop the practice on the feast day of Epiphany of the "illumination," the blessing of the homes and businesses by the priest with holy water. The shopkeepers had complained that the practice was embarrassing to them when performed in the presence of their American customers. He began first by saying, with respect to the *epitaphion* flowers:

> If those, however, who submitted the petition mean to say that the religious custom of Epitaphios flowers should be abolished altogether, I am GLAD that neither the Christians themselves, nor I, though I am a member of the clergy, are the appropriate persons to decide on this; this can only be decided by the higher authority of the Church.[475]

However, it was in his defense of the "illumination," or blessings with holy water, that Father Hadjidemetriou would make his most fervent and passionate remarks on the Orthodox faith:

> If those who signed the petition, though, mean that I should abolish the religious custom of "illumination," because of wrongly understood sense of honor and self respect, as I was unofficially informed, once again, I am GLAD because we are not the right persons to make such a decision. For, if it was up to us, and we had made it a matter of principle to adjust the customs and traditions of our religion to the liking of foreigners, then, we would have modified everything, the one after the other, and very likely, for many of those "modifications" we would not know which one of the so called American Churches to follow. Because the differences that do

exist between those Churches are as many as the number of heads existing in them; and they do laugh at one another. I am exceedingly sorry, Mr. Chairman, because we cling to such ideas, although it is not our job, and we expect to sacrifice the customs and traditions of our religion in the name of a false pride, and for the sake of foreigners. The Americans, on the other hand, do not feel any shame at the drums of the Salvation Army, and the like. Our own compatriots in Macedonia and elsewhere, especially in Asia [Minor], do sacrifice, like brave soldiers, not only the "touchiness," but even their own lives for the sake of the religious freedom, and of their national consciousness; and the fanatical Turks do not recognize, in a most triumphant way, every such freedom.

The words of our Lord Jesus Christ come, now, to my mind, and in all honesty, I do not mean, by citing them, to speak against you, the Greeks who live in the free America; our Lord says: "Whosoever therefore shall be ashamed of Me and of My words in this adulterous and sinful generation; of him also shall the Son be ashamed when He cometh in the glory of His Father with the holy angels." Indeed, Mr. Chairman, could there be a more demonstrative application of the above words than in this occasion? For in this generation, the sinful and slanderous, it appears that we are ashamed for Our Lord's Cross, which we are asked to kiss in the "illumination," and we seek to do away with these things, which we should be proud of, because our fathers have preserved them with fire and sword. That's why, Mr. Chairman, as being the offspring of those fathers, I consider it to be an honor to hold the Cross of Our Lord, as high as it can be, in the illuminations, during Epiphany, when I arrive, with every solemnity, at the workshops of those Orthodox Christians who, just like me, do not wish to be timid about their religion.[476]

After reading the July 1905 letter that Patriarch Joachim had sent to the Church Council and further defending his receipt of the gratuities from the other Greek communities, he launched into an emotional defense of himself and the priesthood, beginning with a recitation of chapter 9 of the Apostle Paul's First Epistle to the Corinthians:

"Am I not an Apostle? Am I not free? Have I not seen Jesus Christ our Lord? Are you not my work in the Lord? If I am not an apostle to others, yet doubtless I am to you. For you are the seal of my apostleship in the Lord."

My defense to those who examine me is this: Do we have no right to eat and drink? Do we have no right to take along a believing wife, as do

also the other apostles, the brothers of the Lord, and Cephas? Or is it only
Barnabas and I who have no right to refrain from working? Who ever goes
to war at his own expense? Who plants a vineyard and does not eat of its
fruit? Or who tends a flock and does not drink of the milk of the flock?…
If we have sown spiritual things for you, is it a great thing if we reap your
material things? If others are partakers of this right over you, are we not
even more?[477]

Before speaking to the priesthood generally, Father Hadjidemetriou
offered a very personal and proud defense of himself:

> *Well, then, Gentlemen, my small profits are rightfully mine. Now, some*
> *people are asking me to sacrifice them. The sacrifice is optional, it cannot*
> *be demanded. Yet although I am a man of sacrifice, Gentlemen, and I have*
> *proven it in numerous occasions in my life, I am now asking you to show*
> *me the need for it. Show me the religious necessity, or the patriotic one, or*
> *any other common necessity, which I should be doing this for, and I will*
> *do it at once; but I do not see any such necessity…. Didn't your priest act*
> *as a collector, when it was needed? Didn't he generate small profits for the*
> *Church, in ways that no one else had thought before, and he did it even*
> *though he was harming his own interests? Wasn't he always the first one*
> *to offer eagerly his mite, in favor of every cause? Isn't he the one who has*
> *been doing all the writing and the related jobs for the Church, during the last*
> *three years, without the slightest benefit?*[478]

As he approached his concluding comments, Father Hadjidemetriou, in
remarks echoing those of the Apostle Paul, made an eloquent appeal for the
dignity of the priesthood and the concerns of their families:

> *Do my accusers think, by any chance, that when one becomes a priest, one*
> *can successfully shake off human needs, such as taking nourishment, using*
> *clothes, etc.? These are needs that not even our Lord had managed to avoid,*
> *though He was God. Do you think that, by becoming a priest, one loses*
> *one's right to live, and to love, and to take care of the family that he has*
> *created in this world? Doesn't a priest have the fundamental rights, that even*
> *the least of the human beings enjoy, after having spent considerable time*
> *of his life sitting on school benches, in the process of becoming a priest? I*
> *am asking you, Gentlemen: If, instead of studying theology, I had chosen*
> *to study medicine, or law, or some other science, wouldn't then, the parents*

Father Constas Hadjidemetriou and Presbytera Maria and their family, circa 1919. *Courtesy of Nick Demetry.*

who reared me, have the right to expect of me to take care of them, in their old age? Wouldn't my wife have the right to expect of me, to provide her with a tolerable life? Wouldn't I have the obligation to bring up my children in a decent way? Does it mean, then, that just because I became a priest, I have been discredited, and all those who depend on me should be deprived of their rights?[479]

He reminded the men that, as most of them were still unmarried, they could not appreciate the special needs and obligations of a head of a family, such as he faced:

Some will argue that I am wasteful because although I am given 20 dollars to pay rent, I chose to pay 30 dollars instead, as I wish not to reside in a chicken coop, but to live in the kind of house that does honor to me, and to the church, and to the Race that I represent, as well. You may be right,

Sirs, because you are not heads of families. It is not difficult, though, to ask someone who is the head of a family, and get informed about the needs of a family in America.[480]

Finally, he closed his lengthy defense, prior to departing the meeting:

Thus, I am worthy of respect, Sirs…. I will, now, leave the meeting, as I do not wish to exert any influence on you…. I will let myself at the mercy of God, and He will not abandon me; if the decision you arrive at is to refuse me the bread of my family, then, I will abide by the hope to find other Christians, who will provide it for me, without complaints, while I will be working for their benefit. I heartily wish that you may never have to remember me. Farewell Gentlemen![481]

How the individual members of the general assembly personally responded to this emotional presentation by Father Hadjidemetriou is not known. Presumably, it swayed them, as they discussed several options, favorable to the priest, that could be pursued in order to "secure the peace in the Community."[482] The matter was referred to the Church Council for further discussions with Father Hadjidemetriou.

The council and the priest reached an agreement under which Father Hadjidemetriou could continue making his rounds to the Greeks in other cities so long as he notified the council and provided it with addresses in each city visited so that he could be reached by telegram if any needs should arise in his Atlanta community while he was absent.[483] However, despite the efforts of both the council and Father Hadjidemetriou to return to their previous relationship, the breach created by the disagreements could not be repaired.

It was also evident that the relatively small Atlanta community would continue its struggle to compensate him enough to allow him to care for the needs of his family. When the much larger Holy Trinity Church in Lowell, Massachusetts, offered him its pastorate, he accepted. He explained that "he has found it difficult to provide for his large family as he should, and he realized that the church here, which is young and few in numbers, could not afford to pay him the salary offered by the Church in Lowell."[484]

At a meeting on March 28, 1909, he informed the council that he was leaving Atlanta, most likely before Easter. The timing of his leaving would pose problems for the community, as it approached the holiest period of the church calendar and the many services that would require the presence of a priest.

In 1908, Patriarch Joachim, facing an uncertain future with the rise of Turkish nationalism under the Young Turks, had transferred the spiritual jurisdiction of the Greek Orthodox churches in America to the Church of Greece.[485] At almost the same time, Greek prime minister Georgios Theotokis had appointed Lambros Koromilas as the Kingdom of Greece's first envoy to the United States. With the patriarch's jurisdictional transfer to the Greek Synod and the absence of any Orthodox hierarchs in the country, Koromilas would assume extraordinary importance for Greek immigrant communities throughout America, even with respect to church affairs.[486]

The general assembly resolved that Koromilas "be asked to designate a Priest for the Community."[487] So, with Father Hadjidemetriou's departure imminent, the Church Council appealed directly to the ambassador for an extension of the date of their priest's transfer. The Atlanta Greeks cabled Koromilas on the same day of Father Hadjidemetriou's announcement: "We are very sorry to see our Priest transferred. However, because of the upcoming holiday season, we are kindly asking you to extend the deadline of his departure, with no harm befalling on him. Reply paid. The Church Council."[488] Father Hadjidemetriou also wrote a letter to his future parish in Lowell, asking its consideration in allowing him to remain in Atlanta until after Easter.[489]

Father Hadjidemetriou presents a sympathetic case. The passionate eloquence of his defense reaches beyond his immediate disagreement with members of the parish over his compensation. It could serve as the lament of all clergy, especially Orthodox priests, to be treated fairly in similar situations. Like all of the early Greek Orthodox priests assigned to the newly developing parishes in the United States, he had come from an Orthodox world radically different from the one in which he was now involved. In Greece and in the Greek lands of Asia Minor, the clergy completely administered the affairs of the church based on the authority derived through apostolic succession. There was no joint lay or parishioner involvement in the administration of the church. The clergy were compensated by the state and were thus shielded from the type of salary dispute that confronted Father Hadjidemetriou. The parish priest's decisions, with the approval of his bishop, were final. There were no lay Church Councils to consult, much less to defer to. In America, or at least in the early Atlanta church, the priest attended the council and general assembly meetings only if invited by the lay leaders, which was not often.[490] Finally, and perhaps most importantly, the Orthodox Church that Father Hadjidemetriou had left behind did not burden him with the ongoing responsibility of soliciting and collecting the funds necessary to operate the church. As the state religion of Greece, the church's operations were almost entirely underwritten with public monies. In Atlanta, this responsibility was assumed by Father Hadjidemetriou with a clear sense of his priestly duties and carried out with an enthusiasm that sustained the Atlanta church through its early, difficult years. We can understand his frustration, then, when he was challenged on the nature and amount of his compensation in a manner inconsistent with the terms that originally had been decided.

The governance of the church in Atlanta would continue in this manner throughout these early years. The lay leaders exercised almost complete control over the daily administration of the church's affairs. As these men understood, the priest's field of responsibility was limited to liturgical and theological matters, his authority confined to issues of the faith. His performance in his ministerial responsibilities was judged not by the church's hierarchs but rather solely by the Church Council. As the president of the council would later express about a potential, new priest: "[The] priest will not come to us for life; he will be here for trial, first. If he does well, he will remain with us indefinitely, and if he doesn't, the Community will make sure to replace him with someone else."[491]

The priest was not expected, unless requested, to involve himself in what were considered "community matters."[492] When a disagreement arose in 1915 between Father Demetrios Petrides and members of the council pertaining to the local chapter of the Pan Hellenic Association, the council was quick to reassert its primary authority and make plain the consequences of his not recognizing that authority: "[W]e should invite the Very Reverend and request of him to no longer speak of matters that are not immediately related to the Ecclesiastic cycle…. Indeed, if the priest does what is required of him, all will be well; otherwise, we will give him the allowed time to look for another Community."[493]

Father Petrides apparently continued to sermonize on "community matters," as the council again reminded him in July 1916 to "stick to the religious issues" and "not deliver speeches with personal character from the pulpit."[494]

Father Hadjidemetriou departed Atlanta soon after Easter, which was on April 11, 1909. In May, the ambassador notified the community that "the candidate recommended by His Excellency" as its priest was Father Basil Lambrides.[495] The appointment of Father Lambrides was approved by the general assembly that same month, as were the terms of his contract.

Born in Varna, Bulgaria, on November 26, 1867, Father Lambrides became the Atlanta church's third priest.[496] He was married to Calliope Pilledes, with whom he had four daughters. Fluent in seven languages, he was educated at the Theological School of Halki and ordained a priest in the church of Hagia Sophia in Constantinople. He pursued further studies at the University of Jena in Germany, where he earned a Doctor of Divinity degree while also studying the principles of the great Swiss educational reformer Johann Pestalozzi.[497] Father Lambrides had first arrived in the United States on Christmas Eve 1905, having been appointed by Patriarch Joachim as the parish priest in Lynn, Massachusetts.[498] After serving that community for about three years, he was assigned to the Annunciation Church in Atlanta.

Unlike the community's arrangement with Father Hadjidemetriou, there would be no further ministering by Father Lambrides to the Greek communities outside Atlanta, nor could he receive any gratuities from the money collected for the *epitaphion* flowers or from the blessings performed on Epiphany.[499] However, the community allowed him to supplement his $1,500 annual income with gratuities he received from christenings, weddings and other religious ceremonies. He was also allowed to keep the money received from special collection trays passed around on several feast days during the year.[500]

However, it became apparent by the next year that the current salary for the priest was inadequate. The issue of the priest being allowed to minister to the Greeks in other communities was revisited. The council reversed its earlier opposition to this and voted to recommend to the general assembly that Father Lambrides be authorized to visit Greeks in other cites on six Sundays per year.[501] When the matter was addressed later that month by the general assembly, there was almost unanimous support for the general idea, with the only differences centered on the exact number of such Sundays.[502] The pragmatic justification for allowing these trips was simple: many of the Greeks in other communities had not only contributed financially to the Atlanta church in the past but also continued to make monthly donations.[503] In addition, as Mr. Avgerinos pointed out, "the Priest should be going out to the Greek expatriates who live in the surrounding areas more often, because…'it is our religious duty to do so.'"[504]

With the arrival of the new priest, the community again began discussing its long-held plans to enlarge the church and to start the Greek school.[505] The general assembly approved the expenditure of $100 for the architectural plans.[506] But these most recent enlargement plans were short-lived. The community decided to defer further action on both the enlargement and the Greek school for a year, as Father Lambrides began experiencing some unexplained health problems.[507]

Father Basil Lambrides and Presbytera Calliope with daughters Helen, Maria and Roxani, circa 1911. *Courtesy of the Annunciation Greek Orthodox Cathedral of Atlanta.*

Several months later, however, a real estate opportunity presented itself to the community that seemed to offer a solution both to the need of the community for a larger church structure and to its desire for the establishment of a Greek school. The State of Georgia had offered for sale an approximate half-acre lot at the corner of Pulliam Street and Woodward Avenue, not far from the existing church.[508] The site was more spacious than the Garnett Street location and could accommodate the construction of both a larger church and a school. The community had never been completely satisfied with its purchase of the Presbyterian church and now saw this as an opportunity for the construction of a church more in keeping with the Orthodox style.

Father Lambrides saw other opportunities as well in purchasing this lot. As reflected in the general assembly's minutes, he "expressed the wish that the day, when all the Greek families in our area, that are presently scattered here and there, will join together and form the Greek quarter around the newly built Church and School, will not be late."[509]

The $6,500 sales price, with $2,000 of that required as a down payment, presented a significant challenge to the church, which at the time had a cash balance of $850 in its account.[510] Further action on the matter was deferred to a special general assembly meeting called three days later. Constantine Athanasopoulos, as president of the Parish Council, presided over the spirited discussion of the lengthy meeting in a conciliatory tone and with a firmness that produced a decorum not always demonstrated when these Greek men gathered to discuss the church's business:

> *I am imploring you in earnest, today, to hear me out carefully and patiently, and without prejudice. To hear me in a spirit of gentleness, of good understanding, of brotherly love, and like people who are proud of, and enthusiastic over every task related to the Community and the Church. Because of these qualities, the Greek community of Atlanta, which is self-respecting, progressive and peaceful, stands rightfully, and with pride, much above the other communities.... I will implore everyone to listen closely to all those who will speak, patiently, and quite attentively through the end, without interruption, and without prejudice. If someone has anything to remark on what is being said, one can request to be allowed to speak, after each address is finished, and not while the speech is in progress.[511]*

When the remarks were concluded and the secret ballots tallied, the assembly had decided by an almost unanimous vote to purchase the property. The enthusiasm generated by the discussion and the final decision produced pledges at the meeting to cover the remainder needed for the initial $2,000 installment for the property.[512]

By at least the first months of 1911, both Father Lambrides and Presbytera Calliope began experiencing serious health problems of an undisclosed nature. Father Lambrides would later describe his medical condition at this time as "barely escaping death."[513] His illness was serious enough that the church was forced to remain closed for more than two months because of his extended hospital stay.[514] The general assembly in March 1911 resolved by acclamation to pay for his medical expenses incurred in his hospitalization.[515] He described Presbytera Calliope as being "afflicted dangerously with a serious and incurable disease."[516]

Their medical conditions continued to deteriorate as a result of the Atlanta climate, and her physician recommended that they relocate to a city with a cooler and drier climate.[517] On Easter Sunday, April 7, 1912, Father Lambrides announced to his parishioners that "because of his, as well as his wife's, gradually declining health, he was obliged, to his great sorrow and against his will, to leave our Community, and seek refuge at some other place, where the climate would be more suitable to his family's health, as he has been advised by his doctors."[518] He officially submitted his resignation to the Church Council in June, saying that "he was resigning his present position, in order to look for some other community, which would be in some place with a colder climate, as much as possible, so that, hopefully, it would be possible for him to be restored to health."[519] He specifically asked that the council send a cable to the Holy Synod of the Church in Athens requesting that he be transferred to the community in Salt Lake City. Father Lambrides' professed sadness at leaving Atlanta was heartfelt, later writing to Metropolitan Meletios of Athens that "had I not become seriously ill…I would have stayed there lifelong."[520]

On June 16, Father Lambrides wrote to the synod, requesting that it authorize his transfer to the Salt Lake City community, for the sake of his and Presbytera Calliope's health, in particular "asking the Synod to consider the very real danger that my Presbytera is in, while she stays here."[521] With still no reply from the synod several weeks later, the council president, Constantine Athanasopoulos, also wrote to Athens imploring the church to approve the transfer that "would save the very life of the Presbytera."[522] The concern of the community for their health was real and the pleading to the synod earnest: "[B]y this, our filial letter, we are respectfully pleading, and supplicating with much humility the Sacred and Holy Synod, which is our Mother in Spirit, to extend to us her motherly love; because although we are far away physically, we still are Her genuine and faithful children, always present in spirit."[523]

By early August, Father Lambrides and the community had still not received a response from the synod about Father Lambrides' transfer to Salt Lake City. Growing ever concerned about the deteriorating health of Presbytera Calliope, he again wrote the synod seeking this approval and notified it of his decision to leave Atlanta on August 28, before he had received the necessary authorization: "Thus, I say, I have the unshakable conviction the Holy Synod…will show kindness to me, and will not interpret the decision, made out of necessity, as disobedience; I say this, because I made the decision to hasten my departure from here, before I take into my hands the venerable approval of the Holy Synod."[524]

Father Lambrides' announcement to the community of his resignation had been made prior to the publication of Dio Adallis's guide, which included a valedictory statement to the priest in his book:

During the early part of this year our beloved pastor, Rev. Basilios Lambrides, had contracted cold, which bade fair, after a series of serious complications, to take him away from us forever. In no other time did the good and true members of his flock manifest the affection they cherished for him, as on this occasion. Nearly every day the progress of his illness was eagerly watched, and verbal bulletins published forth his latest development. We love Father Basilios and are proud of him as our spiritual leader, and father…. Father Basilios loves simplicity, and agrees with Longfellow and Ben Johnson, that "simplicity is a grace." It is, and no one appreciates it better than a great man; it is the attribute of genius—of the man to whom the world is like an open book, reading, as he walks, the hidden secrets of its pages.[525]

With Father Lambrides' resignation, the community was again faced with the task of locating another priest. Father Lambrides suggested that they reach out to Archimandrite Germanos Papapanagiotou, who was serving as the parish priest for the Salt Lake City community to which Father Lambrides was being assigned. At its July 1912 meeting, the council concurred in Father Lambrides' opinion and proceeded to exchange letters with Father Germanos, who expressed his willingness to transfer to Atlanta.[526] As an archimandrite, Father Germanos was a celibate monk-priest, and his status as such raised concerns for some members of the general assembly brought together to approve the council's recommendation.[527] After extended discussion on the advisability of choosing a monk-priest to lead the Atlanta church, the assembly voted unanimously to bring Father Germanos to Atlanta.

However, Father Germanos, "fearing that his coming might cause a division in the Community," would soon reconsider his earlier willingness to come to Atlanta because of the opposition to a celibate priest that was expressed by some.[528] By September, he had declined the offer of the position, at least for the present time. Although there was some support for trying to allay Father Germanos's concerns, the council moved quickly instead to reach an agreement with Father Demetrios Petrides on the same terms and conditions as its agreement with Father Lambrides.[529] Father Petrides had recently resigned his position in Philadelphia, and the Atlanta men were anxious to secure his commitment to their church. The church had remained closed since Father Lambrides' departure in August, and the council reminded the church hierarchs that "the presence of a Priest here was urgent," as the community had been "spiritually orphaned."[530] With the approaching, annual council elections ushering in new church leadership, the community was anxious "to bring this issue to completion," so as to avoid "handing over the Church shut down, without a Priest."[531] Some in the community urged that an offer to Father Petrides be delayed until additional discussions with Father Germanos could be held. But the prevailing sentiment was that "we cannot afford this much longer," as "religious needs come up daily."[532] On September 6, 1912, the general assembly unanimously affirmed the council's decision to extend an offer to Father Petrides to serve as its priest, with members of the assembly repeatedly shouting, "Yes, yes," in support of the decision.[533] His salary would be $110 per month.

Like Father Hadjidemetriou before him, Father Petrides was a native of Samos, born in August 1863 and ordained into the priesthood in 1887.[534] He was a married priest, with children, although his wife, Presbytera Eleni, had died before he immigrated to the United States in 1907. His first parish in America was the Greek Orthodox Church of the Annunciation in Philadelphia. There he befriended a young, black Episcopalian deacon from Jamaica, Robert Morgan.[535] Morgan began attending the Annunciation Church after Father Petrides' arrival and was encouraged to convert to Orthodoxy and become an ordained Orthodox priest. He traveled to Constantinople for his ordination, carrying with him a letter of recommendation from Father Petrides. He was ordained as Father Raphael Morgan, the first black Orthodox priest in the United States.[536]

The transition for this middle-aged priest from the Mediterranean island of his birth to the gritty streets of south Philadelphia, unaccompanied by his wife, was difficult. He bared these feelings in a letter that he wrote in 1910 to the small Greek community in Wilkes-Barre, expressing his intention to celebrate the liturgy with the community: "I will come to celebrate with you 'brave young men' from our unforgettable homeland of Greece…because when I am with you, I forget my old age…and bitterness of the harsh living abroad."[537]

Father Petrides had arrived in Atlanta by September 11, 1912, before he had actually received the official confirmation of his appointment by the synod in Athens as the Atlanta community's new priest. The Atlanta community's urgent need to fill the vacancy created by the departure of Father Lambrides was matched by Father Petrides' desire to leave as soon as possible what had become a difficult ministry at the Philadelphia church:

> [B]*ecause I have suffered enough hardships, and I was sufficiently tormented in Philadelphia, where, I dare say, terrible martyrdom awaits my successor as well, whoever he may be. I wish to find a quiet community; to find peace*

Father Demetrios Petrides, circa 1912. *Courtesy of the Annunciation Greek Orthodox Cathedral of Atlanta.*

and calm, so that I can breathe again, and appease the tempest of my soul, caused by the indescribable hardships that I suffered in Philadelphia. And indeed, Holy Providence came to my help.[538]

After gently chastising both Father Petrides and the Church Council for his move to Atlanta without the "prior…permission of the proper supervising Authority," the synod in its letters of October 12 recognized and confirmed Father Petrides' appointment to the Atlanta church.[539]

In his letter to Metropolitan Theoklitos, chairman of the synod, acknowledging its decision, Father Petrides sought the synod's forgiveness in assuming his new position before receiving hierarchical approval. "I run too fast," he wrote.

> *I have come with the hope that, when the Holy Synod would have learned and sized up all these* [actions], *She would be kind enough to approve of what I did, for my deeds had good motives, and were done for the sake of economy, and not in a rebellious spirit, which is incompatible with my character, my old age, and the total sense existing in me that it is my duty to submit to the Ecclesiastic Authority.*[540]

His arrival in Atlanta came just a few weeks before the onset of the First Balkan War, with the resulting departure from the community of scores of Greek immigrants returning to Greece to take up arms for their native land. As almost all of those returning to Greece were stewards of the church, the financial loss occasioned by these departures on the still struggling church was significant. The preexisting financial difficulties of this immigrant church were exacerbated by the problems caused by the loss of so many of its members to the Balkan war effort in the latter part of 1912 and the first half of 1913. The negative impact of the wars on the Atlanta church's finances was severe and long-lasting. These difficulties would persist throughout the almost five years of Father Petrides' service in Atlanta as priest. As the church treasurer informed the council, "owing to the absence of many of its members, who have gone back in order to fulfill their obligations to their country of origin, the Church revenues have markedly dropped."[541]

When the Austro-Hungarian Empire declared war on Serbia in July 1914 after the assassination of Archduke Franz Ferdinand, precipitating World War I, Greek prime minister Venizelos again ordered a mobilization of Greece's armed forces, as well as the call-up of the immigrant reservists residing in the United States.[542] So concerned was the Church Council about the possible departure from Atlanta of a second wave of fellow immigrants and the resulting effect on the church's finances that it dispatched Consul Vafeiades to Washington for a meeting with the Greek ambassador to "clarify the content" of the notifications sent to the reservists. The council was intent "not to get exposed in time of mobilization as it happened during the previous mobilization [prior to the Balkan Wars]."[543]

As the president, Gerasimos Algers, reminded the members of the community, however, even though the reduction in the church's revenues was the result of the prideful "departure of many for the field of honor," the church's expenses remained the same.[544] The "promotion and the success of the Church" required their continuing financial support, he said, "in the fulfillment of the highest and holy duties towards the Church and religion."[545] The parlous state of the church's finances caused by these departures also affected the church's ability to pay the third, and final, installment on the note for the church property.

With decreased revenues facing the church for the immediate future, the inadequate salary for Father Petrides became an issue for the Church Council just a few months after his arrival. He informed the council in March 1913 that he would be forced to seek another parish if the council was unable to increase his salary.[546] Having earlier lost Father Hadjidemetriou due to financial difficulties and Father Lambrides to illness, the community was resolute in its desire to keep its priest.

The council unanimously voted to increase his salary to $150 per month, which was equal to Father Lambrides' salary before he had departed Atlanta.[547] The general assembly approved the council's decision. The chairman, Pete Vergiotis, urged this approval to an assembly far more receptive than the one to which Father Hadjidemetriou had earlier unsuccessfully pleaded for relief. The chairman reminded those assembled:

> As we are all aware, our Priest, who performs his duties diligently and is worthy of every support and protection, has a large family, and he is the only provider for this family.... [N]eedless to say that it is to our credit and honor to keep our Priest with decorum, and to make sure that he is not in want of even the slightest thing.... I do believe that there is not any one, either among the present members, or among those who are not here now, who does not feel national pride when he can see the Priest go about clean and well dressed, and not deprived of anything, especially in this foreign country, where people are used to seeing their priests live with dignity.[548]

Despite the efforts to maintain the priest's salary at its original level, the continuing financial difficulties of the church in 1915 forced the general assembly to reduce it to $125 per month. Father Petrides, although already experiencing his own personal financial problems, accepted the decision, saying that "when his flock is suffering, he gladly accepts to suffer with them."[549]

The onset of the Balkan Wars resulted in a preoccupation with Greece's fate among the Atlanta Greeks. This preoccupation, coupled with the community's struggles with the departure of so many men to the battlefield, left the council unable to tend to the ordinary business of the church. No council meetings were held during the last five months of 1912. The council was criticized by some in the community for its relative inaction on the church's business during these war months, a criticism that Algers addressed in a general assembly meeting:

> [W]e are all aware that due to the irregular circumstances, and the critical period that the [Greek] nation went through in the recent days, the attention of all, and of everyone individually, was turned towards other, more current events and urgent issues. During these events, the patriotism and the sense of honor of the Community of Atlanta played a leading role, exceeding even that of the Diocesan Communities in America, which number ten or even twenty times higher number of Greek expatriate members. Only our Community was admired for its role by all the Greeks in America, and those in Greece alike, as well as by the foreigners; this is worthy of great praise. No one is ignorant of the fact that during these difficult circumstances, and the times of national action, the Church Council performed its own duty in every single issue and in all circumstances, not to say that it was always the leader.[550]

With Father Petrides' arrival and the conclusion of the wars, however, the community refocused its efforts on the establishment of the community's school. In 1906, E. Basil, eager to assure his *Atlanta Constitution* interviewer of the unconditional determination of the Atlanta Greeks that their children become "thoroughly Americanized," declared that "unlike other foreigners, the Greeks are not teaching their children their native language, but are educating them solely in the English language."[551] However, this was not the case. The establishment of the Greek school had always been one of the community's most important goals, and its development and expansion would remain a priority for the next decade. Father Petrides injected a renewed energy into the effort, just as the Greeks began settling back into their daily routines with the conclusion of the Balkan Wars:

[T]he time was now right to bring the matter of the establishment of the School for consideration, because our Community has an absolute need for the School; and besides, since the much desired peace agreement had been signed, the reasons which had turned the attention of the Community to other, more urgent matters had been finally lifted.[552]

First expressed as a priority in the church's initial bylaws in 1908, the school's creation at that time had been a casualty of the ongoing financial difficulties. The loss of revenue attributable to the return of so many men of the community to fight in the wars of 1912–13 had also hindered any progress, as "the reduction of the revenues was such, that the income was not sufficient to support both the Church and the School."[553] Although the financial position of the church was now only marginally improved, both the council and Father Petrides were fully committed to its establishment. Father Petrides volunteered to teach without compensation until a teacher had been hired.[554] Although opinion in the community was divided, the majority was determined to operate the school through the church's annual operating budget and not through irregular, special collections and fundraisers.

These budget disputes were typical of the kinds of disagreements that occupied the church community in its early years. Nothing more serious than this or the occasional personality conflicts in the congregation or with the clergy ever divided the community. With Orthodox Christian faith tradition thousands of years old and solidly based on biblical and patristic teachings and the canons of the church's early Ecumenical Councils, the basic beliefs of the church were never challenged. The theological disputes of the early twentieth century that would produce rifts in the Presbyterian Church and other Protestant denominations did not exist in the Orthodox Church. Even the Royalist-Venizelist dispute that would divide Orthodox churches in America after World War I was rooted in the politics of Greece.

Gerasimos Algers, a leader in the community and church throughout the early years. *Courtesy of the Annunciation Greek Orthodox Cathedral of Atlanta.*

At the church's general assembly meeting held on December 3, 1913, the community finally took its first concrete steps toward the establishment of the school when it created a twelve-member committee tasked with that responsibility.[555] The high priority placed by the Church Council in establishing the Greek language school was indicative of the changing character of the Greek immigrant community in the city and its evolving needs. For most of its existence in Atlanta since the end of the 1880s, the community was almost completely composed of unmarried men. Between 1905 and 1910, with the increased arrival of Greek women and the resulting marriages to these men, the face of the community began to change. Seventy-six infants and children were baptized between 1906 and 1912.[556] For the first time, the presence of women and children was noted at general assembly meetings in February and August 1913.

The needs of families with children began to predominate, and addressing their needs, most especially through the establishment and expansion of the school, became a primary focus of the church's leaders. There would be very few meetings of the Church Council or the general assembly in the coming years that were not devoted to some extent to matters pertaining to the school. As the presiding chairman, Pete Vergiotis, noted in that year's last general assembly meeting:

> *The present meeting…also has the character of a family meeting, too. That is because today active care will be taken for, and a definite decision will be made about the fate of these small children, who will constitute the next generation. We have the duty to take all the care for this generation to be educated in a way that befits a Greek. We will do this by establishing a School, and constantly preserving it in the most decent way.*[557]

The assembly—including men, women and children—affirmed the recommendations of the council and the newly created school committee regarding the funding of the school. So, on December 21, 1913, five years after the community's initial desires for a school were formally expressed in the church's initial bylaws, the school had become a reality. Addressing the men of the council and the committee but "turning towards the children, sitting nearby," Vergiotis offered his congratulations: "Gentlemen, the work you are undertaking today, and you are doing it because you care for the growth and development of these innocent creatures, is one of the greatest deeds of your lives. The day that the School will be ready, the gratitude of these innocent creatures will be the noblest moral remuneration for you."[558]

Father Demetrios Petrides baptizing Mary Farmakis (Algers) in 1913 in the Garnett Street church. *Courtesy of the Annunciation Greek Orthodox Cathedral of Atlanta.*

The financial commitment of the council and the community to the school was total. The 1914 budget for the complete operation of the church was set at approximately $2,600, while the annual budget for the Greek school was established at approximately $1,800, ambitious goals for a community still feeling the effects of the loss of so many men.[559] In order to be able to adequately fund the operations of both the church and the school at these levels, the council for the first time devised a formal pledge system that was adopted by the general assembly.[560] The system consisted of five classes of giving levels, from $3 to $20 and above, and "declaration" or pledge cards were printed and distributed to the entire community.[561] Because, as Pete Vergiotis explained, "the decent preservation of the Church and the School will mainly depend on this budget," special care was taken in the printing of these pledge cards.[562] A photograph of the church's Annunciation icon was depicted on the front of the form, and an engraver was engaged to complete the printing.[563] The members of the Church Council assumed the responsibility of personally distributing the cards to members of the community and returning to collect the completed forms.[564]

The ongoing financial difficulties in the early Greek Orthodox Church in Atlanta were not unique either to the Atlanta church or, more generally, to other Orthodox churches in America. Other immigrant churches labored under almost identical difficulties. Although the Greeks in Atlanta in these years would devise numerous approaches to addressing these problems, the church in its earliest years never resorted to some of the more aggressive forms of fundraising common in Protestant and Catholic churches, such as pew renting.[565] However, with the increased financial needs resulting from the plans for a school, the church ultimately adopted just such a plan in 1916. The best seats in the sanctuary were numbered and made available to the "regular members" for $1.20 per year and to the "non-regular members" for $12.00 per year; separate, unnumbered seats were kept available for parishioners "who do not wish to comply with this rule."[566]

Just as the council was preparing to initiate the hiring process for selecting a teacher for the school it had just established, it received a letter from the local branch of the Pan Hellenic Association announcing that it had also decided to establish a school and was, therefore, asking for the collaboration of the council.[567] Seemingly surprised by this proposal, the council debated whether even to reply to the association, "as the establishment of the School had already been decided by the Community."[568] However, the council resolved that a reply would be sent and "written in a way that would stop possible tendencies that some members of the [association] may entertain about having any kind of supervision or control over the decisions made by the Community, or by the Church Council on School related matters."[569] It is not known whether the Pan Hellenic Association actually intended its proposal for a Greek language school as a challenge to the council's own plans. Regardless, the council made clear its authority to administer more than just the ordinary affairs of the church. These broader community matters would also come under its purview.

It is also worth noting that throughout these early, financially challenging years, the church continued to assist members of its community in need. Burials were paid for when necessary and outright donations made when cases were presented.[570] Even as the church was gathering its resources for the development of the school, allocations were made in its budget for "the needy members of our Parish that are there, all the time, and they are worthy of our assistance."[571] The church's budget also provided for donations to be made to the state hospital and to the Orphanage of Atlanta.[572]

In the months immediately following the school's establishment, the council began to focus on the facilities necessary for its operation and the hiring of its first teacher. Although the community's initial plans included the construction of a new school building on the grounds of the church, budgetary constraints did not immediately allow this. Instead, the general assembly decided to renovate the church's existing meeting rooms to accommodate the needs of the school.[573] The assembly also approved a salary of sixty dollars per month for the new teacher, Miss Papadimitrakopoulou, and reimbursement for her moving expenses from New York.[574] The council met with the city's school inspector in order to clarify that the school's operation as a private, not public, institution gave the church complete discretion as to the subjects taught, the language utilized for instruction and the general operation of the school.[575]

The teacher was personally introduced to the council at its meeting on September 1, 1914. Once her qualifications were presented to the council and confirmed, her hiring was formally affirmed.[576] After her presentation

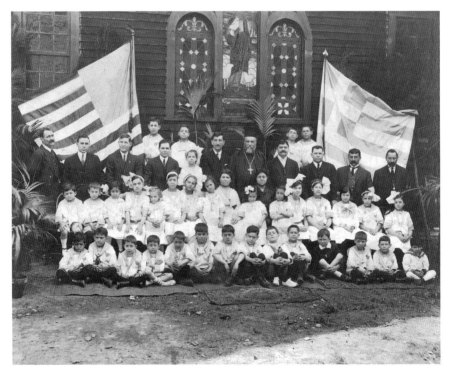

Father Demetrios Petrides with the inaugural class of the Greek community's school, September 1914. *Courtesy of the Annunciation Greek Orthodox Cathedral of Atlanta.*

regarding the schoolbooks and the specifics of the subjects of instruction for the students, the council set the beginning of classes for Wednesday, September 9. With the receipt of a $1,000 donation for the school from the Pan Hellenic Association in New York and the accumulated savings already collected, plans again were made to begin construction of the school building.[577] Property was identified for the location of the school, but the community deferred purchasing the site in the hope that the seller would reduce the sale price.[578]

Although the church continued its financial struggles in these years, there was no slackening in the community's plans to fully develop the school. Enrollment in 1915 approached fifty students.[579] Between Miss Papadimitrakopoulou's introduction to the council in September 1914 and Father Petrides' death in September 1917, there were very few Church Council or general assembly meetings at which the school's affairs did not involve extended discussion. Even with the creation of a school committee designed to oversee the school's operation, it appears there were no school-related issues that were too insignificant for the council or the assembly to consider in detail, from the dates of the school's final examinations to the fees assessed for graduation certificates.[580] The Church Council appointed and met with the committee charged with supervising the school's examinations.[581] Class schedules and school holidays were also established by the council.[582] Even the school's books were ordered by the council.[583]

While the community's external contacts with its Atlanta neighbors continued to emphasize its assimilation into American society, the unceasing and worried focus on the school's development and its importance in maintaining their children's Greek cultural heritage did not abate. A suggestion was made in early 1916 to forego that year's annual Greek Independence Day celebration on March 25 "because the situation in the motherland is irregular, and the families of the mobilized soldiers are ravaged by hunger."[584] Despite the suggestion that the money required for the celebration be sent instead to these families, the community decided to proceed with the annual celebration, as "the teacher had put so much work and effort in preparing, and having the school children learning their poems."[585] The ceremony was to proceed "with every formality," however, with the expenditure not to exceed twenty-five dollars.[586]

The council discussed the alternatives of either constructing the school on the lot near the capitol or building the school adjacent to the church on Central Avenue.[587] The site next to the church was chosen. New appointments were made to the school's supervisory committee.

These were Stephanos Psychalinos, Speros Vryonis, Sotirios Georgiades and Dimitris Psaroudakis, described as "men of letters."[588] The council officially delegated to this committee the authority to administer the affairs of the school.[589] The council president, Gerasimos Algers, announced that the foundation stone of the school would be laid on Sunday, September 3, 1916.[590] George Moore was selected to chair the building committee.[591] For the first time, the community formally expanded its fundraising efforts to include the "American commercial community" with whom Greeks did business, and a $100 contribution for the school from W.L. Lingo was recognized as the first such gift.[592]

A second teacher for the school was hired. Mr. Ioannis Messarchos, responding to an ad the Atlantans had placed in the *National Herald*—a New York–based Greek-language newspaper—was selected over several other applicants.[593] His chief advantage was that he had "only recently arrived from Greece," a fact that prompted the school committee chairman, Stephanos Psychalinos, to tell Messarchos that "we anticipate your teaching to be up-to-date."[594]

Having earlier delegated administrative authority to the school supervisory committee, the council now sought to establish some limits on the committee's independent activities, principally its fundraising activities. The stated motivation was to avoid "any future misunderstandings" and to prevent "a future separation of Church and School."[595] Not unlike the Catholic parochial schools, the daily administration of the school was left to the supervisory committee, but the ultimate "foundation and preservation of the School is due exclusively to the Community. It remains its indispensable possession at all times."[596]

In addition to including the school in the church's operating budget and openly soliciting members of the Atlanta business community, the council continued to entertain other fundraising ideas to support the school financially. These would span a broad cultural spectrum. A series of musical concerts was scheduled, with proceeds divided between the community and the performing musicians.[597] In what was certainly the most unusual fundraising project the community had yet entertained, the council also adopted a proposal to stage a professional wrestling match, again with ticket proceeds earmarked for the school.[598] The most ambitious plan undertaken was to stage two performances of the dramatic play *Esme, i Tourkopoula* ("Esme, the Turkish Girl").[599] Members of the Birmingham Greek community had offered to perform the play in Atlanta, with proceeds divided by both communities to support their respective schools. A special meeting of the Church Council was called to discuss the staging of the play, with invitations extended to members of both *Danaos* and *Agia Ekaterini*. Detailed plans were made regarding promotion of the performances to both the Greek and the broader Atlanta communities, the latter being described as "American merchants, bankers, scientists and politicians."[600]

With the construction of the school building now underway, the council was able to shift its focus to needed improvements in the church building itself and to many other matters requiring the council's action. A Greek iconographer then residing in Atlanta, Constantinos Makris, was chosen to complete the painting of the church's interior, as well as the school rooms.[601] As part of the interior church painting, the council directed that small stars would be painted on the church's ceiling.[602] The council also decided to take advantage of his presence in the city to commission additional icons for the church.[603] Members of the community were given the opportunity to donate an icon, selecting from icons of the Nativity, the Baptism of Christ, the Crucifixion, the Resurrection, the Annunciation and the Last Supper. Vasileios Prylis, one of the council members, proposed that the following quotation be inscribed above the interior of the church entrance: "Where there is faith, there is love; where there is love, there is peace; where there is peace, there is blessing; where there is blessing, God is present; and where God is present, there is no want."[604] The council responded positively to this, agreeing not only to the proposal but also deciding to include the quotation on the church's stationery.

Father Petrides chose this time to make a special request to the council for help in acquiring new priestly vestments. With the community still struggling to underwrite the costs of the school construction and other church improvements, no financial help could be provided. But the women of the community were called on to "make a small sacrifice of this kind for the sake of having our Priest properly vested."[605]

The council president, Gerasimos Algers, also presented to the council the concept of developing for the first time a community register that would assist the church in its organization and growth.[606] As Algers and Dionysios Polychronas, the assistant secretary, envisioned it, the register would include a listing of every member of the Greek community in Atlanta, whether a financial supporter of the church or not. Ages, gender, places of origin, parents' names, addresses, occupations, telephone numbers where available and even "their living habits" would be compiled.[607] The information would allow the council to better identify those not supporting the church, as well as ascertain the future needs of the school.

Algers also saw another purpose in the register: the protection of vulnerable members of the community from the darker impulses of some of their fellow Greeks:

Thus, should any kind of accident ever occur to any of our Community members, the Council will be in the satisfactory position of providing official information to those who are interested in him/her. Because, Gentlemen, mark my words, it is not uncommon that when members of our Community die, and no one knows anything about them or their financial situation, there are those well wishers out there, who act as self appointed relatives, and squander anything that the deceased might have had. I do believe that the Community, in which the deceased people have lived, has the obligation and the duty to intervene, to look into, and safeguard their interests.[608]

Since the church's beginning more than a decade earlier, the community had sought to establish stronger and more formal connections with "fellow Greeks" in Atlanta, who, although not meeting the requirements established by the church's bylaws for membership, nevertheless "continued, even to this day, to offer their mite whenever it is asked of them."[609] Recognizing both their collective contributions and the need to gather information about these Greeks who were "outside of our Community," the council adopted a proposal by Vasileios Efthimiou to produce a detailed ledger of these individuals.[610] Styled by the council as the "Book of the Assisting and Helping Members Outside of the Community," the ledger was also viewed as a tool to more easily enable the church to solicit donations from these nonmembers in the future.[611]

As important as resolving these more ordinary matters had always been to the fabric of the community, an unresolved issue much more critical to the Greeks was securing their own burial grounds. Atlanta was their new home. These immigrants were not returning to Greece, and they were united in the determination to locate and purchase communal plots for their deceased.

Chapter 14

WESTVIEW AND GREENWOOD CEMETERIES

"Weird Greek Ritual to Be Chanted for the Dead"

After the establishment of the church in 1905, the community's foremost priority was the organization of the school. But no less important for these Greeks was deciding where to bury their dead. The members of the community had long since realized that for most of them there would be no return to Greece. Atlanta was their new home, and within three years of the church's founding, they would be searching for permanent space for the deceased.

On December 1, 1901, John Nekas, unmarried, a native of Argos, Greece who was born in 1839, just seven years after Greece secured its independence from the Ottoman Empire, died in Atlanta of tuberculosis.[612] His was the first death of one of the Greek immigrants in the city, and the novelty of his Orthodox funeral prompted the *Atlanta Constitution* to describe it in a headline as a "Weird Greek Ritual to Be Chanted for the Dead."[613] As part of the burial service, a towel was spread over his face, and "wine" was sprinkled on the towel before the coffin was closed and lowered into the grave.[614]

Nekas would be the first of many Greek men, women and children who would die and be buried alone in Atlanta, far from their families in Greece. Over the next two decades, more than fifty Greek immigrants would share the same fate. James Pagonas, who died in 1904, was one of them: "[T]he solemn rites seemed to belong entirely to the old world, and only the rambling of heavy wagons on Houston street or the passing of noisy trolleys on Pryor street, suggested the Atlanta that lay just outside of the half closed doors through which the Georgia sunshine floated to permeate the heavy incense."[615]

It was noted that the congregation attending the funeral was almost entirely composed of men, "and among all these there were not one member of the deceased's immediate connections to mourn his loss." Pagonas died, like so many of these immigrant men would die, unmourned at his funeral by his family, leaving a mother and two sisters in Greece, "still waiting for the return of the son and brother to take them away…to the Georgia sunshine of Atlanta."[616]

With Nekas's death in 1901, the Greek community for the first time was confronted with the responsibility of burying one of its own. The community chose Westview Cemetery for his burial. Westview had been established in 1884 as grave sites had become unavailable in the older Oakland Cemetery. Located on almost six hundred acres of gently rolling terrain in southwest Atlanta, the cemetery was, and remains, the largest cemetery in the Southeast. Members of many well-known and prominent Atlanta families are buried in large family sections marked by elaborate grave markers. Joel Chandler Harris, Asa Candler, Mayor William B. Hartsfield, Robert Woodruff and Henry Grady are just a few of those interred at Westview.

The cemetery had also reserved a section on its premises for the burial of individuals with more limited means. Section 8, known as the old individual grave section, is located on an expansive hillside opposite the hilltop location of the large marble statue of a Confederate soldier. The monument was erected by Atlanta Confederate veterans to mark the graves of more than one hundred of their fellow soldiers killed during the Civil War battle of Ezra Church. The battle had raged over parts of what are now the cemetery grounds, and the Confederate trenches remain on location.

Section 8 holds the remains of scores of Greek, Syrian and Lebanese immigrants, with the vast majority of the grave sites being unmarked.[617] Only seven of the thirty-five known grave sites of Greek immigrants in Section 8 are marked, and these only with small blocks of marble or granite.[618] Neither Nekas's nor Pagonas's grave sites are marked. And for the Greeks buried in Section 8, the designated "individual" grave section, it would remain just that. None of the Greeks buried here is accompanied by any family members. Each is buried alone. Nor is there a "Greek" section on this hillside that would at least allow these immigrants to be buried together. The graves are scattered widely over the entire area of the

Harper's Weekly engraving of Atlanta's Battle of Ezra Church, sketched by Theodore Davis, July 28, 1862. *Courtesy of* Harper's Weekly.

hill. There is one Greek woman buried in Section 8 among these Greek males: Angeliki Kyriakopoulou.

Seven of these graves are the sites of infants and children, none of them older than three at the time of death and none of them buried with their parents. Siblings Constantinos Handelis (nine months old) and his sister, Chrysoula (six months old), as well as Constantina Karagianni (ten months old), are buried separately in unmarked graves in the old pauper's section of the cemetery, known as God's Acre.[619] Without upkeep by either the cemetery or the city, God's Acre is now heavily overgrown with woods and inaccessible to the public.

As the community grew with the ongoing arrival of new immigrants, the burial options offered by Westview Cemetery for continued interments in the individual grave section proved inadequate and unacceptable. The community wanted its own burial grounds for its dead. As early as October 1908, the community was engaged in discussions with Greenwood Cemetery about the purchase of plots for its burials.[620] But it wasn't until the September 1910 meetings of the Parish Council and the general assembly that the community committed itself to the "purchase of a cemetery."[621] Although these unmarried Greek men would continue to die alone for another decade, they would no longer be buried alone but rather in a designated Greek section.

Greenwood Cemetery had been incorporated on December 13, 1904, and was situated only a few miles from Westview Cemetery.[622] Unlike Westview, which served as the final resting place for the leading Atlanta families, Greenwood offered a more modest, if no less attractive, setting for not only Greek but also Jewish and Asian immigrants.[623] The cemetery was receptive to, and perhaps even solicitous of, this immigrant clientele that could so readily commit to the purchase of large sections in these still new cemetery grounds.

On July 28, 1911, the church purchased from Greenwood Cemetery the first plots for "a burial ground for the Greeks of Atlanta," thirty-six in all, for a price of $1,400.[624] In addition, the cemetery conveyed to the church an adjoining strip of land to be used solely for the construction of a chapel.[625]

After the initial purchase in 1911, the need for additional burial plots grew. The members of the Church Council visited Greenwood Cemetery in September 1914 to examine the additional section being considered for purchase.[626] In the following month, the council and the general assembly made their decisions final. The council had earlier appointed the consul Dimitri Vafeiades to explore its options regarding additional burial grounds. He secured a proposal from the cemetery in Marietta for the sale of a section for $5,000, which was significantly more expensive than Greenwood's offer of a large section for $1,750.[627] Under the agreement, Greenwood would undertake "the responsibility of transferring all our dead, buried already in the Cemetery, to this section…and would place four stone signs, in the four corners of the section as a demarcation."[628]

On January 5, 1915, the church accepted this proposal and purchased the offered section. The agreement provided for the church to make a down payment of $125 and monthly payments of $15 over nine years toward the outstanding balance. The church was also given a two-year option to purchase "a like amount of ground" adjoining the purchased land "at the same price." Greenwood also agreed to clean the cemetery of all debris and to mow the lawn. The grounds purchased were apparently in a rough state, as Greenwood committed to removing tree roots and rocks prior to the sale.[629] The burial fees were $5 for adults and $3 for children.[630] This contract included the standard restrictive racial covenant of that time prohibiting the sale of any cemetery plots to "any other than white persons."[631] With the agreement now complete, the Greeks had acquired ample burial plots in a spacious site occupying one of the most elevated locations in the city. This site continues to serve the needs of the city's Greek Orthodox community.

For most of their Atlanta neighbors, the Greeks by this date had ceased being merely a "Greek colony" and had become a community of Greek-Americans. Although not fully integrated or assimilated into the broader society, the Greeks were accepted and, for the most part, respected. If anglicizing their names, becoming naturalized citizens, establishing businesses and consecrating a church were partial payments toward receiving the full acceptance that these Greek immigrants had sought since their first arrival more than twenty-five years before, then certainly securing plots of American soil for their eventual resting places would constitute the final payment in full for that acceptance.

Nonetheless, for the segment of Atlantans who were becoming members of the revived Ku Klux Klan, neither the Greeks nor other less favored immigrants would ever be considered worthy of American citizenship, no matter what steps they took to become part of American society. Rather, they would continue to be viewed as blight on the nation. The Klan's second founding in Atlanta took place about eleven months after the Greeks had completed this latest purchase of the Greenwood burial plots and would affect American society for decades.

Chapter 15

THE RISE OF THE KU KLUX KLAN

"Our Much Boasted 'Melting Pot' Has Turned Out to Be a 'Garbage-Can,' in Which the Nations of the Earth Dump Their Refuse"

With the collapse of the Georgia Immigration Association by 1910 and the completion of the Congressional Dillingham Commission's report on immigration in 1911, a brief lull in the heated anti-immigration rhetoric in the city ensued. However, the 1913 murder of Mary Phagan at the National Pencil Company factory in downtown Atlanta would begin a cascade of events that would include the brutal lynching of Leo Frank and would lead, several years later, to the reestablishment of the Ku Klux Klan on Stone Mountain, less than twenty miles from the city. With the reincarnation of the Klan, another period of sustained vitriol and violence would be ushered in that would continue for several decades. In addition to reviving terror and lynching for the South's blacks, this second iteration of the Klan trained its sights on new targets: Jews, Catholics and southern and eastern European immigrants.

The National Pencil Company began its operations on Forsyth Street in downtown Atlanta in April 1908 in the four-story Venable building that had previously housed a hotel. In August of that year, Leo Frank, born in Texas and the product of a German Jewish family, had been installed as the factory's superintendent by his uncle, Moses Frank, the majority owner of the business and himself a Confederate veteran.[632]

The thirteen-year-old Mary Phagan was one of scores of teenage girls working in the factory in 1913. Her body was found on the morning of April 26 in the factory cellar. She had been strangled the previous day. As noted earlier, one of the earliest suspects in the murder was a Greek employee of a café near the factory. The Pinkerton detectives hired by the company to conduct its own investigation described the murder as having been committed in a "Mediterranean style." The Greek suspect could not be found when the detectives sought to question him. The Pinkerton agents also sought three other Greeks for interrogation who had been observed on the morning of the discovery of the body acting "suspiciously."[633]

But the investigation quickly began to focus on Leo Frank, who was indicted for the murder and brought to trial. Luridly covered by the nation's press, the trial quickly became a sensational story across the nation. Frank was cast as a representative of northern capitalists, a rich northern Jew taking advantage of vulnerable southern girls. Based largely on the questionable and changing testimony of the factory's janitor, Jim Conley, Frank was found guilty of murder by the jury and sentenced to death.

During the appeals process, Tom Watson, the ardent segregationist and anti-Semite, advocated for a revival of the Klan and described Frank as a member of the Jewish aristocracy who had pursued Mary Phagan to a "hideous death":

> *Frank belonged to the Jewish aristocracy, and it was determined by the rich Jews that no aristocrat of their race should die for the death of a working-class Gentile…. [W]hile the Sodomite who took her sweet young life basks in the warmth of Today, the poor child's dainty flesh has fed the worms. Here we have the typical young libertine Jew who is dreaded and detested by the city authorities of the North for the very reason that Jews of this type have an utter contempt for law, and a ravenous appetite for the forbidden fruit, a lustful eagerness enhanced by the racial novelty of the girl of the uncircumcised.*[634]

With his judicial appeals exhausted, in 1915 Frank asked Governor John Slaton to commute his sentence to life imprisonment. The governor, stating that there might have been a miscarriage of justice, commuted Frank's sentence on June 21, five days before his gubernatorial term ended and one day before Frank was scheduled to hang. The Atlanta community was outraged, and the reaction to the commutation was quick and furious. On the evening of the commutation, a mob of about three thousand gathered outside the governor's home in Buckhead, at that time about six miles north of the city.[635] The National Guard was called to protect the governor. For two more days, mobs threatened to enter the governor's home. A score of the governor's friends, armed with shotguns and rifles, had joined the governor's family in the house to offer their protection.[636] On the morning of the third day of the disturbance, a group of about seventy-five men, carrying firearms and dynamite, attempted to enter the home and were surrounded and captured by the guardsmen.

Two months later, Tom Watson told his readers that "another KKK may have to be organized to restore Home Rule." Four days after Watson's published remarks, on August 16, a group of about twenty-five men, including a former Georgia governor, several local elected officials and members of the Cobb County sheriff's office, calling themselves the "Knights of Mary Phagan," kidnapped Frank from the state prison in Milledgeville and drove him about 175 miles back toward a site near the Phagan home.[637] Frank was dressed only in his nightshirt and an undershirt,

The lynching of Leo Frank, August 1915. *Courtesy of Kenan Research Center at the Atlanta History Center.*

and the lynchers tied a piece of brown canvas around his waist like a skirt, handcuffed him and tied his legs at the ankles. He was turned to face the Phagan home and hanged at about 7:00 a.m. on the seventeenth.[638] Much like his contemporary, John Temple Graves, the *Georgian* editor, Watson was unapologetic in his defense of lynching: "This country has nothing to fear from its rural communities. Lynch law is a good sign; it shows that a sense of justice lives among the people."[639]

The firestorm created by the murder of Mary Phagan and the passions unleashed in the lynching of Leo Frank provided the foundation on which the Ku Klux Klan was reestablished in Atlanta in 1915. On Thanksgiving night of that year, three months after Frank's lynching, William Joseph Simmons led a group of men to the top of Stone Mountain, a quartz and granite dome a few miles outside Atlanta. Included in this group were some of the men who had formed the Knights of Mary Phagan. "With a flag fluttering in the wind behind them, a Bible open to the twelfth chapter of Romans, and a flaming cross to light the night sky above, Simmons and his disciples proclaimed the new Knights of the Ku Klux Klan."[640] One week later, the Klan petitioned for a charter of incorporation, which was granted in July 1916.

The first Klan had been established soon after the end of the Civil War by Confederate army veterans. Acting as a vigilante group, the Klan sought to restore white supremacy through threats and violence. Confederate general Nathan Bedford Forrest became the first grand wizard. In the face of prosecution by the federal government, the Klan was broken by the mid-1870s.

This second Klan was organized more in line as a fraternal organization, with all of the external trappings of the Masons and other fraternal orders. In addition to its mission of rolling back black gains through intimidation and renewed violence, this Klan had also developed a strong anti-immigrant agenda aimed at Jews, Catholics and immigrants from southern and eastern Europe. With their increasing numbers, Catholics, and their pope, became the object of the most venomous charges. Caleb Ridley, the Klan's national chaplain and the pastor of Central Baptist Church of Atlanta, described the pope as "some secluded ass on the other side of the world."[641] Atlanta city councilman James Wood, in his campaign for state legislative office, would boast, "I am the original Ku Klux Klansman, and I am proud of it. I belong to everything anti-Catholic I know of."[642]

The Klan was a self-described "army of Protestant Americans."[643] Accordingly, the Klan's appeals were aimed almost exclusively at white

Protestants, who formed almost its entire membership, with Baptists and Methodists composing the overwhelming majority of members. Among the few surviving Klan records are those of the Knox County Klan No. 14 chapter, 95 percent of whose members were Baptist or Methodist.[644] Simmons, the new Klan's founder and first imperial wizard, was an ordained Methodist minister, and ministers from these two denominations were very active in the Klan.

The involvement of these ministers would often give a religious tone to the Klan's activities. Simmons's dramatic prose in describing one of the annual Klan gatherings on Stone Mountain is an example of that:

> *There comes, during our preliminary ceremonies, a moment of marvelous moral tension and exhilaration. The vast throng, with upturned faces, deeply moved to eloquent agony of speechless prayer, catches a glorious inspiration. It comes upon the multitude as a wind moving gently through the forests in the autumn time. Every soul is thrilled. In this conscious moment each man feels as if he were in a holy temple consecrating all that he is and all that he has to a great cause.*[645]

This and other attempts to lay a veneer of civility over the Klan's actions were regularly belied by its acts of violence and intimidation. In presiding over the Atlanta chapter's meetings, Simmons would regularly begin the meetings by placing two revolvers on the table before him and shouting to the members, "Bring on your niggers!"[646]

The national headquarters of the revived Klan, known as the Imperial Palace by its membership, was located on Peachtree Road. Atlanta was also home of the Klan's first local chapter, referred to as the "mother Klan of the Invisible Empire."[647] By 1917, this chapter, officially designated as the Nathan Bedford Forrest Klan Chapter No. 1, was conducting its biweekly meetings on Central Avenue, less than three blocks from the Greek Orthodox church.[648] Little more than one month after its Thanksgiving Day 1915 founding on Stone Mountain, local Klan members were beginning to explain the revived Klan's mission to a broader, though carefully selected, Atlanta audience. The December meeting of the city's United Daughters of the Confederacy chapter included a presentation on the "secret maneuvers" of the new Klan, as well as a reading from a history of the first incarnation of the Klan and an exhibition of one of its original costumes.[649] As it would nationally, the Klan in Atlanta included in its membership many of the city's business and elected leaders. In the next decade, Governor Clifford Walker,

Mayor Walter Sims, Georgia State Supreme Court chief justice Richard B. Russell Sr. and State Attorney General George M. Napier would all become members.[650] At its peak, the Atlanta chapter would boast a membership of more than fifteen thousand.

With the increasing arrival of eastern and southern European immigrants, the Klan saw itself as the primary defender of "pure Americanism," which in its view these new immigrants could never represent. This Klan demonstrated a strong nativist sentiment—a fear of losing power in their country, a fear not unlike the concerns expressed by many in later periods of mass immigration into the United States. Simmons, the Klan's imperial wizard, would verbalize these fears in a remarkable book that he would publish in 1924, *The Klan Unmasked*:

> [W]*e Americans are barely reproducing our numbers on our own soil. In comparison with the colored and foreign elements, our percentage is every year being reduced…. The imbecile and the other feeble-minded, if permitted to do so, multiply much more rapidly than normal persons…. Stop immigration and a homogenous English-speaking nation will again be developed…according to our Anglo-Saxon methods.*[651]

Ku Klux Klan rally on Stone Mountain, 1917. *Courtesy of W.E. Thompson Publishing Company and the Kenan Research Center at the Atlanta History Center.*

Simmons saw this problem as being especially acute in the nation's cities, which he claimed contained populations of only "about fifteen per cent original Americans," and he decried that the "majority of the business class" in these cities would soon "be composed of Greeks, Jews, Germans, Italians and their descendants."[652] Simmons, as others before and after him, believed that these immigrants were simply unable to adopt the values that he saw as uniquely Anglo-Saxon traits. Achieving economic success by itself was insufficient to transform these peoples in his estimation into good Americans.

He singled out the Greek immigrants in particular as lacking the qualities necessary to become good American citizens, citing as the source of his concern the recent Greek referendum to restore to the throne King Constantine, the brother-in-law of German kaiser Wilhelm: "If a vast majority of the Greeks in their home country joyously accept monarchy and Hohenzollernism, how can we expect our Greek immigrants here in the United States to enthuse over our republican institutions? They come like others, as everybody knows, to avail themselves of the opportunity to advance their material interests."[653]

The Klan would establish itself in every section of the nation within a few years of its beginnings in 1915. Fueling a membership that would eventually reach between 4 and 5 million men was its anti-immigration stance. The Klan thrived in areas with relatively small African American populations, even in some large cities. Simmons would devote the publication of another book to the menace that he and the Klan perceived in immigration. Published in 1926, *America's Menace or The Enemy Within* remains a typical nativist screed, recycling the same sentiments expressed by the earlier leaders of the Georgia Immigration Association, with the addition of Simmons's more melodramatic depictions:

> *THE POSITIVE DANGER is the Now well organized activities of this "alien element" (which I designate elsewhere herein as the "common enemy"!) strongly established within our borders and intelligently programmed and shrewdly directed.... It holds politics as a mere plaything and dallies it with begrimed hands of conscienceless venality.... In our great fraternal and civic organizations this "alien element" breathes its blighting breath.*[654]

Not content with the two hundred pages of prose invective that he had hurled at immigrants, Simmons concluded his work with a poem, titled "America, My America," to further drive home his objections:

The Alien's foot is in Thy soil,
Thy life and honor to despoil,
His treach'rous sons who nurse Thy breast
Are never idle, they never rest,
They seek Thy ruin at his behest;
Cast the Alien's curse from off Thy shore,
That guileful guest from out Thy door,
Be peril-free for evermore,
America! My America.[655]

Voices were few in Atlanta and Georgia that would publicly oppose the Klan. It permeated every level of society and, of course, always maintained the threat of violence to those perceived as its enemies. Yet the Greek immigrants of the city responded to the Klan's message with an organizational effort designed to counter the Klan's perception of them. Even though the story of the American Hellenic Educational Progressive Association (AHEPA) is outside the scope of this history, it should be noted that the Greeks of Atlanta in 1922 would establish the Order of AHEPA in direct response to the rise of the Klan. Faced daily for a time with the Klan's presence on the street of their church's location, the founders would use the very language of the Klan in proclaiming AHEPA's purpose to be "advancing and promoting pure and undefiled Americanism among the Greeks of the United States." The Order of AHEPA remains today the preeminent Greek-American organization.

The Klan represented an external threat to the Atlanta Greek community and resulted in the Greeks rallying together in a protective stance, as ethnic minorities in America have almost always done when confronting such real and perceived attacks. Unified as a community both locally in Atlanta and across the nation as AHEPA's membership grew, the Greek immigrants were well equipped to defend themselves. What would pose a much more serious peril to the Greek immigrants were the internal disputes arising out of the divisions between the followers of Eleftherios Venizelos and those loyal to Greece's royal family that would instead tear Atlanta's Greek community apart in the decade after World War I and threaten its existence. The first outward signs of this dispute appeared in March 1917.

CONCLUSION

"I'll Put You Out!"…"No, I Am Not Going Out!"

Atlanta's Greek community, as did Greek communities throughout the
United States, annually prepared (and still does) political, educational
and religious pageants to celebrate March 25, Greece's national celebration
of its independence and the Orthodox Church's celebration of the feast day
of the Annunciation. This day had special relevance for those communities,
such as Atlanta's, that had taken the "Annunciation" name for their church.
Yet despite the importance of this day in the annual calendar, in 1917 the
Church Council initially considered foregoing that year's celebration.

With most members of the council inclined to proceed with a
celebration, the debate revolved around whether to schedule that
celebration for the twenty-fifth, which that year coincided with Lazarus
Saturday, or the following day, on Sunday. The proponents of a Saturday
celebration feared that the Royalist-Venizelist split in the community might
produce disruptive "serious incidents" during the celebration that would
scandalize the Americans who were more likely to attend on a Sunday.
For these proponents, it was better to celebrate the holiday on Saturday, a
working day, so as to minimize the Americans' attendance:

> *Today, the Greek people in our Community are divided into two rival
> sides, the Royalists [the Vasilikos], and the supporters of Venizelos
> [the Venizelikos]; it's only natural that we will have scenes during the*

celebration, and we will be misunderstood by the residents of this place that we live in…the holiday should be observed on the day that it coincides, on Lazarus Saturday, and that's because on that day, being a working day, it will be difficult for many people to come. This way we will avoid the scenes that are likely to happen otherwise.[656]

However, with the issue still undecided, the council met again two days later, and the discussion became more rancorous. The council president, Gerasimos Algers, again urged that there should be no celebration whatsoever:

[T]*he Greek people in our Community are also in discord. Therefore, although our original view was to celebrate the holiday in the most solemn possible way, today, this view has been changed. That is because it is natural to expect that serious incidents will take place, and if they do, the Greeks in America will suffer moral and material damages in the eyes of the people who are offering us hospitality.[657]*

One compromise offered was to celebrate the day "unceremoniously" in the church, in a "religious way" that would minimize the political aspects of the holiday.[658] Others insisted on a more formal celebration as originally planned, both "official and majestic." Even after a consensus developed for the more limited, religious celebration, "forceful" discussion continued between the president and one of the other council members, Theofanis Georgiou, with the meeting secretary diplomatically noting in his minutes the exchange of the phrases, "I'll put you out!" "No, I am not going out!" "Go out yourself!" "You will go out!" and "I'm not going!"[659]

The Church Council met again the next day, for the third time in four days. The council urged the two men to reconcile their differences "for the benefit of the Community and for the love and harmony that exist among us."[660] The men exchanged apologies, with Mr. Algers "asking for [Mr. Georgiou's] forgiveness ten thousand times," and they then "shook hands in reconciliation."[661] The meeting concluded, and "all the councilors, including the two who had just reconciled after their disagreement, were overjoyed."[662]

This first flare-up of the Royalist-Venizelist dispute in the Atlanta Greek community had been quickly and easily resolved. A compromise was reached, apologies were extended and forgiveness was granted. But the underlying disagreements between the two factions remained. Fissures in the community were still present. Six months later, the council's election committee urged those members of the church voting in the council elections to "wisely use our voting right, leaving aside any personal or political preferences."[663] Such easy resolutions in this ongoing dispute would not take place again for more than fifteen years. The passions aroused by this political and class dispute overrode the community's long-standing careful preservation of its good image in the eyes of its Atlanta neighbors. Emotional disagreements, clerical disputes, civil litigation and church closures would become the norm and be played out in public view.

Less than three weeks after the council had debated how the community should observe the March 25 holiday, Father Petrides led his congregation in the midnight celebration of Easter, the great feast day of the Orthodox Church. Some time after the chanting of *Xristos Anesti*, or "Christ Is Risen," by all those present in church in the early morning hours, Father Petrides delivered his Paschal homily. Described by him as a "Festive Speech delivered during the holy night of the Joyous Resurrection of Our Lord and God and Savior Jesus Christ," it would be the last Easter homily he ever gave.[664]

He welcomed his "dear brethren in Christ" with words that stressed the resurrectional message of the evening: "After the heavy and icy cold winter, behold, the sweet and delightful spring has come. After the stormy seas, calmness has followed. After the fearful Passion and painful Death of our Savior, His glorious and joyous Resurrection from the dead dawned upon us again. Death was not His end."[665]

And his later remarks in the sermon almost served as a response to the Atlanta community's real concerns nine years earlier about the ongoing viability of the church it was establishing.[666] In the church's initial bylaws in 1908, the council had included provisions for the disposition of church property in the event that the church was dissolved. But Father Petrides' message on this Easter morning was that, at least for the greater church, with Christ's Resurrection there could be no dissolution: "The perpetuation of His life is the guarantee for the perpetuation of His Church. Among all the social classes in the world, the Church alone is secured against total dissolution."[667]

Father Petrides had struggled with diabetes his entire adult life. Less than six months after the Easter celebration, he succumbed to the disease and died on September 5. So, at this critical time at the onset of serious political discord in the community, the Atlanta Greeks would proceed without the guidance of their priest.

The community underwrote both the costs of his hospitalization and his funeral expenses, "for reasons of honor and gratitude...for our Ever

Memorable Priest."[668] The Church Council also committed to burying him "in the most conspicuous place" in Greenwood Cemetery, a burial spot that visitors to the cemetery today see almost immediately as they enter the gates of the old Greek section.[669] The large marble slab marking his grave is inscribed in poetic Greek with the community's epitaph for their priest:

> *Muses of Elikonas, go into mourning now.*
> *In a mournful voice sing for the Priest*
> *From the island of Pythagoras, the enchanted Samos.*
> *The luminous source of the Greek letters,*
> *Demetrios Petrides, who like Prometheus*
> *Transported from there the fire, and like Orpheus,*
> *Accompanied the music with national speeches,*
> *And his works crowned his religious speeches.*
> *But as he imparted the Divine Fire to those who are here,*
> *The illness like a vulture killed him.*
> *The spirit he delivered to the Creator,*
> *And the remains are guarded under the earth.*
> *And every Orthodox Greek reveres the grave.*

Father Petrides' death in September followed by only a few months the first major eruption of the Royalist-Venizelist dispute in the Atlanta Greek community. For the next fifteen years, the very existence of the church that was founded with such difficulty would be threatened. The Greeks of Atlanta would move into this new era without the experienced pastoral leadership of Father Petrides. Over the span of those years, seven successive priests would struggle with this ongoing crisis, with a measure of calm not returning until the arrival of Father Panos Constantinides in 1933.

Appendix I

GREEK IMMIGRANTS LISTED IN THE 1896 LOCAL CITY OF ATLANTA CENSUS

Name	Age	Gender
Ward 1		
J. Brown	40	Male
K. Constantine	23	Male
Mrs. Constantine	24	Female
T. Frank	18	Male
John Moore	32	Male
Nick Moore	17	Male
Nicholas Solon	26	Male
George Solon	20	Male
Jim Williams	35	Male

Ward 2		
Alex Carter	36	Male
Mary Carter	30	Female
Alice Carter	8	Female
Christ Cochakos	25	Male
Jim Fort	25	Male
Charles Kake	24	Male
Nic Kutres	18	Male

Name	Age	Gender
Vacell Petropol	22	Male
Peter Petropol	16	Male
P. Tripose	50	Male

Ward 5		
James Brown	20	Male
Chris Mitchell	22	Male
George Mooroodis	28	Male
Nicholas Spon	25	Male

Ward 6		
James Akers	18	Male
D. Allesbut	30	Female
Peter Barbour	20	Male
Peter Brown	24	Male
Pano Caralee	27	Male
George Caralee	47	Male
B. Constantine	35	Male
Jean Gickas	50	Male
George Gickas	27	Male
John Handelis	13	Male
D. Handelis	35	Male

Notes: (1) There were no Greek immigrants listed as residing in Wards 3 and 4; (2) The spellings of names in this table are exactly as provided in the census.

GREEK IMMIGRANTS LISTED AS RESIDING IN ATLANTA IN THE 1900 UNITED STATES FEDERAL CENSUS

NAME	AGE	GENDER	MARITAL STATUS	OCCUPATION
WARD 1				
N.N. Pope	22	Male	Single	Merchant
N.L. Pope	13	Male	Single	Merchant
Michael Conomo	36	Male	Single	Restaurant Keeper
Nick Grigarchulos	41	Male	Single	Restaurant Keeper
John Nikas	55	Male	Single	Fruits/Grocer
Jim Malevy	25	Male	Single	Fruits/Grocer
Vict Bolas	21	Male	Married	Fruits/Grocer
George Moore	22	Male	Single	Fruits/Grocer
Crist Moore	15	Male	Single	Fruits/Grocer
John Bekaks	24	Male	Single	Fruits/Grocer
Niklas Pullos	24	Male	Single	Fruits/Grocer
Tom Pratts	24	Male	Single	Fruits/Grocer
Mihles Moore	24	Male	Single	Fruits/Grocer
Paul Moore	18	Male	Single	Fruits/Grocer
Angle Sellas	51	Male	Married	Fruits/Grocer

Name	Age	Gender	Marital Status	Occupation
WARD 4				
John Bachus	27	Male	Single	Fruits/Grocer
Evangelos Hozzepolos	16	Male	Single	Fruits/Grocer
George Bonsabe	28	Male	Single	Fruits/Grocer
Jaues Valwals	20	Male	Single	Fruits/Grocer
WARD 5				
Robert Mitchell	27	Male	Single	Fruits
James Mitchell	16	Male	Single	Candy
George Mitchell	24	Male	Single	Candy
WARD 6				
Mark Drasus*	31	Male	Married	Fruit Dealer
Pete Moore	32	Male	Single	Fruit Dealer
Myte Vergheotes	22	Male	Single	Fruit Dealer
Dernus Thomas	24	Male	Single	Fruit Dealer
John Mitchell	19	Male	Single	Fruit Dealer
James Mitchell	19	Male	Single	Fruit Dealer
John Brown	15	Male	Single	Fruit Dealer
Xenopher Brown	21	Male	Single	Fruit Dealer
Theodore Brown	18	Male	Single	Fruit Dealer
George Caralie	38	Male	Single	Fruit Dealer
Pete Caralie	36	Male	Single	Fruit Dealer
Constantine Petrople	25	Male	Single	Fruit Dealer
Jassiar Mitchell	24	Male	Single	Fruit Dealer
George L. Brown	37	Male	Single	Fruits/Grocer
John Drasas	37	Male	Single	Tailor
Charles Market	32	Male	Single	Fruit Dealer
Cris Constantine	38	Male	Married	Fruits/Grocer
Victor Constantine	30	Male	Single	Fruits/Grocer
Alison Caralee	40	Male	Married	Bartender
Mary Caralee	32	Female	Married	———
Alice Caralee	11	Female	Single	———

Notes: (1) There were no Greek immigrants listed as residing in Wards 2 and 3; (2) The spellings of names in this table are exactly as provided in the census.

* There is a separate listing for a Mack Drasas with the identical date of birth and address in what is apparently a double entry by the census taker for the same individual.

Appendix III

ATLANTA GREEK IMMIGRANTS PETITIONING FOR NATURALIZATION IN FULTON COUNTY SUPERIOR COURT PRIOR TO 1907

NAME	DATE OF PETITION	DATE OF IMMIGRATION	AGE
Vasseleios Foufas/John Moore	8/9/1894	8/1890	24
C. Charalambidis	9/30/1897	5/1892	54
Stylianos Antoniou	9/29/1898	12/1897	21
Evangelos Hatzopoulos	3/5/1901	10/1898	21
George Mavroodis	5/29/1901	2/1890	37
Victor Canares	7/22/1902	6/1897	21
Athen Prates	1/12/1903	10/1896	25
Charles Poulos/Constantine Athanasopoulos	2/24/1904	7/1890	29
James Poulo	4/5/1904	7/1898	26
Chris Carlos	9/13/1904	7/1899	23
Pete Carolee	10/12/1904	1890	40
Eli Chotas	11/8/1905	2/1901	35
Constantine Cosdallas/Costalas	4/19/1906	10/1903	35
Dionis Fotou	4/25/1906	10/1897	38
James Manos	9/10/1906	3/1901	30
Christ Matrangas/Matrangos	10/19/1906	8/1902	22

INCORPORATION DOCUMENT OF THE EVANGELISMOS SOCIETY

Georgia
Fulton County
In Re G. Avgerinos   Ex parte
  J. Stavropulos   Application for Incorporation
  Et al.   as Evangelismos Society

G. Avgerinos, J. Stavropulos, C. Athanasopoulos, Ch. Cochacos, G. Caralee, N. Culukis, C. Charalambidis, C. Mpulos, A. Caralee, P. Verghitis, V. Petropulos, A. Demopulos and S. Pergantes all of said state and County having filed in the office of the Clerk of the Superior Court of said County their petition seeking the formation of a corporation to be known as

      "Evangelismos" Society

for the purpose of promoting the interests and improving the condition of the members of said society, nursing its sick, burying its dead and doing other such like charitable work as well as for the purpose of creating and fostering a feeling of brotherhood among its members, and for other purposes as […] by their petition, and said petitioners having complied with the requirements of the law for such cases made and provided, and the court having satisfied that such application is legitimately within the purview and […] of the Code, the prayers of the petitioners are hereby granted, and the above named persons, their associates, successors and assigns are hereby incorporated under the name and style of "Evangelismos" Society [...] buying, holding, using and disposing of such property, real and personal, and choses in action as may be necessary, of making all contracts and doing all acts and things necessary to carry out the purpose of its organization with all the privileges, powers and corporate authority usually conferred upon corporations of like character.

And petitioners will need pray

Slaton T. Phillips
Attorney for Petitioners

Filed in office Oct. 20th 1902
Arnold Broyles Clerk

Georgia
Fulton County

To the Superior Court of said County G. Avgerinos, J. Stavropulos, C. Athanasopoulos, Ch. Cochasos, G. Caralee, N. Culukis, C. Charalambidis, C. Mpulos, A. Caralee, P. Verghiotis, V. Petropulos, A. Demopulos and S. Pergantis all of said state and County respectfully shows:

(1) That they desire for themselves, their associates and successors to become incorporated as a business and charitable society under the name and style of

Evangelismos Society

(2) The term for which petitioners ask to be incorporated is twenty years with the privilege of renewal at the end of such period.
(3) There shall be no such capital stock.
(4) Membership in such society shall be obtained by election, and the payment of an initiation fee, the manner of which election, and the amount of which fee shall be fixed by the bylaws of said society.
(5) The object of the proposed corporation is [...] and during a period of 20 years with the privilege of renewal at the expiration of that time.

Said corporation is hereby empowered to sue and be sued, to have and use a common seal, to make and enforce bylaws, to own real estate and personal property and is hereby clothed with all other and every right, power, privilege and immunity accorded corporations generally, subject of course to all the restrictions and liabilities fixed by our law.

In […] Court Fall Term 1902 this Nov. 24th 1902
   J. Lumpkin
   Judge Superior Court Fulton County
   Atlanta Circuit

Recorded November 25th 1902
   Arnold Broyles Clerk

Appendix V

ATLANTA GREEK IMMIGRANTS FEATURED AS BUSINESS OWNERS AND MANAGERS IN DIO ADALLIS'S 1912 GREEK MERCHANTS' REFERENCE AND BUSINESS GUIDE

NAME	BUSINESS OPERATED
Pete Alexander	Bell Confectionary Company
James Alexander	New Orleans Café
Charles Alexiou	Columbia Ice Cream Parlors
Gerasimos Algers	Blue Seal Ice Cream Company
Diomides Anastopoulos	Manhattan Café
Andreas Angelopoulos	Whitehouse Ice Cream Parlor
Charles Antoniou	Edgewood Avenue Soda Fountain
Stelios Antoniou	Edgewood Avenue Grocery
George Antonopoulos	New York Fruit Company
John Antonopoulos	New York Fruit Company
Andrew Bakas	Auburn Avenue Soda Fountain
Andrew Baker	Atlanta Lunch Room
Charles Bamboos	Central Avenue Ice Cream Parlors
John Baraklis	Near-Beer Saloon and Pool Parlors
E. Basil/Vasilios Efthimiou	Child's European Hotel and Café
Pete Basil	Ladies' Dining Room
Andrew Berry	Eagle Café/Majestic Theater

NAME	BUSINESS OPERATED
Athanasios Bitsaktzes	Metropolitan Café
And. Blatzos	Edgewood Avenue Soda Fountain
George Blatzos	Silver Moon Restaurant
Sam Bouras	Boulevard Ice Cream Parlors
Denis Brown	Post Office Ice Cream Parlors
James Brown	Edgewood Avenue Groceries
George Breuze	Capital City Fruit Company
Victor Brown	Decatur Street Saloon
George Caltis	Broadway Hotel
Leon Campbell	Blue Seal Ice Cream Company
Andreas Cacarountas	Metropolitan Restaurant
Leonidas Cacarountas	Daylight Restaurant
Alex Carolee	Ivy Street Bar and Pool Room
Athanasios Chakopoulos	Greek-American Grocery Company
Constantinos Charalambides	Harris Street Soda Fountain
Eli Chotas	Eagle Café/Majestic Theater
Nick Chotas	Greater Atlanta Confectionery Company
Christ Cochakos	Central Avenue Ice Cream Parlors
George Colias	Independent Lunch Room
Charles Collias	Union Restaurant
James Cotsovas	Arcade Restaurant
Andrew Dagress	Decatur Street Soda Fountain
Costa Daravingos	Busy Bee Café
Dem. Daules	Peters Street Lunch Room
Deamantopoulos	Plaza Café
Dion Demetery	Produce Farmer
James Demetracopoulos	Pryor Street Fruits
J. Demetriou	Busy Bee Café
George V. Economy	Bell Confectionery Company
George Elson	Piedmont Ice Cream Parlors
John Forlidas	Olympia Barber Shop
Dionysios Fotopoulos	Greater Atlanta Confectionery Company

NAME	BUSINESS OPERATED
Pete Galiatzos	Greater Atlanta Confectionery Company
Andreas George	Broadway Café
F. George	Coney Island Near-Beer Saloon
S.J. Georgiades	Cigar Manufacturer
Charles Geramides	Peachtree Café
Steve Gialelis	Atlanta Shoe Shine Parlors
Gregoropoulos	Edgewood Avenue Lunch Room
G.S. Gregory	American Pool Parlors
Christ Gyfteas	California Fruit Company
Christ Hanjaras	Broadway Café
Constantinos Hanjaras	Red Cross Creamery
John Hanjaras	Decatur Street Saloon
Nick Hanjaras	Red Cross Creamery
Nick James	Wall Street Saloon
V. Kanakopoulos	Independent Lunch Room
Costa Kanellos	Inman Yards Lunch Room
Kaneoglou	Edgewood Avenue Lunch Room
Charles Keramidas	Walker Brothers Groceries
Mike Kollias	Edgewood Avenue Groceries
Koubotos	Koubotos Barber Shop
Nicholaos Kutres	Broad Street Wholesale Fruit
Charles Leres	Bijou Lunch Room
Christ Liappes	Marietta Street Lunch Room
Pete Louis	Louis Café
Pete Louizos	Walker Brothers Groceries
George Macedon	Atlanta Café
George Mallas	Decatur Street Saloon
Nick Mallas	Decatur Street Soda Fountain
Harry Mamos	Coney Island Ice Cream Parlors
Andreas Manos	Atlanta Ice Cream Parlor
Jim Manos	Wholesale Banana Merchant
Marinos	Plaza Café
Christ Matrangos	New Orleans Café

Name	Business Operated
Nick Matrangos	Peachtree Café
George Mavroodis	Marietta Street Fruits and Candies
G. Mennias	Madison Avenue Café
J.V. Mennias	Madison Avenue Café
George Metropapas	Crystal Lunch Room
Angel Mitchell	Arcade Restaurant
George Mitchell	Mitchell's Café
Jim Mitchell	Decatur Street Near-Beer Saloon
Pete Mitchell	Decatur Street Saloon
Victor Mitchell	Riverside Café
George Moore	Central Avenue Ice Cream Factory
Christ Moutzopoulos	California Fruit Company
Nick Nickas	The Home Restaurant
George Nikas	Imperial Fruit Company
A. Panagopoulos	Dixie Café and Restaurant
Jim Papadakes	Edgewood Avenue Restaurant
Alex Papas	———
Pete Pappas	Atlanta Ice Cream Parlors
Phil Pappas	Columbia Ice Cream Parlors
George Pefinis	Bon-Ton Café/New York Café
Nick Pefanes	The Greek Club
Stephen Pergantes	Mitchell Street Soda Fountain
Argyre Pheles	Eagle Café/Majestic Theater
Demetrios Photopoulos	———
Pete Poolos	Pete's Place
Jim Pope	Edgewood Avenue Candies
Nick Pope	Nick's Pool Room
Soterios Pope	Edgewood Avenue Candies
Pete Potagos	Capital City Fruit Company
George Poulos	Hunter Street Soda Fountain
James Poulos	Central Avenue Soda Fountain
John Poulos	Georgia Avenue Soda Fountain
George Pouris	Edgewood Avenue Soda Fountain
Athan Prattes	Budweiser Near-Beer Garden

NAME	BUSINESS OPERATED
George Prattes	Mitchell Street Fruits and Candies
J. Prattes	Mitchell Street Fruits and Candies
Victor K. Preles	Dixie Café and Restaurant
D. Psaroudakis	The Greek Club
D. Psaros	Broad Street Fruits
Eustathios Sardelis	Taxi and Chauffeurs Company
John Sirmas	Peachtree Barber Shop
Angel Smerles	Peachtree Café
Vasilios Soteriou	Edgewood Avenue Soda Fountain
Angel Soteropoulos	Alamo Moving Picture Theatre
Dionisios Souranis	Atlanta Ice Cream Parlors
Speros Stamos	Peachtree Café
V. Stephanides	Atlanta Restaurant
Orestes T. Stephens	U.S. Immigration Inspector
George Themelis	Egyptian Cigarettes Manuf.
Nicholas Tountas	Arcade Restaurant
John Vardouniotes	Mocha Coffee Company
John Varellas	Alabama Street Fruit Store
Paul Varellas	Alabama Street Fruit Store
Pete Vergiotis	Imperial Fruit Company
St. Vergiotis	Ivy Street Bar and Pool Room
Andreas Vergios	People's Lunch Room
George Voulgaris	Walker Brothers Groceries
Dr. Spero G. Vryonis	Physician
D. Zakas	Zakas Bakery
Alex A. Zuzulas	Forsyth Street Soda Fountain

Note: The spellings of names in this table are exactly as indicated in the Adallis merchants guide.

THE SEPTEMBER 1905 LETTER FROM THE CHURCH COUNCIL TO ECUMENICAL PATRIARCH JOACHIM III

Your Holiness:

Your letter dated July 7 has been received. In reply to this letter, we wish to inform you that the community is pleased to be in a position to offer the Priest $1,000 a year, in monthly installments. The Priest will, also, have <u>many extra earnings</u>, that is, from marriages, christenings, deaths, liturgies, etc. The City of Atlanta is the capital of the State of Georgia, and it has 80,000 to 100,000 inhabitants, and 250 to 300 Greeks. Ever since they arrived in Atlanta, these Greeks did not have the chance to attend the Divine Liturgy, due to the lack of a Priest. For that reason, they are obligated to perform their marriages with Ministers of other religions, and they do likewise for the interment of their dead. There are, also, many Greeks in the surrounding areas, the suburbs, from where the Priest will have <u>many earnings</u>, too. For all these reasons, we implore your Divine Holiness to send us an appropriate Priest, who will guide us worthily, and bring us back to our dear Orthodox Church. Because, as we have earlier mentioned, we fear that we will be de-touched from our Holy Orthodox Church, for not having a Priest in our Community.

   As we have mentioned in our previous letter to you, we have put together a sum of money for the construction of a Church, and we are already negotiating the purchase of a building ground. We are, therefore, addressing your Divine Holiness our fervent supplications, asking that you seriously consider all the things mentioned in this letter, find the right Priest for us, and send him over here on time. This way, by his presence and advice, we will be able to construct our Church in short time.

You should, also, rest assured that as soon as the building of the Church is completed, the Greek Orthodox people here will be more generous to the Priest.

Enclosed here, you'll find a remittance of ten dollars, to be used for a telegram, which we will be expecting you to send us, if you consent, after you receive this letter, and have the Priest ready for us. This way, we will also be sending you, by cable, the money that is required for his fare.

We respectfully bow to receive the blessings of Your Divine Holiness.

Acting according to the instructions of the Greek Orthodox Community in Atlanta,

The Church Council.

Note: The emphasis provided by the underscoring in the translation of the letter appears in the original.

Appendix VII

THE DEFENSE OF FATHER CONSTAS HADJIDEMETRIOU PRESENTED AT THE GENERAL ASSEMBLY MEETING ON AUGUST 27, 1908

Estimable Mr. Chairman of the Church Council:

You have informed me, in your invitation, that a number of church members are seeking, by their petition, the following three changes: 1. To recall the right, granted to me by the Regulation, to use 12 Sundays a year for the purpose of holding Liturgical Services in neighboring communities. 2. To do away with the flowers of the Holy Friday. 3. To dispense with the "illumination" [the blessing of homes or work places by the priest], in the feast of Epiphany. Although I am, now, giving my reply in writing regarding the above issues, by this memorandum, I will wait until the next General Assembly, and then, I will verbally elaborate, before the Community on all that is necessary to be said.

It is known that by its letter to the Patriarchate, a copy of which I have enclosed here, the community has undertaken the obligation to give me the opportunity to celebrate the mass and other services, in the surrounding communities, too. This right was given to me due to the inadequacy of my salary, which in other words means that the amount in excess of the salary, needed to me, to make my living, will be supplemented by the Divine Liturgies, and other small profits, coming from the neighboring Greek Communities. A proof of this is provided by the fact that when I first arrived, the then Church Council hurried to publish that it was giving, with pleasure, the right to the priest to call on neighboring Greek communities for their religious needs, thus, making them, too, participants in the religious benefits that the Greeks in Atlanta had been blessed with. Time, however, Mr. Chairman, has shown that the Greeks in America go to the Divine Liturgy only on Sundays. Even here, in this Church, during the feast days of our Lord the Christ, or of the Mother of Our Lord, or of the Saints, when they fall on week days, is it not true that there is just one, or not even one churchgoer attending? In such days, am I not obliged to address the chairs, for lack of any human presence, and pronounce "let us love one another…" or "bow your heads onto the Lord"? Yes, I am. So, it became necessary to have 12 Sundays in a year granted to me, in accordance with the existing Regulations. As you well know, I made an intelligent and advantageous use of those Sundays, managing not only to bring in the amount of money, in excess of my salary, which I need as a family man and as a Priest, but also to bring in, from the neighboring communities, both money and offerings for the church that are equal in value to the total amount of money that I have received as salary, to this day. One could say that for the past three years, the community was not burdened with the payment of a priest's salary. The key witness to what I am trying to say, here, is the Church Book. Therefore, I, as well as the various Church Councils, that served throughout this time, have considered this as being only advantageous to the Community. There are already members of the community, though, who are in disagreement, because they consider the above way as being harmful to the interests of the community. I wish, Mr. Chairman, that the damages, alleged to have occurred until now, could be demonstrated by facts, exactly as I have done for the gains. For, as I was able to demonstrate, already, I can only see important gains for our community, and also for those who live in the neighboring areas, too. These people are not foreigners, after all, and I am well aware that they have organized themselves considerably, in every respect, ever since I have started calling on them, as they, themselves, would declare, too. I am asking, then, Mr. Chairman: Who helped the community of Savannah form, and provide its members with a Church? Who provided the motive for the community of Memphis to form, after all the commendable efforts of Mr. Miltiades Seretis, who is an indispensable witness to all this? The Greeks in that community were not even willing to go to the Liturgy, at first, because they did not know each other. Who organized the community of Augusta, as Mr. K. Athanasopoulos would truthfully testify? Who helped with the formation of the numerous neighboring communities, as Mr. Kyr. Kyriakopoulos, and the communities themselves, would most certainly acknowledge? None other, Mr. Chairman, than your priest, with all his homilies addressed to the Greeks in the surrounding areas. Those homilies, though, would have never been heard by the Orthodox Christians, if they had not been preached on Sundays.

It becomes quite another matter, of course, Mr. Chairman, if, acting selfishly, we choose to forget the responsibility we feel, and have undertaken, for the Greek expatriates, our compatriots. If such an egotistical way of thinking should prevail in the present matter, and if deserting those Greek expatriates who need my support, without help, were to be imposed on me, then, although it would sadden me, still, in order to maintain the love and peace among its members, I would agree to come to an understanding with the community, hoping that those members, who wish to take away my right of using the Sundays in question, are not driven by deceitful purposes, and that their intentions towards the Church and the Priest are, actually, good. For, the Priest is in a position to boast that, to this day, he has done no evil, and he has only, heartily, sought after the benefit of every one; and, if the intentions are truly good, you should be able to supplement my present salary by an amount equal to what I gain when I go to neighboring communities. You are all in a position, I'm sure, to recognize the necessity of this. For, every head of a family would understand that it is required, in order to allow a family man to meet his needs, even more so when this man is a priest, who represents the Church, and the Race. I can assure you that I would be grateful with such an arrangement, at least where the financial aspect of it is concerned, because I will not be obliged to beg for what is necessary for me, to meet my human needs. If the community, however, is in no position to do so, then, I will implore all of you to comprehend that using those Sundays as a means of achieving this, was the only salvation for me, as well as for the community. What was already established should be left as it is, and should continue being in force; it is not prudent to bring something down, when we are in no position to replace it with something else. Moreover, by the letter sent to the Patriarchate, the community has undertaken the obligation to increase my salary, which in itself would be very pleasing to me, if it had happened. Although, however, almost three years have elapsed, acting out of sense of honor, I have never mentioned the subject, until now. This is because I did not wish to become a burden to the community, thinking that any good thing that may happen to me should only be the result of the same consciousness and it should be offered with pleasure.

If, on the other hand, in spite of the fact that you are not in a position to increase my salary, you still insist in taking away from me the Sundays in question, this will only mean that, actually, it is not pleasing to you to have me as your priest. If this is so, there is no need for excuses; the community can say it overtly, and you can rest assured that I will not attempt to stay by force. I will seek a position elsewhere in America. Should that happen, I will only ask of you to be patient until I find such a position, which, I hope, will be easily done. Because, if my education itself is not given a chance to help me in this, then God will provide for me according to the best intentions of my heart. In this case I can only wish you to find a successor who will be better than me, so that you will never need to remember me; and even from far away, I will not stop to wish the best for your community, as I do for all the communities that I have served until now.

As for the issue of the flowers of the *Epitaphios* I will say this: The books of the Church will demonstrate that all the money earned from the flowers, in the first and third year, I donated to the Church on my own account, in spite of my personal needs; I have only kept, for my own benefit, the money earned from the flowers in the second year. I happen to think that the way I acted should have given the community reason to thank and congratulate me rather than to cause glares of jealousy, and criticism, and even more so, considering the fact that my small profits in Atlanta can be counted on the fingers of one hand. If those, however, who submitted the petition mean to say that the religious custom of *Epitaphios* flowers should be abolished altogether, I am GLAD that neither the Christian themselves, nor I, though I am a member of the clergy, are the appropriate persons to decide on this; this can only be decided by the higher authority of the Church.

As for the "illumination" in the feast of Epiphany, I will say this: As far as the monetary aspect of it is concerned, I am willing to accept any kind of arrangement, which will provide my compensation in a different way. If those who have signed the petition, though, mean that I should abolish the religious custom of "illumination," because of wrongly understood sense of honor and self respect, as I was unofficially informed, once again, I am GLAD because we are not the right persons to make such a decision. For, if it was up to us, and we had made it a matter of principle to adjust the customs and traditions of our religion to the liking of foreigners, then, we would have modified everything, the one after the other, and very likely, for many of those "modifications" we would not know which one of the so called American Churches to follow. Because the differences that do exist between those churches are as many as the number of heads existing in them; and they do laugh at one another. I am exceedingly sorry, Mr. Chairman, because we cling to such ideas, although it is not our job, and we expect to sacrifice the customs and traditions of our religion in the name of false pride, and for the sake of foreigners. The Americans, on the other hand, do not feel shame at the drums of the Salvation Army, and the like. Our own compatriots in Macedonia and elsewhere, especially in Asia Minor, do sacrifice, like brave soldiers, not only the "touchiness," but even their own lives for the sake of the religious freedom, and of their national consciousness; and the fanatical Turks do not recognize, in a most triumphant way, every such freedom.

The words of our Lord Jesus Christ come, now, to my mind, and in all honesty, I do not mean, by citing them, to speak against you, the Greeks who live in the free America; our Lord says: "Whosoever therefore shall be ashamed of me and of my words in this adulterous and sinful generation; of him also shall the Son of man be ashamed when he cometh in the glory of his Father with the holy angels." (Mark 8,38)

Indeed, Mr. Chairman, could there be a more demonstrative application of the above words than in this occasion? For in this generation, the sinful and adulterous, it appears that we are ashamed for Our Lord's Cross, which we are asked to kiss in the "illumination," and we seek to do away with these things, which we should be proud of, because our fathers have preserved them with fire and sword. That's why, Mr. Chairman, as being the offspring of those fathers, I consider it to be an honor to hold the Cross of Our Lord, as high as it can be, in the illumination, during Epiphany, when I arrive, with every solemnity, at the workshops of those Orthodox Christians who, just like me, do not wish to be timid about their religion. I would, certainly, not pay a visit to the shops of those who regard it as a decline in their dignity. This can be arranged; those who do not wish to have the illumination can simply declare this. Where religious matters are concerned, as in the present case, so long as even one person wishes to preserve his religious customs, none of the others, even more so the Priest, of course, have the right to prevent him from doing so. This is one issue that can not be resolved by the principle of the "will of the majority."

So, Mr. Chairman, as far as the financial aspect of this matter is concerned, I will accept any arrangement that will allow me to have a more dignified way of life; but as for the religious aspect of it, I can not accept any annulment or reform, because it is part of my duty to preserve everything that was entrusted to me by my Church. I will, however, respectfully accept any decision or special instruction coming from the Higher Authority of the Church. Most importantly, though, what I would really like to call your attention on, as well as the attention of the Council and of the Assembly, is the following: You should make every effort that all decisions regarding the Regulation, are based on the general consent, and they are made by the entire community, or at least by a large majority of it. This will only be possible if the General Assembly is attended by a large number of members. Otherwise, every decision that you arrive at will only represent a part of the members, and, as such, it will always cause the reaction of those who were not there when the decision was made. It is self-understood, and unnecessary for me to emphasize that in a democratic and constitutional administration, the decisions are made by the rule of the majority, and the minority has always the obligation to submit and accept the decisions made by the majority. Otherwise, laws can never be made, nor can they be observed, and order can never prevail. Everyone becomes a self-appointed chief, recognized but by himself; such a situation is simply called, and it is in fact, anarchy.

Moreover, I am wishing the best to you all, and remain, always with love, a willing supplicant in the name of the Lord

Very Reverend Constas Hadji Demetriou

[At this point, Father Hadjidemetriou read the September 1905 letter (Appendix VI) sent by the Church Council to Patriarch Joachim III. Upon completing the reading of this letter, he resumed his defense by reading the lengthy written remarks that he had prepared especially for the general assembly.]

Gentlemen:

All three points made in the petition are on the one hand of religious nature, and of financial on the other. The religious aspect of these issues is in the jurisdiction of the Church Authority, only. No one else is allowed to have even the slightest intervention. The financial aspect of these points, though, matters to me, and to the Church, as well. The Church, of course, belongs to you; but, I dare say that it belongs to me too, not to a lesser extent, considering, that I have contributed to it not only in person, but also, most of the money that came from the neighboring communities, outside the city, together with all the votive offerings. You can very well look down upon the money that I bring from the neighboring communities, of course, and you may say "the Church has no need for it, it can rely on its own children." I am afraid, though, that the same logic does not apply to me, unless you are willing to maintain that you are my children, too, and that you will take care of my needs, as well. If not, then, I am the one who has the duty and the right to use the small profits as I choose. No one else. Do you want to be assured that this is so? Then listen to what the Apostle Paul has to say, in his Epistle to the Corinthians:

Am I not an apostle? Am I not free? Have I not seen Jesus Christ our Lord? Are you not my work in the Lord? If I am not an apostle to others, yet doubtless I am to you. For you are the seal of my apostleship in the Lord.

My defense to those who examine me is this: Do we have no right to eat and drink? Do we have no right to take along a believing wife, as do also the other apostles, the brothers of the Lord, and Cephas? Or is it only Barnabas and I who have no right to refrain from working? Who ever goes to war at his own expense? Who plants a vineyard and does not eat of its fruit? Or who tends a flock and does not drink of the milk of the flock?

Do I say these things as a mere man? Or does not the law say the same also? For it is written in the law of Moses, "You shall not muzzle an ox while it treads out the grain." Is it oxen God is concerned about? Or does He say it altogether for our sakes? For our sakes, no doubt, this is written, that he who plows should plow in hope, and he who threshes in hope should be partaker of his hope. If we have sown spiritual things for you, is it a great thing if we reap your material things? If others are partakers of this right over you, are we not even more?

Nevertheless, we have not used this right, but endure all things lest we hinder the gospel of Christ. Do you not know that those who minister the holy things eat of the things of the temple, and those who serve at the altar partake of the offerings of the altar? Even so the Lord has commanded that those who preach the gospel should live from the gospel. [I Corinthians 9: 1-14]

It has been said, Gentlemen, that I have the magical ability to *read prayers over* those who come to serve in the Church Council, and turn them into unquestioning supporters. Although you see each one of these members protest against this allegation, as any conscientious person would do, yet, I don't believe that you suppose that Apostle Paul, too, had *prayers read over* him. For, I was not present in this world during Apostle Paul's life time, nor was anyone else of my generation.

Well, then, Gentlemen, my small profits are rightfully mine. Now, some people are asking me to sacrifice them. The sacrifice is optional, it cannot be demanded. Yet, although I am a man of sacrifice, Gentlemen, and I have proven it in numerous occasions in my life, I am now asking you to show me the need for it. Show me the religious necessity, or the patriotic one, or any other common necessity, which I should be doing this for, and I will do it at once, but I do not see any necessity. On the contrary, I can see this is a mere eccentricity, since by asking me to do so, you are looking down upon that other money, which I bring to the Church by making use of those 12 Sundays to call on the neighboring communities.

That goes to say, that those who are asking for this are lacking in good intentions, and it makes me wonder whether there is any esteem for me, as a person. Now, if the answer is Yes, I thank you very much. If the answer is No, then, I have to ask Why? Is it because I am not worthy of your esteem, or is it simply because "this is how we want it to be?" If the answer is "this is how we want it to be," then, I have nothing to say; it is impossible to convince someone who does not want to be convinced, even by clear reasoning. If the whole thing, however, is simply due to ignorance, then, allow me to explain to enlighten those who ignore facts. I am really sorry to have to blow my own trumpet, but I am not to be blamed for it, because I consider it necessary for all of you to get to know your priest, especially because the possibility exists that this may be the last time that you hear your priest's voice in this church. I will start by saying the following:

In order to enjoy the general appreciation and approval, a person has to be motivated by good intentions, to have the appropriate education and abilities, and to be a man of good character, as well. To prove that your priest is endowed with these gifts, I do not really have to use proofs that you are not familiar with. The fact that the heart of your priest is filled with good intentions, not only for the religion and the motherland, but also, for the community, as well as for every single individual, is demonstrated by the great willingness that he has shown in every matter, including those that are not in the circle of his regular duties. I am asking you, then:

Didn't your priest act as a collector, when it was needed? Didn't he generate small profits for the Church, in ways that no one else had thought before, and he did it even though he was harming his own interests? Wasn't he always the first one to offer eagerly his mite, in favor of every cause? Isn't he the one who has been doing all the writing and related jobs for the church, during the last three years, without the slightest benefit? Didn't he play a leading part in every national matter? Or, was it ever a private individual who asked for a personal favor and did not find the priest willing to help? His diploma provides the answer to the question, whether his education is suitable or not. Likewise, the remarkable respect that he enjoys among the literary people, both in America, and in Europe, provides testimony to this. Testimony for his abilities is furnished by the letter of the

Ecumenical Patriarch, who wrote to the previous chairman of the Council, saying "You have got my best cleric"; it is also provided by the letter of recommendation. In that letter a specific mention was made to his success, achieved under the supervision of the Patriarchate. Moreover, the love he enjoys in all the surrounding communities is a testimony in itself. Further testimony to his abilities is provided by the fact that he has managed to bring from the surrounding communities to the Church sums of money equaling the total amount of money that he has received as salary in the last three years. You should, also, remember that the Community of Atlanta occupies a high place among the Greeks abroad. Finally, what sums it all up is the brilliant success that your priest had in ever kind of business he undertook; this, in itself, bears testimony to his abilities. Now, in order to form your opinion about your priest's <u>character</u>, you should ask yourselves if you have ever seen him being greedy, acting unfairly, being quarrelsome or spiteful, or being a scoundrel, or impolite, undignified, voluptuous, or drunkard. Can you recall any incident where you have not seen him—overcoming all human weakness—try hard to be a model for the faithful, in every respect?

The only thing, Gentlemen, that some people—a very small number—have learned to say well, just like a lesson, and they have made it like "chewing gum" in their mouths (something repeated very frequently and mechanically) is the slogan that the priest is "avaricious." Do you really comprehend the meaning of this word? Avaricious is someone who is a money lover. The person, then, who is greedy has a thirst for money. He tries to collect it, and hold on to it; he is afraid to spend even pennies of it. Tell me, if you please, when did your priest exhibit lust for acquisition of wealth? I would say that there are quite a few people attending this meeting who are aware of the opposite; and I mean that, many times, even though I was entitled to it, and was exhorted to do so, I did not take the money. The Church Books will testify to the fact that, several times, not just once, I presented the Church, of my own initiative, with the small profits that I earned, and with money in cash, too. Maybe those who are accusing me view the acceptance of a salary on my part, and the occasional acceptance of my, seldom, small profits as greediness. These are within my rights, and I expect to live from this income alone, since I do not run any other kind of business on the side. Do my accusers think, by chance, that when one becomes a priest, one can successfully shake off human needs, such as taking nourishment, using clothes, etc? These are needs that not even our Lord had managed to avoid, though He was God. Do they think that, by becoming a priest, one loses one's right to live, and to love, and to take care of the family that he has created in this world? Doesn't a priest have the fundamental rights, that even the least of the human beings enjoy, after having spent considerable time of his life sitting on school benches, in the process of becoming a priest? I am asking you, Gentlemen: If, instead of studying theology, I had chosen to study medicine, or law, or some other science, wouldn't then, the parents who reared me, have the right to expect of me to take care of them, in their old age? Wouldn't my wife have the right to expect of me to provide her with a tolerable life? Wouldn't I have the obligation to bring up my children in a decent way? Does it mean, then, that just because I became a priest, I have been discredited, and all those who depend on me should be deprived of their rights? If you think that this is so, then why are you speaking against the illiterate clergy? You are, then, demonstrating by your opinions, and your ways, that you are worthy only of such a clergyman.

Aren't you?

Yet, I have never exhibited thirst for money, and did not seek to become wealthy; tell me, if you please, has any of you ever seem me affectionately caress the money in my hands, when it was rightfully given to me for the work I had done, in the most dignified way? Or rather, let someone show me the excess money, that as a money loving man, I am supposed to have. Your wealth, Gentlemen, is calculated in positive hundreds of dollars, whereas mine, in negative hundreds of dollars. If I were avaricious, I ought to have, at least, some excess money. You may claim, of course, that I am wasteful, and I spend all my money; but if this is so, I cannot be greedy, too, at the same time. I assure you, Gentlemen, that I am neither wasteful nor a lover of money. I am simply a dignified person. Some will argue that I am wasteful because although I am given 20 dollars to pay rent, I chose to pay 30 dollars, instead, as I wish not to reside in a chicken coop, but to live in the kind of house that does honor to me, and to the Church, and to the Race that I represent, as well. You may be right, Sirs, because you are not heads of families. It is not difficult, though, to ask someone who is the head of a family, and get informed about the needs of a family, in America. Thus, I am worthy of respect, Sirs. If you truly wish to hold me in esteem, I do thank you. If you do not wish to, it doesn't matter, because, after all, neither am I bound to you by crown [married to you], nor are you to me. Besides, I heard someone say that you are considering a less costly priest, and that's alright. You can certainly hire that priest, who will cost you less money. I am expensive, and I am most glad of it. Because an expensive item cannot be eaten by the dogs. Yet, although expensive, I have been the cheapest one for you: and to be precise, the one for free, because, to this day, I did not cost anything to the Community.

In the end, I am sorry, but I cannot accept any decision that would reduce the bread of my family. This is my answer to you, and I beg of you to discuss it among yourselves in a peaceful manner, putting your hands over your hearts. I will, now, leave the meeting, as I do not wish to exert any influence on you, and even more so, because I am alleged to have the magical power of convincing by *reading prayers over* people, and the like. I will let myself at the mercy of God, and He will not abandon me; if the decision you arrive at is to refuse me the bread of my family, then, I will abide by the hope to find other Christians, who will provide it to me, without complaints, while I will be working for their benefit. I heartily wish that you may never have to remember me.

Farewell, Gentlemen!

Appendix VIII

CHANTERS OF THE ATLANTA GREEK ORTHODOX CHURCH, 1906–1917

Theofanis Georgiou Gounaris	February 1906
Theofanis Georgiou Gounaris	April 1906
G. Stroumboulis	December 1908
Theofanis Georgiou Gounaris	June 1909
G. Harharides	August 1915
Theofanis Georgiou Gounaris	August 1915
Aristomenis Klamarias*	November 24, 1916
Theofanis Georgiou Gounaris	September 2, 1917

Note: The dates listed indicate the date of the Church Council or general assembly minutes in which each individual is described as the church's chanter.

*Mr. Klamarias became the church's first left-side chanter during this month, as Theofanis Gounaris continued to serve as the primary chanter.

CHURCH COUNCILS OF THE ATLANTA GREEK ORTHODOX CHURCH, 1906–1917

SEPTEMBER 7, 1905
Nicholas Papademetropoulos
Leonidas Kyriakopoulos
Georgios Papageorgakopoulos
Constantine Athanasopoulos
Stavros Gialelis
Evangelos Botsaris
Dionysios Fotopoulos

FEBRUARY 28, 1906
Nicholaos Kouloukis
Leonidas Kyriakopoulos
Constantine Athanasopoulos
Georgios Papageorgakopoulos
Stavros Gialelis

MARCH 16, 1906
Constantine Athanasopoulos
Leonidas Kyriakopoulos
Stavros Gialelis
I. Eikonomopoulos

Nicholaos Matrangos
Dionysios Fotopoulos

APRIL 29, 1906
Constantine Athanasopoulos
Nicholaos Kouloukis
Dionysios Fotopoulos
I. Eikonomopoulos
Leonidas Kyriakopoulos
P. Bitsakis
Stavros Gialelis

MAY 27, 1906
Constantine Athanasopoulos
Dionysios Fotopoulos
Stavros Gialelis
Nicholaos Kouloukis
I. Eikonomopoulos
Nicholaos Matrangos

MAY 28, 1907
Nicholaos Kouloukis
Vasileios Euthymiou
Demetrios Manos
V. Petropoulos
Georgios Koriopoulos
Dionysios Pendovolas
Christos Karachalios

AUGUST 19, 1907
Constantine Athanasopoulos
Nicholaos Kouloukis
Dionysios Fotopoulos
Dionysios Pendovolas
Nicholaos Matrangos

AUGUST 27, 1907
Stephanos Psychalinos
Georgios Kouloukis
Georgios Karalis

Panagiotis Papanikolopoulos
Stavros Gialelis

JUNE 21, 1908
Christos Karachalios
Petros Mitsanis
Panagiotis Vergiotis
Georgios Papageorgakopoulos
Nicholaos Matrangos
Leonidas Kyriakopoulos
Charalambos Christopoulos

JULY 2, 1908
Stephanos Psychalinos
Panagiotis Papanikolopoulos
Georgios Papageorgakopoulos
Georgios Kouloukis
Dionysios Fotopoulos

AUGUST 21, 1908
Nicholaos Kouloukis
Thanos Tsakopoulos
Petros Mitsanis
Panagiotis Papanikolopoulos
Nicholaos Gregoropoulos
Christos Cotsakis
Nicholaos Tountas

NOVEMBER 29, 1909
Gerasimos Algers
Stephanos Psychalinos
Georgios Gregorakis
Angelis Moukios
Christos Karachalios
D. Constandopoulos
Panagiotis Papanikolopoulos

APRIL 22, 1911
Constantine Athanasopoulos
Gerasimos Algers

Angelis Moukios
Andreas Angelopoulos
Elias Tsatas
Nikolaos Tountas

SEPTEMBER 6, 1914
Panagiotis Papanikolopoulos
Constantine Athanasopoulos
Elias Tsatas
Georgios Blatsos
Andreas Angelopoulos
Andreas Dagres
Vasileios Prylis

NOVEMBER 23, 1916
Gerasimos Algers
Vasileios Efthymiou
Vasileios Prylis
Theofanis Georgiou
Stephanos Psychalinos
Spyros Vryonis
Demetrios Psaroudakis

MARCH 29, 1917
Gerasimos Algers
Vasileios Efthymiou
Theofanis Georgiou
Angelis Moukios
Panagiotis Vergiotis
Georgios Papageorgakopoulos
Vasileios Prylis

Note: It is uncertain how many council members served on the Church Councils from 1906 until March 1908, when the initial set of church bylaws was adopted. Although the existing lists in the record almost uniformly provide seven members, the meeting minutes of at least one Church Council meeting imply a council of eleven members. The bylaws adopted in March 1908 formalized a seven-member council, to be elected every two years. Despite the clarity of the bylaws provision, retrieving accurate and complete council lists from the council and general assembly minutes is not an easy task. Membership on the council in the early years was very fluid, with members resigning and others being appointed with some regularity. Often, men (there is no record of any women being elected to the Church Council in the period from 1906 to 1917) would be elected without being aware that their names had been offered as candidates, resulting in their being unable to assume office because of personal or business obligations. This would often produce two council listings within one or two months of each other, one providing the names of those elected, and the other listing the names of those able to serve, which would include the new appointees. At least in the earliest years, prior to the adoption of the bylaws, it also appears that new councils were chosen sometimes as often as every few months. Also, there are occasional gaps in these minutes, leading to the likely result that not all council listings have been preserved. This table simply records as carefully as possible the council listings that are in the record. Thus, it is almost certainly incomplete. The dates given in this table are the dates in the various archival records (either the Church Council or general assembly meeting minutes, the church charter or the church treasury book) in which the particular council listing is provided.

Appendix X

PRESIDENTS OF THE GREEK ORTHODOX CHURCH COUNCILS, 1906–1917

Constantine Athanasopoulos	1905–6
Nicholas G. Kouloukis	1906–9
Constantine Athanasopoulos	1910–12
Gerasimos Algers	1912–14
Constantine Athanasopoulos	1914
Eli Chotas	1915–16
Gerasimos Algers	1916
Vasileios Efthymiou	1917
Stefanos Psychalinos	1917–18

WESTVIEW CEMETERY REGISTER FOR GREEKS BURIED IN SECTION 8 AND GOD'S ACRE, 1901–1914

NAME	DATE OF DEATH	AGE AT DEATH	BURIAL PLOT
John Nekas	12/1/1901	62	8/2-A/100
John Bekakas/ Bikukas	9/6/1902	28	8/R-H/4
James Pagonas	4/9/1904	37	8/R-C/25
Angeliki Kyriakopoulou	2/24/1905	32	8/R-1/13
John Badalias	4/24/1907	23	8/R-1/5
Harry Chlovitis	6/6/1907	35	8/R-1/11
Thomas Evangelinos/ Evangelos	9/18/1907	22	8/R-2/2
Vasileios Magritis	4/13/1908	70	8/R-1/2
Nick Gerasanos	7/24/1908	28	8/R-3/21
N. Pistolimou	1908	29	unknown
Alexandros Koutroulis	7/28/1909	33	8/R-5/22
Victor Geraketes	6/14/1910	1	8/R-T/19
Vasoulis Theodosiou	6/14/1910	15 months	unknown
Konstantinos Handelis	7/8/1910	9 months	GA/13-B/27
Alexandros _____	7/28/1910	33	82.5-22
Dionysios Barros	8/9/1910	21	8/R-8/9
Kalliopi Manou	11/21/1910	16 months (removed)	8/R-T/30

Name	Date of Death	Age at Death	Burial Plot
Georgios Pandovolos	5/23/1911	6 months	8/R-V/13
George Mavroudis	6/26/1911	42	8/R-11/9
Georgios Memos/Manos	8/26/1911	30	8/R-13/5
Giannoula Bouloukas	9/2/1911	3	8/R-W/13
Panag. Papastathopoulos	9/7/1911	24	8/R-13/9
Theodoros Denezakos	9/29/1911	39	8/R-13/14
G. Iosyf Siasas	1911	5 months	unknown
Nikolaos Manedakis	11/29/1911	39	8/R-14/3
G. Dollis/Katsoulas	12/10/1911	29	S.8-24, 8
I.A. Mantis	1911	35	8/R-10/9
Chrysoula Handeli	6/24/1911	6 months	GA/13-J/35
Constandina Karagianni	7/1/1911	10 months	GA/13-E/36
Sam Soules	1/1912	27	8/R-14/13
Eirini Psychalinou	7/6/1911	8 months	8/R-V/25
Andrew Stephanopoulos/ Stefinies	7/23/1912	25	8/R-15/25
Panos Apostolopoulos	6/18/1913	38	8/R-18/14
Tom Pappas	7/2/1913	18	8/R-18/19
George Hangrioannis	3/1914	44	8/R-20/22

FINANCIAL CONTRIBUTORS TO THE ATLANTA GREEK ORTHODOX CHURCH AS LISTED IN THE CHURCH'S TREASURY BOOK FROM JUNE 1906–JUNE, 1907

Panagiotis Alapandis
Demetrios Alexandrou
Konstantinos Alexiou
Theodoros Anagnostopoulos
Eustratios Antoniou
Stylianos Antoniou
Ioannis Antonopoulos
Dionysios Apostolopoulos
Andreas Athanasopoulos
Panagiotis Athanasopoulos
Vasileios Athanasopoulos
Christos Avrotis
Ioannis Begesiotis
Anastasios Bieras
Konstantinos Blatzos
Georgios Blatzos
Gregoris Blatzos
Demetrios Boukatelis
Anastasios Boutos
Minas Christopoulos
Anastasios Christou
Panagiotis Danikas
Kyriakos Deligiannis

Demetrios Demetrakopoulos
Christos Dgorezos
Demetrios Diangelis
Ioannis Diplaris
Konstantinos Drakopoulos
Georgios Eustathiou
Kourios Eustratios
Vasileios Euthymiou
Ioannis Fotopoulos
Ioannis Fourlides
Nicholaos Fourlides
Garitza brothers
Vasileios Gatzanis
Georgopoulos brothers
Stavros Gialelis
Athanasios Giambanis
_____ Giannaros
Panagiotis Girangas
Vasileios Gogias
Augustis Goulimis
Ioannis Goulimis
Georgios Gouras
Andreas Goutos

Nicholaos Gregoropoulos
Georgios Grammatikopoulos
Anastasios Grilas
Father Constans Hadjidemetriou
Demetrios Hantzaras
Nicholaos Hantzaras
Theodoros Hantzaras
Demosthenes Iliakopoulos
L. Iliakopoulos
Nicholaos Iliakopoulos
Petros Kallianos
Demetrios Kalovedouris
Konstantinos Kanelleas
Georgios Kapouralis
Christos Karachalios
Konstantinos Karachouras
Panagiotis Karalis
Stylianos Karalis
Konstantinos Karatas
Demetrios Katsoulas
Vasileios Katsoulas
Ilias Kavouras
Georgios Kimbouropoulos
Petros Kimbouropoulos
Athanasios Kiousis
Demetrios Kolyvanis
Nicholaos Kokotzis
Michael Kolikoniaris
Charalambos Konstantinopoulos
Demetrios Konstantopoulos
Georgios Koriopoulos
Georgios Kouloukis
Nicholaos Kouloukis
Eustratios Koundourelis
Panagiotis Kourlabas
Georgios Kylikas
Leonidas Kyriakopoulos
Theodoros Kyriakopoulos
Ladas brothers

Demetrios Lambrinos
Andreas Lazaris
Christos Liapis
Panagiotis Liapis
Alexandros Linardos
Konstantinos Louis
Louizou brothers
Panagiotis Lysandros
Ioannis Manglaras
Vasileios Manos
Konstantinos Makris
Minas Margaritis
Demetrios Matsoulas
Demos Michalakakis
Andreas Milias
Nicholaos Misombis
Evangelos Mitropapas
Georgios Mitropapas
Panagiotis Mitsanis
Nicholaos Molias
Demetrios Moundreas
Ioannis Nikas
Andreas Panagakopoulos
Demetrios Pantazopoulos
Ioannis Papadimitriou
Demetrios Papadakis
Andreas Papadopoulos
Panagiotis Papadopoulos
Georgios Papagiannis
Georgios Papanastasiou
Nikitas Papanikolopoulos
Panagiotis Papanikolopoulos
Georgios Papoutsalaras
Nicholaos Paraskevopoulos
Georgios Patapis
Demetrios Pefanis
Georgios Pefanis
Dionysios Pendovolas
Georgios Petropoulos

Ioannis Petroulas
Konstantinos Petroutzis
Demetrios Polychronopoulos
Thomas Psadourakis
Athanasios Prattis
Georgios Prattis
Vasileios Psaras
Athanasios Pournaras
Nicholaos Pournanas
Michael Praktikakis
Vasileios Prylis
Stephanos Psychalinos
Nicholaos Saravakos
Georgios Seimenis
Ioakim Serafeimides
Miltiades Seretis
Ioannis Sirmakezis
Nicholaos Sivilas
Demetrios Skamentos
Vasileios Skandalis
Nicholaos Skandangos
Stavros Sotiropoulos
Vasileios Spanogiannis
Athanasios Spyropoulos
Nicholaos Spyropoulos
Panagiotis Spyropoulos
Ioannis Stalimeros
Ioannis Syrmas
Evangelos Themistoklis
Konstantinos Theodorakopoulos
Michael Theodosiou
Georgios Theoharis
Georgios Tsamouklas
Georgios Tsouroulas
Christos Tsousis
Demetrios Tziroulas
Ioannis Tzouraklas
Christos Vachliotis
Anastasios Valeras

Ioannis Valliotis
Konstantinos Vasileiou
Georgios Velis
Vasileios Velis
Georgios Venias
Dionysios Visvardis
Demetrios Vlachos
Dionysios Zakas
Vasileios Zakas
Ilias Zervas
Georgios Zervis
Panagiotis Zervis

NOTES

Introduction

1. *Atlanta Constitution*, December 16, 1887, 5. Muhler was also described as being Greek in all of the *Constitution*'s stories about this match and others. In an article on February 4, 1889, the *New York Times* gave Greek George's name as "Tedory George Costaky," a phonetic rendering of Theodoris George Costakis.
2. Ibid.
3. Ibid., December 17, 1887, 4.
4. Ibid., December 21, 1887, 4.
5. Ibid., December 26, 1887, 5.
6. Ibid., December 20, 1887, 5; December 26, 1887, 5.
7. For a thorough and interesting discussion of the prominence of Greek professional wrestlers in the late nineteenth and early twentieth centuries, see Steve Frangos's article "Costakis: A Gentleman Sportsman," *National Herald*, August 23–29, 2014, 1, 7.
8. Concordia Hall was constructed in 1892 at the corner of Mitchell and Forsyth Streets by the membership of the Concordia Association. The association was composed of German and Hungarian Jews seeking to preserve their cultural heritage through the staging of musical and dramatic performances. The membership would later establish the Standard Club, a Jewish country club. The Concordia Hall façade today is part of Hotel Row, in a designated Landmark District in downtown Atlanta that was listed on

the National Register of Historic Places in 1989. Part of the original swan neck pediment with a sculpted lyre is still a part of the façade.

9. *Atlanta Constitution*, December 28, 1887, 5.

10. Ibid.

11. Ibid., January 10, 1888, 5.

Chapter 1

12. Saloutos, *Greeks in the United States*, 29.

13. *Atlanta Constitution*, September 13, 1911, 14.

14. Adallis, *Adallis Greek Merchants' Reference Book*, 63.

15. Moskos, *Greek Americans*, 11; Immigration and Naturalization Service, 1976 Annual Report, 87–88.

16. Moskos, *Greek Americans*, 25.

17. Ibid., 33–34.

18. These men were Evangelos Athanasopoulos, Elias Karahalios, Christos Karalis, Dimitrios Karalis and Efthimios Mitropapas. Ship manifest for SS *La Savoie*, October 21, 1906, Ellis Island website. Constantine Athanasopoulos had adopted the name Charles Poulos in Atlanta, and it is with this name that he is identified in the manifest record. His brother is also identified as Evangelos Poulos.

19. Church Council Meeting Minutes, June 29, 1916.

20. See the 1920 United States census and the Danaos Ledger Book, 2–10, 41–45.

21. Interview with Cleo Janoulis Edwards.

22. *Atlanta Constitution*, August 10, 1889, 5. Charles Brown comes to us in the historical record as the victim of an assault at his fruit stand by Reuben Simpson. Simpson was arrested and charged with attempted murder. He was found guilty of assault and battery and fined fifty dollars. Fulton County Superior Court Criminal Minutes, 1889–94, vol. 1, 11.

23. See the Treasury Book of the Greek Orthodox Church, 1905–17, 42–54.

24. 1910 United States Census.

25. *Atlanta Constitution*, October 7, 1912, 3; Centennial Anniversary Album of the Atlanta Annunciation Greek Orthodox Cathedral, 51–52.

26. Church Council Meeting Minutes, November 3, 1915.

27. Danaos Charter of Incorporation. The incorporators were Pete Mitchell, Thomas Tascopoulos, B. Georgopoulos, James Manos, George Pope and Peter Brown.

28. The exact date of the founding of *Agia Ekaterini* is uncertain. Although it was not officially incorporated until October 26, 1921, it was established

sometime in early 1917. The Church Council minutes of March 9, 1917, describe *Agia Ekaterini* as a "newly founded Association." Both Danaos and *Agia Ekaterini* still exist today.

29. Fiftieth Anniversary Album of the Atlanta Annunciation Greek Orthodox Church, "Santa Ekaterini Fraternity" (unpaginated).

30. Church Council Meeting Minutes, May 11, 1915.

31. Ibid., October 5, 1916.

32. Saloutos, *Greeks in the United States*, 46.

CHAPTER 2

33. Benjamin Hill had served in the Confederate senate and been an ally and supporter of Jefferson Davis. This statue was later removed from this street location and placed in the northern wing of the Georgia State Capitol, where it remains today.

34. Rogers, *History, Confederate Veterans' Association*, 11.

35. Ibid.

36. Swan, *Chicago's Irish Legion*, 166.

37. Smith, *Church that Stayed*, 11. The site of Sherman's headquarters in 1864 is now the location of Atlanta City Hall.

38. Martin, *Handbook of the City of Atlanta*, 32, 47.

39. Garrett, *Atlanta and Environs*, vol. 2, 204; Local 1890 Census of City of Atlanta.

40. United States Census Bureau.

41. Burns, *Rage in the Gate City*, 3.

42. Mebane, "Immigrant Patterns in Atlanta 1890 and 1896," 43, 48; Local 1896 Census of City of Atlanta.

43. Mebane, "Immigrant Patterns in Atlanta 1890 and 1896," 4.

44. Martin, *Handbook of the City of Atlanta*, 99.

45. *Report on Population of the United States at the Eleventh Census*, clxxiv.

46. Rogers, *History, Confederate Veterans' Association*, 19.

47. Ibid., 26. A statue of Gordon is located today on the grounds of the Georgia state capitol.

48. *Atlanta Constitution*, March 17, 1893, 7.

49. Acts of the Georgia General Assembly, 1893, vol. 1, 114. This licensing exemption did not apply to the sale of "whiskey, sewing machines or lightning rods."

50. *Atlanta Journal*, August 4, 1902, 7.

CHAPTER 3

51. Chandler, *Travels in Greece*, 119.

52. Letter of John Adams to Robert Livingston, July 14, 1783, the Library of Congress. Adams was equally caustic and dismissive of others he considered to be outside the circle of his self-described "natural aristocracy" of which he was a part. After attending Mass at the Catholic Church of St. Mary in Philadelphia in October 1774, Adams wrote to his wife, Abigail, describing his experience: "This afternoon, led by Curiosity and good Company, I strolled away to Mother Church, or rather Grandmother Church, I mean the Romish Chappell. Heard a good, Short moral Essay upon the Duty of Parents to their Children, founded in Justice and Charity, to take care of their Interests temporal and spiritual. This afternoons Entertainment, was to me, most awful and affecting. The poor Wretches, fingering their Beads—chanting Latin, not a Word of Which they understood—their Pater Nosters and Ava Maria's. Their holy Water—their Crossing themselves perpetually—their Bowing to the Name of Jesus, wherever they hear it—their Bowings, and Kneelings, and Genuflections before the Altar. The Dress of the Priest was rich with Lace—his Pulpit was Velvet and Gold. The Altar Pice was very rich—little Images and Crucifixes about—Wax Candles—lighted up. But how shall I describe, the Picture of our Saviour in a Frame of Marble over the Altar at full Length upon the Cross, in the Agonies, and the Blood dropping and Streaming from his Wounds. The Musick consisting of an organ, and a Choir of singers, went all the afternoon, excepting sermon time—and the assembly chanted—most sweetly and exquisitely. Here is every Thing which can lay hold of the Eye, Ear, and Imagination. Every Thing which can charm and bewitch the simple and ignorant. I wonder how Luther ever broke the spell." Adams, *My Dearest Friend*, 49.

53. See the opening quote of this history for the more extensive Jefferson excerpt from his letter to Adamantios Korais.

54. Journal of the United States Senate, January 2, 1824, 70.

55. Annals of Congress, May 19, 1827.

56. Ibid., December 29, 1823.

57. Constitution of the Immigration Restriction League, 1911.

58. Reports of the Immigration Commission, 1911.

59. Immigration Restriction League's Numerical Restriction Bill, 1918.

60. *Atlanta Constitution*, July 13, 1907, 1; July 15, 1907, 3; *New York Times*, July 15, 1907.

61. *New York Times*, February 21, 1909.
62. Ibid.
63. Janes, *Manual of Georgia*, 1–2.
64. Ibid., 27.
65. Acts of the Georgia General Assembly, 1866, vol. 1, 70.
66. Ibid., 1869, vol. 1, 26.
67. Ibid., 1871, vol. 1, 318.
68. Ibid., 1872, vol. 1, 378.
69. *Proceedings of the First Annual Session of the Southern Immigration Association*, 100.
70. *Atlanta Constitution*, February 27, 1884, 4.
71. Ibid.
72. Ibid., January 18, 1888, 7.
73. *Proceedings of the Southern Interstate Immigration Convention*, 3.
74. Ibid., 4.
75. *Proceedings of the First Annual Session of the Southern Immigration Association*, 5.
76. Ibid., 343.
77. *Proceedings of the Southern Interstate Immigration Convention*, 13–14.
78. Acts of the Georgia General Assembly, 1882, vol. 1, 184.
79. *Proceedings of the Southern Interstate Immigration Convention*, 32.
80. Ibid., 7.
81. Gorman, *Handbook of Talbot County, Georgia*, 24.
82. Singleton, *Putnam County, Ga.*, 4.
83. Ibid., 90–92.
84. Acts of the Georgia General Assembly, 1890, vol. 1, 459.
85. Ibid., 1893, vol. 1, 493.
86. Georgia Immigration and Investment Bureau, *Georgia*, 5.
87. Acts of the Georgia General Assembly, 1894, vol. 1, 104.
88. Georgia Immigration and Investment Bureau, *To Build Up Georgia*, 3–5.
89. *Atlanta Constitution*, May 6, 1891, 4; Hertzberg, *Strangers within the Gate City*, 119.
90. Williams, *Shadow of the Pope*, 103–4.
91. *Atlanta Constitution*, December 4, 1895, 7.
92. Ibid., January 30, 1897, 2.
93. Ibid., July 1, 1897, 4.
94. Ibid., August 16, 1897, 4.
95. Ibid., July 8, 1903, 6.
96. *Our Baptist Young People and American Citizenship*, 11.
97. *Atlanta Constitution*, November 3, 1905, 3. See also May 15, 1897, 9; October 21, 1897, 12; January 27, 1898, 7; June 8, 1900, 5; October 26, 1900, 7; March 13, 1901, 10; May 3, 1901, 9.

98. *Sunny South*, May 24, 1902, 3; *Atlanta Constitution*, May 25, 1902, A3.

99. *Atlanta Constitution*, February 9, 1902, 17.

100. Ibid., October 15, 1905, C2.

101. Ibid., July 15, 1905, 4.

102. Ibid., June 8, 1905, 6.

103. Ibid.

104. Ibid.

105. *Printers Ink* 60, no. 6 (August 7, 1907): 14–15.

106. Ibid.

107. Ibid.

108. *Textile World Record* 33 (1907): 84.

109. *Atlanta Constitution*, March 19, 1905, D2.

110. Ibid., June 4, 1905, A4.

111. Ibid.

112. Ibid., May 18, 1905, 5.

113. *Atlanta Georgian*, June 9, 1906, 16.

114. Ibid.

115. Ibid.

116. *Immigration*, June 6, 1907 (there is no pagination before page 8).

117. Ibid., 16–17.

118. Ibid., 14.

119. Ibid., 18.

120. *Atlanta Georgian*, November 11, 1906, 2.

121. Ibid.

122. *Atlanta Constitution*, March 10, 1907, C4.

123. Ibid.

124. Ibid., February 3, 1907, A4.

125. Ibid., B8.

126. *Fibre and Fabric* 45 (February 9, 1907): 3.

127. Ibid.

128. *Atlanta Constitution*, February 3, 1907, B8.

129. *Immigration*, 15.

130. *Atlanta Constitution*, February 21, 1907, 6.

131. Ibid., November 24, 1906, 7; December 29, 1906, 7.

132. Acts of the Georgia General Assembly, 1894, vol. 1, 104.

133. *Atlanta Constitution*, December 29, 1906, 7.

134. Ibid., November 6, 1906, 6.

135. Ibid., March 4, 1907, 3.

136. See *Immigration*.

137. *Atlanta Constitution*, March 7, 1907, 7.

138. Ibid.

139. *Evening Argus*, December 10, 1906, 1.

140. *Atlanta Constitution*, May 5, 1907, E3.

141. Ibid.; February 27, 1907, 6.

142. Ibid., November 4, 1906, F7.

143. Ibid., May 5, 1907, E3.

144. Ibid.

145. Ibid., August 4, 1907, 7; December 14, 1907, 4.

146. Ibid., December 12, 1907, 14.

147. *Cleburne New Era*, February 2, 1907.

148. *Atlanta Constitution*, May 15, 1907, 9.

149. Ibid., February 3, 1907, B8.

150. Ibid.

151. Ibid., August 4, 1907, 7.

152. Ibid.

153. *Atlanta Georgian*, June 5, 1906, 6.

154. Ibid.

155. Ibid.

156. Ibid., June 13, 1906, 6.

157. Ibid.

158. *Atlanta Constitution*, July 14, 1907, D3.

159. Ibid., June 27, 1907; April 29, 1908, 6.

160. Ibid., December 2, 1905, 7.

161. Ibid., April 29, 1908, 6.

162. Ibid.

163. Ibid.

164. Ibid., July 20, 1910, 4.

165. Ibid.

166. Ibid., April 29, 1908, 6.

167. Ibid., January 6, 1913, 4.

168. Ibid., February 1, 1912, 1; February 22, 1913, 4.

169. Ibid., November 28, 1909, C2.

Chapter 4

170. See Atlanta Chamber of Commerce, *Atlanta*.

171. *Atlanta Journal*, July 9, 1906, 3. In July, prior to the Democratic primary, Smith prominently placed a daily statement in the *Journal*'s pages. Titled

"Hoke Smith on Disenfranchisement," he promised that if elected, he would "urge with all my power THE ELIMINATION OF THE NEGRO FROM POLITICS AS THE BEST POSSIBLE SOLUTION OF THE RACE PROBLEM, FOR BOTH WHITES AND BLACKS." See *Atlanta Journal*, July 3, 1906, 8; July 4, 1906, 6.

172. *Atlanta Georgian*, June 9, 1906, 12.

173. Ibid., September 5, 1906, 4; *Atlanta Constitution*, September 5, 1906, 3.

174. *Atlanta Georgian*, September 4, 1906, 4.

175. *New York Times*, August 12, 1903.

176. Burns, *Rage in the Gate City*, 17.

177. Allen, *Without Sanctuary*, introduction by Leon Litwack, 8–9.

178. Ibid.

179. *Atlanta Georgian*, August 21, 1906, 6.

180. Ibid.

181. Ibid.

182. Ibid.

183. Ibid.

184. Ibid., September 1, 1906, 2.

185. Ibid., August 22, 1906, 6.

186. *Atlanta Constitution*, September 23, 1906, 4.

187. Ibid.; September 23, 1906, B3.

188. Ibid., September 23, 1906, B4.

189. *New York Times*, September 24, 1906.

190. *Atlanta Evening News*, September 24, 1906. See also Burns, *Rage in the Gate City*, 124.

191. See *New York Times*, September 24–25, 1906.

192. *Atlanta Georgian*, September 24, 1906, 3.

193. Grimke, *Atlanta Riot*, 4, 8.

194. Miller, "An Appeal to Reason," 1.

195. Johnson, *Book of American Negro Poetry*, 49.

196. *New York Times*, December 28, 1906.

197. Informational card promoting the Civic Leagues, 1911, Georgia State Archives.

198. Northen, *Evolution of Lawlessness and Unchallenged Crime*, 10.

CHAPTER 5

199. *Atlanta Constitution*, January 28, 1894, 21.

200. Ibid., March 9, 1892, 2.

201. Ibid., February 25, 1895, 3.

202. Ibid., February 16, 1890, 3.

203. Georgia Immigration and Investment Bureau, *Georgia*, 33.

204. Garrett, *Atlanta and Environs*, vol. 1, 204.

205. Cooper, ed., *Progress* 2, no. 4 (September 1910): 12.

206. *Atlanta Constitution*, February 16, 1890, 4.

207. Ibid. See also *Atlanta Georgian*, January 6, 1909, 2; September 11, 1908, 1.

208. *Atlanta Georgian*, January 6, 1909, 2; October 4, 1911, 12.

209. Ibid., January 6, 1909, 2.

210. *Atlanta Constitution*, January 28, 1894, 21.

211. Ibid.

212. Ibid.

213. Ibid.

214. Ibid., September 26, 1896, 7; *Atlanta Georgian*, May 13, 1909, 1.

215. *Atlanta Constitution*, April 22, 1901, 7.

216. Ibid., August 10, 1889, 5; Fulton County Superior Court Criminal Minutes, 1889–94, vols. 1–3, Fall Term, 11–12.

217. *Atlanta Georgian*, May 13, 1909, 1.

218. *Atlanta Constitution*, November 8, 1896, 20; September 15, 1895, 17.

219. Ibid., August 28, 1892, 2; July 22, 1894, 16; January 12, 1897, 10.

220. Ibid., December 22, 1896, 12.

221. Ibid., September 15, 1895, 17; November 8, 1896, 20.

222. Ibid., July 2, 1899, 10; June 5, 1895, 9.

223. Ibid., June 16, 1895, 3.

224. Ibid., May 18, 1910, 5.

225. Ibid., March 9, 1892, 2; August 7, 1894, 8.

226. Ibid., July 9, 1897, 6.

227. Ibid., April 22, 1901, 7.

228. Ibid.

Chapter 6

229. *Atlanta Constitution*, August 10, 1889, 5; October 5, 1889, 8.

230. Atlanta City Council Meeting Minutes, October 5, 1896.

231. Ibid., November 2, 1896.

232. Ibid., March 1, 1897.

233. Ibid., April 5, 1897.

234. *Atlanta Constitution*, September 13, 1897, 6.

235. Ibid., August 31, 1899, 9.

236. Atlanta City Council Meeting Minutes, April 1, 1901.

237. Ibid., May 6, 1901.

238. *Greek Star*, April 22, 1904, A2.

239. *Atlanta Constitution*, March 6, 1901, 9.

240. Atlanta City Council Meeting Minutes, August 4, 1902.

241. Ibid.

242. Ibid.

243. Ibid., October 6, 1902.

244. Ibid.

245. Ibid.

246. *Atlanta Constitution*, October 7, 1902, 9.

247. Ibid.

248. Ibid.; Atlanta City Council Meeting Minutes, December 5, 1904; May 1, 1905; April 5, 1909.

249. The Atlanta City Council at this time was a bicameral body. It was composed of two separate boards. There was a ten-member board of aldermen, with one alderman representing each of the city's ten wards, and a twenty-member council. The boards met independently. The aldermanic board was abolished in 1954.

250. Atlanta City Council Meeting Minutes, May 16, 1910.

251. *Atlanta Constitution*, May 18, 1910, 5.

252. *Atlanta Georgian*, May 17, 1910, 1.

253. *Atlanta Constitution*, May 17, 1910, 1.

254. *Atlanta Georgian*, May 25, 1910, 3.

255. Atlanta City Council Meeting Minutes, June 6, 1910.

256. See Church General Assembly Meeting Minutes, October 18, 1909; October 31, 1909; November 29, 1909.

CHAPTER 7

257. Adallis, *Adallis Greek Merchants' Reference Book*, 24.

258. Ibid., 43.

259. Dolan, *Immigrant Church*, 34.

260. See *Atlanta Georgian*, November 16, 1911, 8; *Atlanta Constitution*, July 31, 1910, A8.

261. *Atlanta Constitution*, July 31, 1910, A8.

262. Church Council Meeting Minutes, January 24, 1911.
263. *Atlanta Georgian*, November 16, 1911, 8.
264. See Adallis, *Adallis Greek Merchants' Reference Book*.
265. Church Council Meeting Minutes, April 22, 1911.
266. Adallis, *Adallis Greek Merchants' Reference Book*, 18.
267. Ibid., 6, 8, 40.
268. Ibid., 21.
269. Ibid.
270. Ibid., 45.
271. Ibid., 8, 9, 14, 17.
272. *Atlanta Constitution*, May 18, 1910, 2.
273. Adallis, *Adallis Greek Merchants' Reference Book*, 49.
274. *Atlanta Constitution*, October 30, 1912, B3.
275. Ibid., May 24, 1913, B6.
276. Ibid., October 23, 1912, A11.
277. Ibid.
278. Ibid., March 20, 1913, 16.

Chapter 8

279. Adallis, *Adallis Greek Merchants' Reference Book*, 67.
280. *Atlanta Constitution*, October 31, 1911, 1.
281. Declaration of Intention and Petitions for Naturalization of the Fulton County Superior Court, vols. 1 and 2. Prior to 1907, the naturalization process for immigrants was completed in a state's local court system. Subsequent to this date, the process became the responsibility of the Unites States District Courts.
282. *Atlanta Constitution*, April 26, 1908, 7.
283. Ibid.
284. Adallis, *Adallis Greek Merchants' Reference Book*, 19.
285. Ibid., 42.
286. Ibid., 43.
287. Ibid., 23.
288. Ibid., 25.
289. Ibid., 29.
290. Ibid., 30.
291. Ibid., 61.
292. Ibid., 40.

293. Ibid., 41.

294. Ibid., 48.

295. Ibid., 52.

296. Ibid., 55.

297. Ibid., 31.

298. Ibid., 40.

299. Ibid., 25.

300. Ibid., 61.

301. Ibid., 60–61.

302. *Atlanta Constitution*, October 28, 1906, B6.

303. Ibid.

304. Ibid.

305. Ibid., May 21, 1910, 6.

306. Ibid.

307. Ibid., April 19, 1911, 3; April 17, 1911, 1.

308. This building still stands on Luckie Street in downtown Atlanta and is used today as a concert hall.

309. Church Council Meeting Minutes, May 18, 1913.

310. Ibid., March 2, 1917.

311. Ibid., November 26, 1908.

312. *Atlanta Georgian*, March 14, 1908, 7; *Atlanta Constitution*, March 16, 1908, 5; March 18, 1908, 7.

313. *Atlanta Constitution*, April 19, 1906, A5.

314. Ibid., May 8, 1913, 5; May 9, 1913, 4.

315. Ibid., May 8, 1913, 5.

316. Ibid., May 9, 1913, 4.

317. Ibid., May 18, 1913, 1.

318. Ibid., May 15, 1914, 7.

319. Saloutos, *Greeks in the United States*, 99–100.

320. Ibid., 102–3; *Atlantis*, December 26, 1908.

321. Saloutos, *Greeks in the United States*, 103.

322. Ibid.

CHAPTER 9

323. *Atlanta Constitution*, July 28, 1912, 12C.

324. Ibid., March 8, 1897, 1.

325. Ibid.

326. Ibid., April 26, 1897, 5.

327. Ibid., May 1, 1897, 7.

328. Ibid., April 20, 1897, 4.

329. Ibid., April 24, 1897, 2.

330. Ibid., April 26, 1897, 5.

331. Ibid., March 8, 1897, 1.

332. Fraser, *Pictures from the Balkans*, 12.

333. *Atlanta Constitution*, April 10, 1902, 7.

334. Ibid.

335. Ibid., October 7, 1912, 3.

336. Ibid.

337. Ibid., October 15, 1912, 13.

338. Church Council Meeting Minutes, January 12, 1913.

339. Ibid., February 26, 1913.

340. *Atlanta Constitution*, October 15, 1912, 13.

341. Ibid.

342. Ibid., October 7, 1912, 3.

343. Ibid., November 10, 1912, A7.

344. Church General Assembly Meeting Minutes, December 3, 1913.

345. Ibid., February 9, 1913.

346. Ibid.

347. Church Council Meeting Minutes, March 20, 1913.

348. Church General Assembly Meeting Minutes, March 23, 1913.

349. The exact date of the establishment of the Greek Consulate in Atlanta is unknown, although it was certainly in existence by March 1913. Vafeiades would create an uproar in the Atlanta Greek community almost four years later with an article he authored for publication in January 1917 in the *Atlantis*, a Greek-language newspaper. Critical of the Atlanta Greek community for being "divided," the article stirred the Church Council to prepare a published response to what it considered a "villainous defamation." For good measure, the council described the vice-consul as being divisive, a non-contributor to the church, unsupportive of the school and a profiteer. Church Council Meeting Minutes, January 21, 1917. The *Atlantis* ceased publication in 1973.

350. Church General Assembly Meeting Minutes, March 23, 1913.

351. *Atlanta Constitution*, March 20, 1913, 16.

352. Ibid., December 27, 1911, 4.

353. Church General Assembly Meeting Minutes, August 20, 1913.

354. Church Council Meeting Minutes, August 14, 1913.

355. Ibid., October 21, 1914.

356. *Atlanta Constitution*, June 6, 1917, 7.

357. Ibid.

358. Ibid.

359. Ibid., April 26, 1915, 7.

CHAPTER 10

360. 1920 Greek Census, statistics of the Peloponnesus, 294–96. The 1920 census shows the total population of the Peloponnesus to be 945,204, 942,180 of whom were Greek Orthodox Christians. There were 2,350 Catholics, 160 Protestants, 171 Muslims and 94 Jews. The census also lists 59 individuals as being "Schismatic," who were most likely Old Calendarists—those Greek Orthodox Christians who still followed the old Julian calendar and were not in communion with the Orthodox Church of Greece. This Orthodox dominance was even more pronounced in the small villages in the interior. The same census for Tripolis shows a population of 12,067, 12,059 of whom were Greek Orthodox, 7 Catholic and 1 Protestant.

361. Church General Assembly Meeting Minutes, August 27, 1908.

362. *Atlanta Constitution*, February 20, 1913, 5.

363. See *Eighty-eighth Report of the American Board of Commissioners for Foreign Missions*.

364. Ibid., xi.

365. Xenides, *Greeks in America*, 70.

366. Ibid.

367. Ibid., 66.

368. Ibid., 132–33.

369. Ibid., 129.

370. Interview with Mary Algers Farmakis, October 20, 2010; Fiftieth Anniversary Album of the Annunciation Greek Orthodox Church, "History of Our Community" (no pagination).

371. *Atlanta Constitution*, June 26, 1900, 9.

372. Ibid.

373. Ibid.

374. Ibid.

375. *Atlanta Constitution*, December 2, 1901, 5.

376. Samonides, "First Greek Orthodox Hierarch to Visit America."

377. Namee, "Fr. Kallinikos."

378. *Atlanta Constitution*, September 8, 1902, 7; September 10, 1904, 9; April 11, 1904, 2.

379. *Atlanta Constitution*, April 11, 1904, 2.

CHAPTER 11

380. Annunciation Greek Orthodox Cathedral of Atlanta, Ex Parte Application for the Incorporation as Evangelismos Society, October 20, 1902.

381. Church General Assembly Meeting Minutes, June 5, 1908.

382. This address requires some explanation. At least since the publication of the community's Fiftieth Anniversary Album in 1955, the street address of this commercial space first used for church services has been identified as 111½ Whitehall Street. A photograph of the building itself almost always accompanies this particular history. However, the current research shows that both the 111½ address and the building shown in the photograph are incorrect. Because of the configuration of the buildings on that block of Whitehall Street, the address of 111 or 111½ Whitehall simply did not exist at that time. Moreoover, the address for the building shown in this photograph was actually 79 Whitehall Street, so that building likewise has been misidentified. There is no independent record of either the 111 Whitehall or the 79 Whitehall addresses ever being associated with the community. In 1926, the street addresses on Whitehall were renumbered so that the building photographed became 111 Whitehall. This is almost certainly how this long-standing confusion partially arose. Instead, the address of the actual building in which the hall was converted to the community's chapel in 1905 was 113 Whitehall Street, with 113½ representing the upper floor. There is independent evidence in the record of the community's use of the space at this address. This building has been demolished, but the current street address for its former location is 149 Peachtree Street. A photograph of this building is included in this book. See Sanborn Fire Insurance Maps, Atlanta, Georgia, 1899, sheets 7, 9, 11 and 12, and Sanborn Fire Insurance Maps, 1911, vol. 3, sheet 311 and vol. 4, sheet 465; *Atlanta Constitution*, April 9, 1906, 8, and March 24, 1913, 2; Fiftieth Anniversary Album of the Annunciation Greek Orthodox Church, "History of Our Community" (no pagination).

383. Church General Assembly Meeting Minutes, June 5, 1908.

384. Samonides, "Father Christos Angelopoulos (1867–1933)"; ship manifest, SS *La Gascogne*, May 24, 1903.

385. Letter of Father Angelopoulos to Archbishop Athenagoras, April 22, 1931.

386. Ibid.

387. Ibid.

388. Ibid.

389. *Atlanta Constitution*, September 14, 1903, 2.

390. Ibid., April 12, 1904, A1.

391. Church General Assembly Meeting Minutes, August 8, 1908.

392. The minutes of the Church Council and church general assembly throughout this history consistently use the term "Church Council" to describe the administrative board of the church, except for an approximately two-year period in 1909–10. In this period, the Church Council begins using the term "Administrative Board" to label itself. The council members throughout the period covered by this history interchangeably use the terms "warden" and "councilor" to describe individual members of the council.

393. Church General Assembly Meeting Minutes, August 8, 1908; Treasury Book of the Annunciation Greek Orthodox Church, entries on August 26 and August 30, 1905, 3.

394. 1905 letter to Ecumenical Patriarch Joachim III, recorded in Church General Assembly Meeting Minutes of August 8, 1908.

395. Ibid.

396. Treasury Book of the Annunciation Greek Orthodox Church, entries on August 26 and August 30, 1905, 3.

397. Application for Charter of Incorporation as Greek Orthodox Church of Atlanta, November 7, 1905.

398. Ibid. At a meeting of the Church Council on December 14, 1916, the council chairman, Gerasimos Algers, announced that this 1905 charter of the church's incorporation, long thought to be lost, had been found. He had placed it in safekeeping among his personal papers years before but had forgotten about it until he uncovered it on the day before the meeting. He presented the charter to the members of the council, none of whom "knew that it even existed." They responded with palpable joy for the return of the charter, which they considered "the most valuable possession of the Community." The charter remains in the archives of the church.

399. Application for Charter of Incorporation as Greek Orthodox Church of Atlanta, November 7, 1905; Centennial Anniversary Album of the Atlanta Annunciation Greek Orthodox Cathedral, 43–44.

400. Interview with Nick Demetry on December 16, 2013; unpublished research by William H. Samonides on the early Greek Orthodox priests of America.

401. Interview with Nick Demetry.

402. Unpublished research by William H. Samonides.

403. Interview with Nick Demetry.

404. *Atlanta Constitution*, March 26, 1906, 6; *Atlanta Georgian and News*, January 6, 1909, 2.

405. *Atlanta Georgian and News*, April 10, 1908, 7.

406. The Treasury Book of the Annunciation Greek Orthodox Church, entry for October 14, 1905, 3.

407. The following items were ordered: "5 Church oil lamps, 1 censer, 1 cassock, and 2 gold embroidered cloth covers, 1 chalice, 1 discarion, 1 asteriskos, 1 communion spoon, 1 lance, 1 sponge, 1 zeon, 1 artophorion, 1 sprinkler, 1 small seal, 1 antimension (the other was a present by the Patriarch). And the following books: 12 menaion (one for every month), of small size, and 12 menaion of large size, 1 pentakostarion, 1 euchologion, 1 big Gospel, 1 Apostol (readings), 1 typika, 1 book of the hours, 1 paracletikon, 1 Triodion, 1 Psalter. Also, 1 large vessel for Holy Myron, 9 Icons (the other two were given as presents by the Patriarch)." The Treasury Book of the Annunciation Greek Orthodox Church, 3.

408. Church Council Meeting Minutes, February 26, 1906; March 28, 1906.

409. Ibid., February 28, 1906; Church General Assembly Meeting Minutes, March 18, 1906; Church Council Meeting Minutes, April 3, 1906.

410. See the Treasury Book of the Annunciation Greek Orthodox Cathedral, 2. This date was according to the Julian calendar followed by the Greeks at that time.

411. Church Council Meeting Minutes, March 28, 1906.

412. The Treasury Book of the Annunciation Greek Orthodox Church, 3; *Atlanta Constitution*, March 26, 1906, 6. Hunter Street is now Martin Luther King Jr. Drive, and the lot purchased there by the Greeks is now the site of the offices of the Georgia Building Authority, at 1 MLK Jr. Drive.

413. *Atlanta Constitution*, March 26,1906, 6.

414. Ibid.

415. Church Council Meeting Minutes, February 28, 1906. The members of the church committee responsible for the purchase of the Presbyterian church were Constantine Athanasopoulos, chairman, Nick Pope, Nick Matrangos, Stavros Gialelis, John Poulos and Dionysios Fotopoulos.

416. Church General Assembly Meeting Minutes, March 18, 1906. The church was located on the southwestern corner of Garnett Street and Central Avenue. While this church has always been referred to as the Garnett Street church by the Greek community and likewise described that way in the records of the Presbyterian church, the street address of the church was 181 Central Avenue.

417. *Atlanta Georgian and News*, July 12, 1906, 2; *Atlanta Constitution*, July 12, 1906, 6.

418. Church Council Meeting Minutes, September 17, 1908.

419. Contract for the sale of the Garnett Street church property, July 9, 1906; Church General Assembly Meeting Minutes, July 15, 1906. The attorney for the Presbyterian church in this transaction was Hugh M. Dorsey, who would later prosecute Leo Frank for the murder of Mary Phagan and serve as Georgia's governor for two terms from 1917 to 1921. Dorsey also represented the Greek Orthodox Church in a number of legal matters throughout the years, including its incorporation in 1905.

420. Church General Assembly Meeting Minutes, July 15, 1906.

421. 1895 Deed from Florence Warner to the Associate Reformed Presbyterian Synod of the South, May 30, 1895; Abstract of Title, Property of Board of Trustees of the Associate Reformed Presbyterian Church of the South, June 16, 1906. At the time of the transfer of the property from Florence Warner to the Presbyterian church, Central Avenue was named Lloyd Street, and the church lot was described as being at the corner of Garnett and Lloyd Streets. Upon the sale of its church, the Presbyterian congregation moved from this location to another downtown location on Whitehall Street, followed by a move to North Highland Avenue in what was then a suburb of Atlanta. The congregation is now located in Grayson, Georgia, using the name of Highlands Presbyterian Church, in order to reflect the denomination's Scottish heritage.

422. Church Council Meeting Minutes, July 14, 1914; November 11, 1916.

423. *Atlanta Constitution*, July 12, 1906, 6.

424. Church Council Meeting Minutes, May 10, 1906.

425. Ibid., July 26, 1906.

426. Ibid. These icons remain in the church archives today.

427. Church Council Meeting Minutes, July 26, 1906.

428. Church General Assembly Meeting Minutes, March 18, 1906.

429. The Treasury Book of the Annunciation Greek Orthodox Church, 5.

430. The Church of Greece adopted a revised Julian calendar in 1923 following a synod in Constantinople in May of that year.

431. *Atlanta Constitution*, January 7, 1909, 9; January 3, 1911, 1; *Atlanta Georgian and News*, January 6, 1909, 2.
432. *Atlanta Constitution*, January 7, 1909, 9.
433. *Atlanta Georgian and News*, January 18, 1908, 8.
434. *Atlanta Georgian*, June 17, 1907, 1.
435. Ibid.

Chapter 12

436. Church Council Meeting Minutes, February 28, 1906; April 3, 1906. The first two sacristans of the church were Constantine Theodosiou and D. Panagiotopoulos.
437. Church General Assembly Meeting Minutes, May 28, 1907.
438. The Treasury Book of the Annunciation Greek Orthodox Church, entry for February 6/21, 4; Church General Assembly Meeting Minutes, March 18, 1906. In addition to Brownsville, Father Hadjidemetriou, Constantine Athanasopoulos and Kyriakos Kyriakopoulos visited and collected donations in Augusta, Savannah, Jacksonville, Tarpon Springs, Tampa, Pensacola, Mobile, New Orleans, Montgomery, Birmingham, Memphis, Nashville, Chattanooga and Knoxville.
439. The Treasury Book of the Annunciation Greek Orthodox Church, entry for February 6/21, 1906, 4.
440. Church Council Meeting Minutes, May 31, 1907.
441. Ibid., June 18, 1907. Tardiness by the council members at their meetings was apparently chronic, and each late-arriving member was fined five dollars. As Father Hadjidemetriou, in his capacity as recording secretary, dryly noted in his minutes for the meeting of June 12, 1907: "Everybody was present in this meeting, except for Mr. G. Kouloukis. However, the 'Romeiko' [contemporary Greek habits] was amply manifested: nine members arrived after 10 am, and consequently they had to pay the fine that was agreed on. Therefore, the Church had a 45 dollar gain."
442. Church Council Meeting Minutes, June 18, 1907.
443. Ibid.
444. Church General Assembly Meeting Minutes, August 2, 1908.
445. Church Council Meeting Minutes, August 21, 1908.
446. Church General Assembly Meeting Minutes, August 16, 1908.
447. The Treasury Book of the Annunciation Greek Orthodox Church, 42–54.

448. Church Council Meeting Minutes, May 29, 1907.

449. Ibid.; May 31, 1907.

450. Church General Assembly Meeting Minutes, April 6, 1908.

451. Ibid., Articles 2 and 15 of the Regulation.

452. Ibid., Articles 5 and 15 of the Regulation.

453. Ibid., Article 1.

454. Church Council Meeting Minutes, August 19, 1917.

455. Ibid., August 29, 1908.

456. Church General Assembly Meeting Minutes, April 6, 1908, Article 4.

457. Ibid., Article 11.

458. Ibid.

459. Ibid.

460. Ibid., Article 10.

461. Ibid., Articles 10 and 7.

462. Ibid., Article 7.

463. Ibid., Article 28.

464. Church General Assembly Meeting Minutes, April 16, 1909.

465. Ibid., May 20, 1909. The National University in Athens was founded in 1837 and is the oldest university in Greece.

466. Church General Assembly Meeting Minutes, April 6, 1908, Article 6.

Chapter 13

467. Church Council Meeting Minutes, August 25, 1908.

468. Ibid.

469. Ibid.

470. Church General Assembly Meeting Minutes, August 27, 1908.

471. Ibid.

472. Ibid.

473. Ibid.

474. Ibid.

475. Ibid.

476. Ibid.

477. At this point, the minutes simply indicate that Father Constas read from Chapter 9 of the Apostle Paul's First Epistle to the Corinthians. The passage is not reproduced in the minutes. This quoted New King James Version comes from *The Orthodox Study Bible*, courtesy of Thomas Nelson Inc.

478. Church General Assembly Meeting Minutes, August 27, 1908.

479. Ibid.

480. Ibid.

481. Ibid.

482. Ibid.

483. Church Council Meeting Minutes, September 22, 1908.

484. *Atlanta Georgian and News*, April 12, 1909, 3.

485. Efthimiou and Christopoulos, *History of the Greek Orthodox Church in America*, 5, 11, 63–66. The Patriarchate's jurisdiction over the church in America was reestablished by Patriarch Meletios in 1922, soon after his election as Ecumenical Patriarch. *Idem.*, 15–16. Even after the jurisdictional transfer to the Synod of Greece in 1908, the Atlanta church continued to include a contribution for the Ecumenical Patriarchate in its annual budget. See Church Council Meeting Minutes, December 25, 1913.

486. Saloutos, *Greeks in the United States*, 98–117.

487. Church General Assembly Meeting Minutes, April 16, 1909.

488. Church Council Meeting Minutes, March 28, 1909.

489. Ibid., March 29, 1909.

490. Ibid., March 1, 1915.

491. Church General Assembly Meeting Minutes, July 21, 1912.

492. Church Council Meeting Minutes, September 11, 1914.

493. Ibid., May 11, 1915.

494. Ibid., July 31, 1916.

495. Church General Assembly Meeting Minutes, May 20, 1909.

496. Father Lambrides was the son of Alexios and Marica Constantinou Lambrides. His wife, Presbytera Calliope, was the former Calliope Pillides, and their four daughters were Roxani, Helen, Maria and Cleo. He died in Washington, D.C., on January 8, 1921, and is buried at Forest Hills Cemetery in Boston, Massachusetts.

497. Adallis, *Adallis Greek Merchants' Reference Book*, 59.

498. Letter of Father Lambrides to Metropolitan Meletios, September 27, 1916.

499. Church General Assembly Meeting Minutes, May 20, 1909.

500. Ibid.

501. Church Council Meeting Minutes, September 6, 1910.

502. Church General Assembly Meeting Minutes, September 25, 1910.

503. Ibid.

504. Ibid.

505. Church Council Meeting Minutes, November 3, 1910.

506. Church General Assembly Meeting Minutes, January 29, 1911.

507. Ibid., March 26, 1911.

508. Ibid., May 21, 1911.

509. Ibid.

510. Ibid.

511. Ibid.

512. Ibid.

513. Letter of Father Lambrides to Metropolitan Meletios, September 27, 1916.

514. Letter of Father Lambrides to the Holy Synod of Athens, Greece, June 6, 1912.

515. Church General Assembly Meeting Minutes, March 26, 1911.

516. Letter of Father Lambrides to the Holy Synod of Athens, Greece, June 16, 1912.

517. Ibid.

518. Church General Assembly Meeting Minutes, May 19, 1912.

519. Church Council Meeting Minutes, June 18, 1912.

520. Letter of Father Lambrides to Metropolitan Meletios, September 27, 1916.

521. Letter of Father Lambrides to Metropolitan Theoklitos of the Holy Synod of Athens, Greece, June 16, 1912.

522. Letter of Constantine Athanasopoulos to the Holy Synod of Athens, Greece, August 8, 1912.

523. Ibid.

524. Letter of Father Lambrides to the Holy Synod of Athens, Greece, August 15, 1912.

525. Adallis, *Adallis Greek Merchants' Reference Book*, 59–60.

526. Church Council Meeting Minutes, July 12, 1912.

527. Church General Assembly Meeting Minutes, July 21, 1912.

528. Ibid., September 6, 1912.

529. Ibid.

530. Ibid.; Letter of Constantine Athanasopoulos to Metropolitan Theoklitos of the Holy Synod of Athens, Greece, September 11, 1912.

531. Church General Assembly Meeting Minutes, July 21, 1912; September 6, 1912; Letter of Constantine Athanasopoulos to Metropolitan Theoklitos of the Holy Synod of Athens, Greece, September 11, 1912.

532. Church General Assembly Meeting Minutes, July 21, 1912; September 6, 1912; Letter of Constantine Athanasopoulos to Metropolitan Theoklitos of the Holy Synod of Athens, Greece, September 11, 1912.

533. Church General Assembly Meeting Minutes, September 6, 1912.

534. Unpublished research by William H. Samonides on the early Greek Orthodox Priests of America; interview with Aleck Janoulis, November 18, 2013.

535. Namee, "Stormy Petrel of the Cloth," podcast on Father Demetrios Petrides.

536. Ibid.

537. Dimopoulos, *Brief Historical Survey.*

538. Letter of Father Petrides to Metropolitan Theoklitos of the Holy Synod of Athens, Greece, September 14, 1912.

539. Letter of the Holy Synod of Athens, Greece, to the Atlanta Church Council, October 12, 1912.

540. Letter of Father Petrides to Metropolitan Theoklitos of the Holy Synod of Athens, Greece, November 26, 1912.

541. Church Council Meeting Minutes, April 15, 1913.

542. The mobilization was ordered in fulfillment of Greece's treaty obligations to Serbia established in the Greek-Serbian Alliance of 1913. Under the alliance, both nations committed to come to each other's aid in the event of an attack by a third power.

543. Church Council Meeting Minutes, November 14, 1914.

544. Church General Assembly Meeting Minutes, February 23, 1913.

545. Church Council Meeting Minutes, April 15, 1913.

546. Ibid., March 15, 1913.

547. Ibid.

548. Church General Assembly Meeting Minutes, May 15, 1913.

549. Church Council Meeting Minutes, March 1, 1915.

550. Church General Assembly Meeting Minutes, May 12, 1913.

551. *Atlanta Constitution*, October 28, 1906, B6.

552. Church Council Meeting Minutes, November 28, 1913.

553. Church General Assembly Meeting Minutes, December 3, 1913.

554. Ibid.

555. Ibid. Members of that twelve-member committee included Gerasimos Algers, Eli Chotas, S. Markides, Georgios Blatsos, Panagiotis Papanikolopoulos, Demetrios Constandopoulos, Panagiotis Vergiotis, Constantine Athanasopoulos, Angelos Moukios, Diomidis Anastopoulos and D. Hadjidemetriou. At the same time that the Greek community was working to establish a modern Greek school for its children, the city's board of education made the decision to abolish the study of ancient Greek at Boy's High, one of the city's top high schools. *Atlanta Constitution*, April 24, 1913, 5; April 29, 1913, 8.

556. Sacramental Register of the Annunciation Greek Orthodox Church of Atlanta, 8–13.

557. Church General Assembly Meeting Minutes, December 21, 1913.

558. Ibid.

559. Church Council Meeting Minutes, December 25, 1913.

560. Ibid., December 8, 1913; Church General Assembly Meeting Minutes, December 21, 1913.

561. Church General Assembly Meeting Minutes, December 21, 1913; Church Council Meeting Minutes, December 25, 1913.

562. Church General Assembly Meeting Minutes, December 21, 1913.

563. Church Council Meeting Minutes, December 25, 1913. This large icon remains in the archives of the church today.

564. Church Council Meeting Minutes, January 23, 1914.

565. Dolan, *Immigrant Church*, 47–52.

566. Church Council Meeting Minutes, October 5, 1916.

567. Ibid., March 15, 1914.

568. Ibid.

569. Ibid.

570. Ibid., July 6, 1914; July 14, 1914; August 4, 1914.

571. Ibid., December 25, 1913.

572. Ibid.

573. Ibid., June 4, 1913; June 26, 1913; Church General Assembly Meeting Minutes, July 1, 1914.

574. Church General Assembly Meeting Minutes, July 1, 1914.

575. Church Council Meeting Minutes, June 26, 1914.

576. Ibid., September 1, 1914.

577. Ibid., October 21, 1914.

578. Ibid., December 8, 1914.

579. Ibid., September 19, 1915.

580. Ibid., June 10, 1915.

581. Ibid., June 9, 1917.

582. Ibid., September 19, 1915.

583. Ibid., August 18, 1916.

584. Ibid., January 31, 1916.

585. Ibid.

586. Ibid.

587. Ibid., March 23, 1916.

588. Ibid., August 18, 1916.

589. Ibid., October 12, 1916.

590. Ibid., September 1, 1916.

591. Ibid., October 31, 1916.

592. Ibid., September 1, 1916.

593. Ibid., November 18, 1916.

594. Ibid.

595. Ibid., November 19, 1916.

596. Ibid.

597. Ibid., December 28, 1916.

598. Ibid., December 14, 1916.

599. Ibid., March 6, 1917; March 7, 1917; March 9. 1917. The play, a story of the love between a Turkish girl and a Greek freedom fighter at the start of the Greek War of Independence, was written by the playwright Spyridonas Peresiadis. It was made into a Greek film in 1974.

600. Church Council Meeting Minutes, March 9, 1917.

601. Ibid., October 26, 1916.

602. Ibid., November 11, 1916.

603. Ibid., October 26, 1916.

604. Ibid. The quote is attributed to Leo Tolstoy.

605. Church Council Meeting Minutes, December 1, 1916.

606. Ibid., October 26, 1916.

607. Ibid.

608. Ibid.

609. Ibid., December 28, 1916.

610. Ibid.

611. Ibid.

CHAPTER 14

612. Fulton County Certificate of Death of John Nekas, December 1, 1901.

613. *Atlanta Constitution*, December 2, 1901, 5.

614. Ibid.

615. Ibid., April 12, 1904, A1.

616. Ibid.

617. Westview Cemetery Burial Ledger.

618. Ibid.

619. Ibid.

620. Church Council Meeting Minutes, August 30 1908.

621. Ibid., September 6, 1910; Church General Assembly Meeting Minutes, September 25, 1910.

622. Ex Parte Application for Incorporation as Greenwood Cemetery, December 13, 1904.

623. The Greek and Jewish communities still regularly bury their dead in Greenwood, with both communities having opened additional sections in recent years.

624. Sales Agreement between Greenwood Cemetery and the Greek Orthodox Church, July 28, 1911. The plots were located in columns 36, 37 and 38.

625. Sales Agreement between Greenwood Cemetery and the Greek Orthodox Church, July 28, 1911. Construction of this chapel was not begun until 1928, when the project was undertaken by the Greek Ladies Auxiliary Society.

626. Church Council Meeting Minutes, September 11, 1914.

627. Ibid., October 21, 1914. The Church Council minutes provide that the section purchased at Greenwood comprised two hundred square feet. However, the legal description in the January 5, 1915 sales agreement indicates that the square section purchased measured two hundred feet *per side*, or forty thousand square feet.

628. Church Council Meeting Minutes, October 21, 1914. There were a few Greek burials at Greenwood prior to the community's initial purchase of plots in 1911, so the "transfer" of the deceased "buried already in the Cemetery" almost certainly applies to those burials before 1911. The "four stone" columns remain today, and a plaque attached to one of the entrance columns is dedicated to the "Greenwood Committee of 1912." It lists as members of the committee Father Demetrios Petrides, Charles Poulos (Constantine Athanasopoulos), Gerasimos Algers (Avgerinos), Angelo Moukios, Andreas Angelopoulos, Eli Chotas, George Kouloukis and Nick Tountas.

629. Church Council Meeting Minutes, October 21, 1914.

630. Sales Agreement between Greenwood Cemetery and the Greek Orthodox Church, January 5, 1915.

631. Ibid.

Chapter 15

632. Oney, *And the Dead Shall Rise*, 8–11.

633. *Atlanta Constitution*, May 18, 1913, 2.

634. Woodward, *Tom Watson*, 378.

635. Powell, *I Can Go Home Again*, 289–91.

636. Ibid. One of the governor's friends who had chosen to help defend Governor Slaton and his family in their home was Justice Arthur Gray Powell. The judge later reflected that his weapon of choice was a shotgun, as "there is nothing like a shotgun loaded with buckshot to repel a mob." Powell, *I Can Go Home Again*, 290.

637. MacLean, *Behind the Mask of Chivalry*, 12.

638. *New York Times*, August 18, 1915. The once rural location where Frank was lynched is now in a busy commercial area dominated by strip malls. A commemorative plaque identifies the location, which is near Cobb County's most well-known landmark, the "Big Chicken" sign of a fast-food restaurant.

639. Woodward, *Tom Watson*, 432.

640. MacLean, *Behind the Mask of Chivalry*, 5.

641. Jackson, *Ku Klux Klan in the City*, 34.

642. Ibid., 39.

643. MacLean, *Behind the Mask of Chivalry*, 12.

644. Jackson, *Ku Klux Klan in the City*, 63.

645. Simmons, *Klan Unmasked*, 105.

646. Jackson, *Ku Klux Klan in the City*, 31.

647. Simmons, *Klan Unmasked*, 31.

648. See Atlanta City Directories, 1917–18.

649. *Atlanta Constitution*, December 31, 1915, 4.

650. MacLean, *Behind the Mask of Chivalry*, 17.

651. Simmons, *Klan Unmasked*, 111, 248–49.

652. Ibid., 112.

653. Ibid., 117.

654. Simmons, *America's Menace*, 31, 36–37.

655. Ibid. Several verbatim lines from different stanzas of the poem have been compressed into this excerpt.

Conclusion

656. Church Council Meeting Minutes, March 27, 1917. The March 27 date recorded for the council meeting followed the dating of the Gregorian calendar. The church still followed the old Julian calendar for its feast days, so March 27 was actually March 14 for its purposes. Hence, March 25 was still a date in the future.

657. Church Council Meeting Minutes, March 29, 1917.

658. Ibid.

659. Ibid.

660. Ibid., March 30, 1917.

661. Ibid.

662. Ibid.

663. Annunciation Greek Orthodox Cathedral of Atlanta, Book of the General Assembly Meeting Minutes, August 6, 1917, 2.

664. Petrides, *ΕΚΚΛΗΣΙΑΣΤΙΚΟΙ ΛΟΓΟΙ ΚΑΙ ΔΙΑΛΕΞΕΙΣ*, from "Ecclesiastical Sermons and Lectures," 177–81.

665. Ibid.

666. Ibid.

667. Ibid.

668. Church Council Meeting Minutes, September 11, 1917.

669. Ibid.

BIBLIOGRAPHY

Primary Sources

Abstract of Title, Property of Board of Trustees of the Associate Reformed Presbyterian Church of the South, June 16, 1906.

Acts of the Georgia General Assembly. Georgia Legislative Documents Archive Collection, 1890–1917. Georgia Archives.

Adallis, Dio. *Adallis Greek Merchants' Reference Book and Business Guide.* Atlanta, GA, 1912.

The American Board of Commissioners for Foreign Missions Eighty-eighth Report. Grand Rapids, Michigan, October 4–7, 1898. Congregational House, Yale University Divinity Library.

Annals of Congress, 1789–73. Library of Congress.

Annunciation Greek Orthodox Cathedral of Atlanta. Book of the General Assembly Meeting Minutes for the Year 1917.

———. Charter of Incorporation of the Annunciation Greek Orthodox Church of Atlanta, September 7, 1905.

———. Charter of Incorporation of the Evangelismos Society, November 25, 1902.

———. Charter of Incorporation of the Grecian Club, February 18, 1910.

———. Charter of Incorporation of the Panargiakos Society Danaos, April 22, 1908.

———. Church Council Meeting Minutes of the Annunciation Greek Orthodox Church, 1906–17.

———. Danaos Ledger Book of Receipts and Expenses, 1919–41.

———. Ex Parte Application for Incorporation as Evangelismos Society, October 20, 1902.

Atlanta Chamber of Commerce. *Atlanta: A Twentieth Century City.* N.p.: Byrd Printing Company, 1904.

Atlanta City Council Meeting Minutes, 1885–1917. The Atlanta History Center.

Atlanta City Directories, 1890–1917. Kenan Research Center, Atlanta History Center.

Atlanta Constitution. Atlanta Journal Constitution Historic Archives. http://pqasb.pqarchiver.com/ajc_historic/search.html.

Atlanta Evening News Archives.

Atlanta Georgian. Georgia Historic Newspapers. http://atlnewspapers.galileo.usg.edu/atlnewspapers/search.

Atlanta Georgian and News. Georgia Historic Newspapers. http://atlnewspapers.galileo.usg.edu/atlnewspapers/search.

Atlanta Independent. Historical Newspapers Online. http://news.google.com/newspapers?nid=0KrOiVmbFBYC.

Atlanta Journal Archives. Atlanta History Center.

Atlantis. New York Public Library. A Greek-language newspaper.

Barrett, Charles S. *The Mission, History and Times of the Farmers Union.* N.p.: Marshall & Bruce Company, 1909.

Chandler, Richard. *Travels in Greece.* N.p.: Clarendon Press, 1776. Reprinted by Elibron Classics, 2005.

Cleburne New Era. Heflin, Alabama.

Constitution of the Immigration Restriction League, 1894. Harvard University Library.

Contract for the sale of the Garnett Street church property, July 9, 1906. Annunciation Greek Orthodox Cathedral of Atlanta.

Cooper, Walter G., ed. *Progress.* Official Organ of the Atlanta Chamber of Commerce, 1909–10. Atlanta History Center.

Correspondence Files of Ecumenical Patriarch Joachim III, 1901–12. Archives of the Ecumenical Patriarchate, the Phanar, Istanbul.

Declaration of Intention and Petitions for Naturalization of the Fulton County Superior Court. Vol. 1, 1878–1903. Georgia Archives.

———. Vol. 2, 1890–1906. Georgia Archives.

Deed of the Garnett Street church property from Florence Cowles Warner to the Associate Reformed Presbyterian Synod of the South, May 30, 1895. Annunciation Greek Orthodox Cathedral of Atlanta.

Ellis Island Passenger Records. www.ellisisland.org.

Ellis Island Port of New York Passenger Records. Ship manifest for SS *La Gascogne*, May 24, 1903. www.ellisisland.org.

Evening Argus. Owosso, Michigan.

Fibre and Fabric: A Record of Progress in American Textile Industries 45 (February 9, 1907).

Fraser, John Foster. *Pictures from the Balkans.* N.p.: Cassell and Company Ltd., 1906.

Fulton County Corporate Charter Ledger, 1890–1920. Archives of the Clerk of the Fulton County Superior Court.

Fulton County Office of Vital Records. Archives of the Clerk of the Fulton County Superior Court.

Fulton County Superior Court Criminal Minutes, 1889–94. Vols. 1–3. Archives of the Clerk of the Fulton County Superior Court.

General Assembly Meeting Minutes of the Annunciation Greek Orthodox Church, 1906–1917. Annunciation Greek Orthodox Cathedral of Atlanta.

Georgia Immigration and Investment Bureau. *Georgia: Its Resources, Conditions and Opportunities, Preliminary Pamphlet.* N.p.: G.W. Harrison, 1898. Available at the Georgia Archives.

————. *Georgia: Its Resources, Conditions and Opportunities, Preliminary Pamphlet.* N.p.: G.W. Harrison, 1894. Available at the Atlanta History Center.

————. *To Build Up Georgia.* N.p., 1895. Available at the Georgia Archives.

Gorman, O.D. *Handbook of Talbot County, Georgia.* Prepared for the Georgia Bureau of Immigration, 1888. Available at the Georgia Archives.

Greek Star Archives.

Grimke, Francis J., Reverend. "The Atlanta Riot: A Discourse." University of Georgia, 1906.

Immigration. An address delivered by Honorable G. Gunby Jordan, president of the Georgia Immigration Association, at the Convention of the Georgia Bankers' Association, at Macon, Georgia, June 6, 1907. N.p.: Gilbert Printing Company, 1907. Available at the Cornell University Library.

Immigration Restriction League's Numerical Limitation Bill, 1918. Harvard University Library.

Indenture for the Garnett Street church property between the United Presbyterian Church of North America and the Associate Reformed Presbyterian Synod of the South, July 18, 1906. Archives of the Annunciation Greek Orthodox Cathedral of Atlanta.

Indenture for the Garnett Street church property between the Werner family and the Associate Reformed Presbyterian Synod of the South, June 21, 1906. Archives of the Annunciation Greek Orthodox Cathedral of Atlanta.

Janes, Thomas P., Commissioner. *A Manual of Georgia for the Use of Immigrants and Capitalists.* Atlanta: Georgia Department of Agriculture, G.W. Harrison, 1878.

Johnson, James Weldon, ed. *The Book of American Negro Poetry.* N.p.: Harcourt, Brace and Company, 1922.

Journals of the Senate of the United States of America, 1789–1873. Library of Congress.

Le Petit Journal. October 7, 1906. Paris, France.

Letter of Constantine Athanasopoulos to Metropolitan Theoklitos of the Holy Synod of Athens, Greece, September 11, 1912. Archives of the Greek Orthodox Archdiocese of Athens, Greece.

Letter of Constantine Athanasopoulos to the Holy Synod of Athens, Greece, August 8, 1912. Archives of the Greek Orthodox Archdiocese of Athens, Greece.

Letter of Father Basil Lambrides to Metropolitan Meletios of Athens, September 27, 1916. Archives of the Greek Orthodox Archdiocese of America.

Letter of Father Basil Lambrides to the Holy Synod of Athens, Greece, August 15, 1912. Archives of the Greek Orthodox Archdiocese of Athens, Greece.

Letter of Father Basil Lambrides to the Holy Synod of Athens, Greece, June 16, 1912. Archives of the Greek Orthodox Archdiocese of Athens, Greece.

Letter of Father Christos Angelopoulos to Archbishop Athenagoras, April 22, 1931. Archives of the Greek Orthodox Archdiocese of America.

Letter of Father Demetrios Petrides to Metropolitan Theoklitos of the Holy Synod of Athens, Greece, November 26, 1912. Archives of the Greek Orthodox Archdiocese of Athens, Greece.

Letter of the Holy Synod of Athens, Greece, to Father Demetrios Petrides, October 12, 1912. Archives of the Greek Orthodox Archdiocese of Athens, Greece.

Letter of the Holy Synod of Athens, Greece, to the Atlanta Church Council, October 12, 1912. Archives of the Greek Orthodox Archdiocese of Athens, Greece.

Library of Congress, Prints and Photographs Online Reading Room.

Local 1890 Census of City of Atlanta. Atlanta History Center, Box 3, Row 1, Section G, Shelf 5, AHS.

Local 1896 Census of City of Atlanta. Atlanta History Center, Box 1, Row 1, Section G, Shelf 5, AHS.

Martin, Thomas. *Handbook of the City of Atlanta.* Issued by the Atlanta City Council and the Atlanta Chamber of Commerce. N.p.: Southern Industrial Publishing Company, 1898.

Miller, Kelly. "An Appeal to Reason: An Open Letter to John Temple Graves." Howard University and University of Georgia, 1906.

Ministry of Interior, Department of Public Economy and Statistics. Statistics of Greece, population census of April 15–16, 1889. 1890.

———. Statistics of Greece, population census of December 19, 1920, the statistical results for the Peloponnesus. 1929.

New York Times Article Archives.

1900 Federal Census. National Archives and Records Administration.

1910 Federal Census. National Archives and Records Administration.

Northen, W.J. *The Evolution of Lawlessness and Unchallenged Crime.* N.p., 1911. Georgia Archives.

Omaha Daily News Archives.

Our Baptist Young People and American Citizenship: An Address by W.J. Northen, Hot Springs, Arkansas, May 10, 1900. Georgia Archives.

Petrides, Demetrios, Father, Protopresbyter. *ΕΚΚΛΗΣΙΑΣΤΙΚΟΙ ΛΟΓΟΙ ΚΑΙ ΔΙΑΛΕΞΕΙΣ.* N.p.: Ο ΚΟΣΜΟΣ, 1917. This book of selected "Ecclesiastical Sermons and Lectures" of Father Demetrios was published in 1917 shortly before his death, when he served as the *Proistamenos* of the Atlanta church. He dedicated the book in memory of his deceased wife, "to the holy shade of my unforgettable Presbytera, Eleni."

Powell, Arthur G. *I Can Go Home Again.* Chapel Hill: University of North Carolina Press, 1943.

Printers Ink: A Journal for Advertisers 60, no. 6 (August 7, 1907). New York.

Proceedings of the First Annual Session of the Southern Immigration Association, Nashville, Tennessee. N.p.: R.H. Howell & Company, 1884. Available at Harvard University Library.

Proceedings of the Southern Interstate Immigration Convention, Montgomery, Alabama. N.p.: Wilmans Brothers, 1888. Available at Harvard University Library.

Report on Population of the United States at the Eleventh Census, Part II. Washington, D.C.: Government Printing Office, 1897.

Reports of the Immigration Commission. Washington, D.C.: Government Printing Office, 1911. Available at Harvard University Library.

Revolutionary Diplomatic Correspondence of the United States. Vol. 6. Library of Congress.

Rogers, Robert L., comp. *History, Confederate Veterans' Association of Fulton County, Georgia.* Atlanta, GA: V.P. Sisson, 1890.

Sacramental Register of the Annunciation Greek Orthodox Church of Atlanta, 1906–1922. Archives of the Annunciation Greek Orthodox Cathedral of Atlanta.

Sales agreement between Greenwood Cemetery and the Greek Orthodox Church, January 5, 1915. Archives of the Annunciation Greek Orthodox Cathedral of Atlanta.

Sales agreement between Greenwood Cemetery and the Greek Orthodox Church, July 28, 1911. Archives of the Annunciation Greek Orthodox Cathedral of Atlanta.

Sanborn Fire Insurance Maps for Georgia Towns and Cities, 1884–1922. Digital Library of Georgia, www.dlg.galileo.usg.edu.

Simmons, William Joseph. *America's Menace or The Enemy Within (An Epitome).* N.p.: Bureau of Patriotic Books, 1926.

———. *The Klan Unmasked.* N.p.: W.E. Thompson Publishing Company, 1924.

Singleton, D.T., comp. and ed. *Putnam County, Ga. and Its Resources: A Guide to Immigration.* N.p., 1895. Available at the Georgia Archives.

Sunny South. Georgia Historic Newspapers. http://atlnewspapers.galileo.usg. edu/atlnewspapers/search.

Textile World Record 33 (1907).

Thomas Jefferson Papers Series 1. General Correspondence, 1765–1826. Library of Congress.

Treasury Book of the Annunciation Greek Orthodox Church, 1905–17. Annunciation Greek Orthodox Cathedral of Atlanta.

Wells-Barnett, Ida B. *Lynch Law in Georgia.* N.p., 1899.

Westview Cemetery Burial Ledger, 1890–1917. Westview Cemetery, Atlanta, Georgia.

Xenides, J.P., Reverend. *The Greeks in America.* N.p.: George H. Doran Company, 1922.

SECONDARY SOURCES

Allen, James. *Without Sanctuary: Lynching Photography in America.* N.p.: Twin Palms Publishers, 2000.

Atlanta Annunciation Greek Orthodox Cathedral. *Eighty Years in Atlanta: A Celebration of Our Cultural Heritage.* Atlanta, GA: self-published, 1985.

Burns, Rebecca. *Rage in the Gate City: The Story of the 1906 Atlanta Race Riot.* Athens: University of Georgia Press, 2009.

Centennial Anniversary Album of the Atlanta Annunciation Greek Orthodox Cathedral. Atlanta Annunciation Greek Orthodox Cathedral, 2007.

Clark, Christopher. *The Sleepwalkers: How Europe Went to War in 1914.* New York: HarperCollins Publishers, 2012.

Dedication Album of the Consecration of the Atlanta Annunciation Greek Orthodox Cathedral, 1970.

Dimopoulos, George, Father, comp. *A Brief Historical Survey.* The Greek Orthodox Community of the Annunciation, Wilkes-Barre, Pennsylvania, 2012.

Dolan, Jay P. *The Immigrant Church: New York's Irish and German Catholics, 1815–1865.* Notre Dame, IN: University of Notre Dame Press, 1983.

Eckert, Ralph Lowell. *John Brown Gordon: Soldier Southerner American.* Baton Rouge: Louisiana State University Press, 1993.

Efthimiou, Miltiades B., Reverend, and George A. Christopoulos. *The History of the Greek Orthodox Church in America.* Greek Orthodox Archdiocese of North and South America, 1984.

Ellis, Ann W. "The Greek Community in Atlanta, 1900–1923." *Georgia Historical Quarterly* 58, no. 4 (Winter 1974): 400–8. Georgia Historical Society.

Fiftieth Anniversary Album of the Atlanta Annunciation Greek Orthodox Church, 1955.

Franklin Garrett Atlanta Necrology Database. Kenan Research Center, Atlanta History Center. http://garrett.atlantahistorycenter.com.

Frazier, John W., and Eugene L. Tettey, eds. *Race, Ethnicity and Place in a Changing America.* N.p.: Fio Global Academic Publishing, 2006.

Garrett, Franklin M. *Atlanta and Environs: A Chronicle of Its People and Events.* Vols. 1 and 2. Athens: University of Georgia Press, 1969.

Geiger, Linda Woodward, and Meyer L. Frankel. *Index to Georgia's Federal Naturalization Records to 1950.* Georgia Genealogical Society, 1996.

Greek Orthodox Archdiocese of America. www.goarch.org.

Hertzberg, Steven. *Strangers within the Gate City: The Jews of Atlanta, 1845–1915.* N.p.: Jewish Publication Society of America, 1978.

Highlands Presbyterian Church Grayson, Georgia. http://www.highlandsarp.org.

Hogan, Margaret A., and C. James Taylor, eds. *My Dearest Friend: Letters of Abigail and John Adams.* Cambridge, MA: Belknap Press of Harvard University Press, 2007.

Immigration and Naturalization Service. 1976 Annual Report. Washington, D.C. Government Printing Office, 1976.

Jackson, Kenneth T. *The Ku Klux Klan in the City, 1915–1930.* New York: Oxford University Press, 1967.

Kennedy, W.W., ed. *The Sesquicentennial History of the Associate Reformed Presbyterian Church.* N.p.: Presses of Jacons Brothers Printers, 1951.

MacLean, Nancy. *Behind the Mask of Chivalry: The Making of the Second Ku Klux Klan.* New York: Oxford University Press, 1994.

Mebane, Ann Fonvielle. "Immigrant Patterns in Atlanta, 1880 and 1896." Master's thesis, Atlanta History Center, 1967.

Moskos, Charles C. *Greek Americans: Struggle and Success.* 2nd ed. N.p.: Transaction Publishers, 2005.

Namee, Matthew. "Fr. Kallinikos: The First Greek Priest in America?" Orthodox History, 2009. Orthodoxhistory.org.

———. "The Stormy Petrel of the Cloth." Podcast on Father Demetrios Petrides. Orthodoxhistory.org.

National Herald.

Oney, Steve. *And the Dead Shall Rise: The Murder of Mary Phagan and the Lynching of Leo Frank.* New York: Pantheon Books, 2003.

Orthodox Observer.

Perlmutter, Philip. *Legacy of Hate: A Short History of Ethnic, Religious and Racial Prejudice in America.* N.p.: M.E. Sharpe Inc., 1999.

Preservation of American Hellenic History. www.pahh.com.

Saloutos, Theodore. *The Greeks in the United States.* Cambridge, MA: Harvard University Press, 1964.

Samonides, William H., PhD. "Father Christos Angelopoulos (1867–1933)." Unpublished.

———. "The First Greek Orthodox Hierarch to Visit America." *Orthodox Observer* 78 (November, 2013).

———. "In the Tradition of St. Paul, Fr. Christos Angelopoulos." *Orthodox Observer* 77 (November, 2012).

———. Unpublished research on the early Greek Orthodox priests of America.

Scott, Dr. Carole E., and Dr. Richard D. Guynn. *The Disappearance from Georgia of the Farm Union.* 1997. www.westga.edu/~bquest/1997/farmer.html.

Sewter, E.R.A., trans. *The Alexiad of Anna Comnena.* N.p.: Sewter, Penguin Books, 1969.

Sklavounos, Yorgo. "A Model of Ethnic Development: The Greek American Community of Atlanta, Georgia." Master's thesis, Georgia State University, 1979.

Smith, John Robert. *The Church that Stayed: Central Presbyterian Church, 1858–1978.* Atlanta, GA: Atlanta Historical Society, 1979.

Swan, James B. *Chicago's Irish Legion: The 90th Illinois Volunteers in the Civil War.* Carbondale: Southern Illinois University Press, 2009.

Tatsios, Theodore George. *The Megali Idea and the Greek-Turkish War of 1897: The Impact of the Cretan Problem on Greek Irredentism, 1866–1897.* Boulder, CO: East European Monographs, 1984.

Unites States Census Bureau. Statistical Abstract of the Unites States, 2003.

Vann Woodward, Comer. *Tom Watson: Agrarian Rebel.* New York: Oxford University Press, 1938.

Williams, Michael. *The Shadow of the Pope.* New York: McGraw-Hill Book Company Inc., 1932.

INTERVIEWS

Demetriades, Charlotte. Regarding Constantine Athanasopoulos, December 13, 2013.

Demetry, Nick. Regarding Father Constas Hadjidemetriou, December 16, 2013.

Edwards, Cleo Janoulis. February 8, 2014.

Farmakis, Mary Algers. Regarding Gerasimos Algers, October 20, 2010.

Janoulis, Aleck. Regarding Father Demetrios Petrides, May 3, 2012.

Pantelis, Helen. May 19, 2015.

Ross, Daphne. Regarding Father Basil Lambrides, October 14, 2013.

INDEX

ABOUT THE AUTHOR

Although not a native Atlantan, Stephen Georgeson has lived in Atlanta for almost fifty years and has been a member of the Annunciation Greek Orthodox Cathedral of Atlanta throughout those years. Born in Chattanooga, Tennessee, he is the grandson of four Greek immigrants. His grandparents Aristomenes and Vasiliki Georgeson helped establish the early Greek community in Oakland, California, and his grandparents Pete and Mary Gulas did likewise in Chattanooga.

Georgeson is a graduate of the McCallie School in Chattanooga and received a BA from Emory University. In addition, he is a graduate of the University of Tennessee College of Law. For many years, he has had his own firm and serves as a lobbyist for several companies and organizations.

He is an Archon of the Ecumenical Patriarchate and a member of the Order of Saint Andrew the Apostle.

He has served the Atlanta Annunciation Cathedral in many capacities. He has been a member of the Parish Council for several years and served as president for four years. He was vice-chairman of Project Faith, which spearheaded the expansion of the cathedral campus by adding an office wing, a ballroom, meeting rooms and a gymnasium. He started the Cathedral History and Archives Committee, which sparked his interest and subsequent research for this book.

Georgeson's interests include travel, reading and Byzantine history. Throughout his life, his greatest sports idol has been Willie Mays.